Y0-BSU-822

America Under Siege

This country has to face the fact
that we're under an invasion.

— Mayor Ed Koch
New York City

Available at special quantity discount for bulk purchases for gift-giving, sales promotions, fund-raising for community organizations, PTAs, churches, congregations, and scout groups. Also for educational use for businesses, schools, colleges and other parents' groups. For more details, write to Light Publishing House, P.O. Box 2629, Daly City, California 94017.

TOM J. ILAO

America Under Siege

Foreword
by

Joseph P. Russoniello
United States Attorney
Northern District of California
U.S. Department of Justice

LIGHT
PUBLISHING HOUSE
San Francisco • California

Editing and production by The forWords Company

Copyright ©1988 by Tom J. Ilao

All rights reserved. Written permission must be secured from the publisher
to use or reproduce any part of this book, except for brief quotations
in critical reviews or articles.

International Standard Book Number: 0-9621101-0-8

Library of Congress Catalog Card Number: 88-82217

Published in San Francisco, California by Light Publishing House

Printed in the United States of America

To my wife, Lolita, and my children, Francis Thomas, Margaret Mary and Jeremiah — for their support, love, and encouragement. They make everything inspiring and worthwhile.

To my father who taught us what integrity means. And to my late mother for her moral guidance.

To all members of law enforcement agencies for their efforts and sacrifices, and so that those who laid down their lives did not die and labor in vain.

To the countless men and women involved in drug crusades.

To the counselors and volunteers in the rehabilitation and prevention centers throughout the nation and around the world.

To all the young people who are the future leaders of America.

And to all the parents in whose hands the fate of our young children lies.

ACKNOWLEDGMENTS

Grateful acknowledgment is made to the following for permission to reprint from copyrighted materials and artworks:

"The Moral of the Story," by Gary Bauer is reprinted from *Policy Review*, Issue No. 38 (Fall 1986). *Policy Review* is a publication of The Heritage Foundation, Washington, D.C.

"Thoughts on Freedom, Two Essays," by Lorin McMackin. Copyright © 1982 by the Board of Trustees, Southern Illinois University. Reprinted by permission of the publisher.

"Healing the Unaffirmed," by Conrad W. Baars and Anna Terruwe. Copyright © 1976 by Alba House, New York (Society of St. Paul).

"Promise Yourself," *The Optimist Creed*, permission to reprint granted by The Optimist International.

"Who's cool today — and who isn't," by John Kelly. Reprinted by permission of Mr. Kelly and *U.S. News & World Report*, through Robert J. Ames, Administrative Editor. Appeared in the *Rostrum* column, April 20, 1987.

"Fried Egg" advertisement reprinted by permission of the advertising agency of Keye/Donna/Pearlstein, Los Angeles, and the Partnership for a Drug-Free America, New York.

"Don't Wreck It With Drugs," by the U.S. Marine Corps. Permission to reprint granted by D.H. Caudill, Lieutenant Colonel, Washington, D.C.

"The Incorruptible Man," *Newsweek*, October 10, 1966. Permission to reprint granted by Norbert Hofman, Jr.

My profound gratitude to the following persons and organizations that made this book possible:

Attorney Joseph P. Russoniello for writing the Foreword and sending materials from the U.S. Department of Justice; Otto Moulton, Committees of Correspondence, Inc., for granting the permission to reprint articles in the Appendices section; Sr.

Anne Hehir, former principal, St. Finn Barr School, San Francisco, for the booklet *What Works: Schools Without Drugs*, published by the U.S. Department of Education; Paula J. Swink, program director, Alcohol and Drug Rehabilitation Center, Peninsula Hospital, Burlingame, California; Beverly Kinnard, drug educator and producer of educational tapes and films for schools and organizations; and Thomas C. Atwood, managing editor, *Policy Review*; James E. Braibish, editor, *Optimist* magazine; Rev. Anthony L. Chenevey, S.S.P. of Alba House, New York; Anja Koot of Personal Growth Project, San Rafael, California; Gipsey Hicks of Southern Illinois University Press; Brenda Rogers, The Media-Advertising Partnership for a Drug-Free America; and Julie Kiricoples, Committees of Correspondence, Inc.

The three major television networks for sending the following transcripts: ABC News 20/20 on "Losing America's War: The Heroes and the Hype," aired on May 7, 1987, hosted by Hugh Downs and Barbara Walters; CBS News Special, "48 Hours on Crack Street," broadcast on September 19, 1986 by Dan Rather; the NBC News Special on "Cocaine Country," anchored by Tom Brokaw, September 5, 1986; and an ABC News Special, "Drugs: A Plague on the Land," Peter Jennings, April 10, 1988.

Materials and news clippings were given unselfishly by Bro. Cornelius Hubbuch, CFX, Jesuit School of Theology, Berkeley, California; Bert Marantal; Rudy H. Concepcion; Tony Da Silva; and Paulette Borg.

The encouragement of Fr. Christopher Cartwright, S.J., executive director, Campus Ministry Office, University of San Francisco; Sr. Hilda McGinnis, director, Permanent Diaconate, Archdiocese of San Francisco; Gualbert R. Gabriel, vice president, marketing, O'Manna Financial Corporation; Alice Bulos, community leader, San Mateo County; Augustus M. Stella, Jonathan Mariano and many others. They have my gratitude.

And finally, to my wife for her patience during the long hard months of research and writing and to my children for keeping me on top of the drug scene.

FOREWORD

Like the weather, drug abuse is one of those issues that everyone has an opinion about, but that no one seems to be able to do much about. Well, that proposition is only partly true. We *can* do something about it. In fact, each of us *must* do something about it. First and foremost, we need to understand the facts about this problem.

For one thing, it won't just go away. For another, it's likely to get much worse if we neglect it any longer. Law enforcement can't solve the problem by itself. Even use of the military to stop the flow of drugs into the U.S. is problematic. Successfully interdicting all the drugs that are imported won't solve the problem — we grow or manufacture enough right here in America to satisfy the world's demand. Legalization would be the worst course for us to pursue. It would make all of us parties to and responsible for the painful destruction of fellow Americans.

If law enforcement supported by the military can't win this battle, how can we as average citizens be expected to succeed? A good part of the answer is contained in this book. It asks the question, "Why are so many people hooked on drugs?" and offers some insight as to how they can get unhooked and stay that way and, especially important, how people who are concerned about this subject can help.

In my opinion, it's "must" reading for anyone who wants to know the truth about drug abuse in America today and what strategies can be deployed to deal effectively with it.

Joseph P. Russoniello, U.S. Attorney
Northern District of California
U.S. Department of Justice

CONTENTS

PREFACE

The world has seen nothing like it — corporate America menaced, people plunged into bankruptcy, respectable people in all walks of life corrupted, driven to suicide, homes and families and friendships destroyed. No scourge on earth has done so much to dehumanize young and old alike than this army of deadly poisons that is besieging our country today. This book is about America Under Siege from drugs — about what these drugs and the people behind them are doing to us — and what we can do about it.

I wrote this book with a sense of urgency and dread in the face of this unfolding American tragedy, haunted by the lines of John Donne: "Any man's death diminishes me, because I am involved in Mankind; and therefore never send to know for whom the bell tolls; it tolls for thee." It is my hope that these words will deeply impress in us the truth that we are all affected by someone's becoming a victim — or a monster — because of drug abuse. Many of us are unaware that we have long been under siege and that millions have become unwilling pawns and puppets in a war that knows no boundaries.

This is a shared crisis. I believe that it is in the realization that we are community that we can find our lasting hope. It is by working together that we can confront this deadly menace — the twin forces that are slowly but surely encroaching upon every area of our lives: the enemy among us, and the enemy within us.

We are losing the fight against the former, as agents of the U.S. Drug Enforcement Agency have admitted, but we will win the war if we take care of the enemy within — *us*. We must realize that drug trafficking is flourishing because it's our problem, not the traffickers'. We created the demand for their products. The fact is, *if there's no demand, there's no supply*. We must curtail our insatiable appetite for any kind of drugs, or the vicious cycle will never end. We will only see more crime, more death, more drug addicts added to the legions we already have. We will surely see a new way of life forced upon us by drug dealers and pushers, a way of life without precedent for Mankind. And what a way of life it would be!

We cannot pretend that we don't know; we cannot make believe that nothing is happening around us, because something is definitely happening. We cannot just sit and watch TV and read news reports about victims dropping like flies. We must not let drug gangs and thugs roam our streets and neighborhoods, turning them into battlefields, while we do nothing but lament.

Our nation is being forced to turn on itself — but only because we allow it. Think about Americans losing the freedom that has been so hard won. We don't realize the value of freedom until we lose it — and are we to lose it to become slaves to a national disgrace called drug addiction? We see millions of fellow Americans risking that freedom in the most unrestrained, destructive, wasteful way. We must be vigilant in order to safeguard our freedom if we want to "secure the blessings of liberty to ourselves and our posterity" and not leave behind us a scarred and brain-damaged generation to become the leaders of this nation.

As often repeated in this book, we can find the solution, not so much by an open declaration of war against the outside forces, but by looking within ourselves. If we honestly plumb the depths of our being and examine ourselves seriously, then we can put an end to this problem.

But this is easier said than done. First, let's begin to become part of the solution. It is my hope that the two chapters in this book, "The Citadel Within" and "The Only Solution" will provide the inspiration to many who seek for the answer. We must realize that while there are always alternatives in life, there is but one Way. It is my heart's desire that my efforts will help put out the fire of rampant drug abuse or at least will keep it from raging further. Together, we can turn back the enemy that is besieging our country and ravaging our citizens.

I leave you with the paraphrased words of Edmund Burke: The only thing necessary for the triumph of evil is for good men and women to do nothing.

Tom J. Ilao
San Francisco, California
December 22, 1988

Part One
The Enemies Among Us

1

STATE OF SIEGE

Drug use threatens the health and safety of millions of Americans. Drugs in one way or the other are victimizing all of us. It's time to make illegal drugs "Public Enemy No. 1."

— President Ronald Reagan

— The Great American Tragedy —

Illegal drug use is as pervasive as the news reports and headlines we hear and read almost everyday. One major TV network, ABC, had aired drug-related topics 29 times[1] on its *Nightline* news program between November 16, 1981 and January 19, 1988 — a period of more than six years, an average of almost five shows a year. That doesn't include the network's other programs nor those aired by other major TV stations. The reality of drug abuse permeates our daily consciousness. How *really* serious is the problem? How does it affect us, and especially our young children?

"American youth, in the last 20 years," says Dr. Robert L. DuPont, Jr., "have made themselves guinea pigs in a *national experiment*[2] of unprecedented proportions ... When the full impact of this experiment is assessed, it will, I am convinced, be seen as a national tragedy of immense proportions."[3] And *Time* magazine reported: "Crack's corruption of children is, in the Bible's phrase, a millstone around the neck of American society."[4] I believe we cannot fault the youth alone — the adult users are

---

1. "Drugs: A Plague on the Land," transcript of ABC News Special, April 10, 1988, narrated by Peter Jennings, p.15.
2. My italics for emphasis.
3. *Getting Tough on Gateway Drugs*, by Robert L. DuPont, Jr., M.D., 1984.
4. "Kids Who Sell Crack," *Time*, May 9, 1988.

equally responsible. The reality is: we are a dope-ridden society or perhaps *even* — as Steve Howe (former Los Angeles Dodgers pitcher) expressed it — "We are a society awash in drugs."

To understand the drug scene today, it is useful to review some key news events in the last 20 years which will help us see that the current problem has been building for some time. These events may even bring back memories for some of us.

January 1970. Music and peace were the themes of the Woodstock folk-rock festival that brought more than 400,000 young people to the green slopes of Bethel, New York. But what disturbed the adult segment of the nation's population was the cloud of marijuana smoke ... Indeed, as one student put it, the smoke was so heavy that "you could get stoned just sitting there breathing."[5] The same magazine also covered this story: "As bullets ricochet from the moldering bricks, junkies nod in doorways ... This is Hunts Point,[6] a neighborhood of roughly 20,000 people whose life style is largely determined by heroin addicts ... they are brazen and bold ... Non-addict residents of Hunts Point sit behind closed doors wedged tight with iron bars bolted to the floor, literally living in a state of siege."[7]

June 1970. "The 60-pound wisp of a boy is twelve years old, barely four feet tall ... the child is a junkie. He has not only used heroin but also taken part in muggings and sold drugs to his friends to support his habit ... The boy is one of the youngest addicts to surface for treatment in a terrifying wave of heroin use among youth ... Long considered the affliction of the criminal, the derelict, the debauched, heroin is increasingly — and invisibly — attacking America's children ... something frightening is sweeping into the corridors of U.S. schools and onto the pavements of America's playgrounds."[8]

December 1970. Dr. Stanley F. Yolles, former director of the National Institute of Mental Health, has estimated that the number of Americans who have tried pot at least once may

---

5. "Marijuana: How Dangerous Is It?" by Steven M. Spencer, *Reader's Digest*, January 1970.
6. Hunts Point is a suburb of New York City.
7. "The Horrors of Heroin," condensed from *The New York Times*, by Richard Severo, *Reader's Digest*, January 1970.
8. "Kids and Heroin," condensed from *Time*, *Reader's Digest*, June 1970.

be as high as 20 million.[9] The Pentagon says that about 30 percent of the U.S. troops in Vietnam have tried it, and most observers consider this estimate conservative. In several large universities where surveys have been taken, the proportion of undergraduate users tops 50 percent and is rising.

March 1972. "A chilling look at a $5.5 billion business that makes heroin our largest consumer import — and Public Enemy No. 1. It is a hard fact that the vast heroin distribution machinery in the United States is expanding at an alarming rate."[10]

September 1978. According to the National Institute on Drug Abuse (NIDA), about seven million people in the United States have used PCP — three times the number for heroin (2.3 million), not far behind cocaine (9.8 million). [In 1977] PCP took an estimated 100 lives and sent more than 4,000 victims to hospital rooms. The executive vice president of the American Medical Association has declared PCP a "prime medical concern" while NIDA has named it the country's new top-priority problem drug.[11]

May 1982. Methaqualone tablets — Quaaludes or "ludes" as the kids call them — are causing more deaths from overdose, accident and suicide than "speed," LSD, "angel dust" or even heroin. More common than cocaine and, some authorities say, more dangerous than heroin, methaqualone is now taken by young Americans more frequently in many areas than any other illicitly supplied drug except marijuana. In 1981, they consumed about a billion tablets averaging $6 each, making this drug a $6-billion-a-year business. Methaqualone's skyrocketing use has triggered an epidemic of horror.[12]

And for every year since then there are similar stories — in many ways a continuing sequel from the past — only now the magnitude of the problem is greater, the statistics more frightening.

We see the symptoms of its tragic consequences, especially among the young, in increased teenage suicides, school dropouts, runaways, homeless teenagers, teenage pregnancies, gang violence and killings. We see a nation suffering from a

9. "What To Do About Marijuana," condensed from *Newsweek*, *Reader's Digest*, December 1970.
10. "Inside Heroin, Inc.," by Nathan M. Adams, *Reader's Digest*, March 1972.
11. "Angel Dust — The Unpredictable Killer," by Florence Isaacs, *Reader's Digest*, September 1978.
12. "Deadlier than Heroin," by Jean Carper, *Reader's Digest*, May 1982.

deadly affliction — slowly being decimated by an epidemic, caused by killer drugs that are sold openly, unabashedly with impudence everywhere. And consumed by buyers with unremitting passion.

— So High a Price to Pay —

The cost to human lives of drug-related incidents is hard to quantify. The following tragedies and incidents which became national news and headlines were directly or indirectly related to this insidious problem:

❏ In Sacramento, California, bodies began showing up in alleys, in ditches and behind apartment buildings where drugs were sold. Police called a press conference to focus on the danger of "tar heroin," a drug so strong that users were found dead with the needle still in their arms.[13]

❏ 130 people were arrested in a drug probe of truckers in California where dealers brazenly advertised their wares on Citizen Band radio to truck drivers passing the drug bazaars set up at roadside stops. "These are unguided missiles, lethal weapons that threatened the safety of every driver," declared State Attorney General John Van de Kamp. In 1986, truck drivers under the influence of drugs and alcohol caused 27 fatal accidents in the state.[14]

❏ Detroit is experiencing an epidemic of children shooting children. Are drugs related to this? FBI agent John Anthony and others claim that the widespread sale and use of crack has promoted warfare among young, heavily-armed drug dealers. Says Anthony, "I remember when carrying a gun was pretty heavy stuff. Now you get 14- and 15-year-old kids carrying guns."[15]

❏ In Chase, Maryland on January 4, 1987 a Conrail engine rear-ends a passenger train: sixteen dead, 170 injured. Urine tests taken after the crash show that Conrail

13. "The Seamier Side of Sacramento," *The San Francisco Chronicle*, July 13, 1987.
14. "Drug Probe of Truckers," *The San Francisco Examiner*, January 27, 1988.
15. *Time*, December 22, 1986.

engineer Ricky Gates had used marijuana sometime prior to the crash.[16]

❏ A PSA airliner crashes with 43 aboard including suspect David Burke. A gun found in the wreckage was believed to be the one used in killing the suspect's former boss, Ray F. Thomson of USAir, PSA's parent company. Investigators were considering the possibility that the pilot and co-pilot had also been shot. The suspect was a former drug dealer who lived in grand style, using his airport connections to move cocaine in quantity. The crash involving innocent victims was triggered with the firing of the suspect by his former boss who caught him stealing flight cocktail receipts.[17]

Those are some news items I culled at random to show the pernicious effect on those affected by illegal drugs. There have been other plane crashes where cocaine was found in the dead pilot's body, near-misses involving air controllers using cocaine and hashish, reports of two-thirds of the nation's nuclear plant workers found stoned on the job. They are everywhere, people entrusted with the safety of the public and people in every profession. It could be your own auto mechanic or driver, stockbroker, dentist or your personal physician. The problem is so widespread that it permeates every business, profession, and economic, political and social group. We are all touched by this deadly menace and this dark side of the American dream.

We see clearly the dehumanizing effects of illegal drugs. They are killing people and turning people into killers. Those who cannot leave home without them have to maintain a constant high if that means stealing, mugging, murdering for it. Some are the unfortunates in our midst who are living on the streets and in the abandoned buildings of our cities, scouring the sidewalks and alleys for drug money. Some sell their babies for cocaine, steal the lifetime savings of their parents, pay food stamps for them and crawl through dirt looking for crack crumbs. This is the most debasing of human tragedies.

16. "Drugs: A Plague on the Land," op. cit.
17. "A Life of Charm and Violence," *The San Francisco Chronicle*, December 10, 1987.

And those who are enterprising are turning buildings and apartment complexes, in many inner cities, into "dope supermarkets." Like the notorious Jamaican gang, they operate and sell in several U.S. cities — managing their "branches" like a legitimate chain operation. As a correspondent from ABC News reported: "If this were McDonald's or Wendy's we would call it franchising but we're not talking hamburgers." Indeed we are not talking about hamburgers and french fries, we are talking about enormous profits being made in cocaine and crack transactions. And it's not just some sleazy characters in this deadly business game for quick profit, but also people in respected professions lured by the excessive rewards and even by the risks. They are lawyers, doctors, pharmacists, engineers, diplomats, servicemen, teachers, judges, airline pilots, corporate executives, businessmen, and politicians.

Most appalling are the latest "entrants" in this growing industry — youngsters who know how to run a business so efficiently that "it's almost a corporate mentality," as *Time* observes. Indeed, "the drug trade," reports *Time* in a cover story, "has become the nation's newest — and most frightening — job program. In some cities, the crack trade may be one of the bigger job programs for youngsters."[18]

Hard hit by the drug problem, in terms of dollar loss, is corporate America — with one out of eight employees afflicted at a cost of between $45 billion and $85 billion a year[19] or even more. The U.S. Chamber of Commerce, in 1986, estimated that drugs in the workplace cost U.S. companies $60 billion in lost productivity. Among the symptoms identified: poor performance, a surge in accidents and absenteeism, skyrocketing health care bills, blackmail, theft, industrial espionage, violence and drug dealing on the job. Substance abuse in the workplace covers the full spectrum of mind-altering chemicals that threaten the health and safety of everyone, including alcohol, barbiturates, amphetamines, marijuana, heroin and cocaine. "Cocaine alone," says actor Stacy Keach, "is estimated as a $20 billion to $30 billion industry and if listed would rank the eighth

---

18. "Kids Who Sell Crack," *Time*, May 9, 1988.
19. "Getting High on the Job," NBC News, September 8, 1985, Stacy Keach, host.

largest among the Fortune 500."[20] Noting the corrupting influence of the drug, he reported:

> And cocaine could be partly responsible for the multi-million dollar bank run which paralyzed 71 Ohio savings institutions in March 1985. The run was touched off by the failure of ESM Government Securities, a Fort Lauderdale company. According to the Securities and Exchange Commission, ESM engaged in a pattern of fraud, hiding losses of almost 200 million dollars and, according to the testimony in a Florida court and a copyrighted story in the *Miami Herald*, corporate practices included whirlwind vacations, expensive luxuries and wild cocaine parties.

"The production, distribution and sale of illegal drugs," says Buck Rodgers, former IBM executive, "is one of the biggest industries in the country today and it's going at a rate any legitimate business would envy. It's estimated that in 1986, Americans spent more than $110 billion on illegal drugs. To put that figure in perspective, the total equity of the six largest U.S. companies comes to just $116 billion."[21] Beverly Kinnard, well-known drug educator, put this figure slightly higher: "When we spend $120 billion a year going out of the country to purchase illegal drugs and it goes to nations who are not always friendly to us, it may buy weapons to use against us — nothing comes back but a chemical that destroys our most vital natural resource, our young leaders of tomorrow, our kids of today."[22]

We spend staggering amounts contributing to the hidden costs of rehabilitation and institutionalization for drug users, offenders and addicts. This is a continuous drain on the taxpayer's money. We all are paying for this. One area we cannot put an estimate on is the time and effort taken away from paid staff and volunteers who otherwise could be working on what is productive and necessary. The most vital services affected are our educational system, the criminal and justice system and the health care delivery system. We know from what statistics tells us that they are already overburdened and the cost to these vital systems is very hard to determine.

20. Ibid.
21. *Getting the Best Out of Yourself and Others*, by Buck Rodgers, 1987.
22. "Marijuana and the Destruction of Family," by Beverly Kinnard, from address given at Marijuana Dependence: A National Conference, October 3-4, 1986, San Francisco, Calif.

Carl T. Rowan, writing for *Reader's Digest* in 1983, summed up the reality of the drug scene in this excerpt from his thought-provoking article, "The Drug Scourge Must Be Stopped":

> As surely as if they were nuclear bombs from a dreaded enemy, the tons of heroin from Asia, the mountains of cocaine from Bolivia and Peru, the endless supply of marijuana, Quaaludes and other illicit drugs from Colombia — and from American farms and laboratories — are wrecking this society. Indeed, no Soviet espionage team could weaken America's military preparedness to the extent that drug abuse is rendering us naked to our enemies.
>
> The curse of drugs has seeped down through our colleges and high schools into our elementary schools. Illegal drugs are playing havoc with the business communities, with sales of marijuana, heroin and cocaine commonplace on Wall Street. Drug abuse has become the scourge of professional athletics, the curse of our entertainment world from Hollywood to Broadway, a shame of Congress.
>
> It is a tragedy that touches every type of family in this land.[23]

— Facts and Statistics —

Abraham Lincoln once said, "I am a firm believer in the people. If given the truth, they can be depended upon to meet any national crisis. The great point is to bring them the real facts." A poll conducted by CBS News and the *New York Times*[24] revealed that the problem that Americans consider most important is the drug crisis — more so than unemployment, the Federal deficit or even issues of war and peace. The overall concern about the drug problem is more than justified as we see this growing crisis everywhere, exemplified by this local report: In Sacramento, California, the murder rate has doubled, gang warfare has intensified. Drug dealing is so bad in some parts of town that street corner vigilantes patrol with picket signs saying, "Crack: Slavery is back." The crack problem alone has spread like wildfire and is killing with a devastating vengeance.

In San Francisco Bay Area cities, from police stations to detoxification centers, the fight against crack has severely strained money and manpower in communities that already

---

23. "The Drug Scourge Must Be Stopped," by Carl T. Rowan, *Reader's Digest*, August 1983.
24. Survey conducted May 9-12, 1988.

have financial problems. In the street, accelerated enforcement has sent police budgets soaring. In the courts, judges, prosecutors and youth counsellors are struggling under staggering caseloads. In the jails, crack offenders have worsened an already serious overcrowding problem. In treatment facilities, many abusers of the drug cannot obtain immediate care because of tight budgets.

A report by the *San Francisco Chronicle*[25] offers these grim statistics:

➪ It costs $8.5 million a year, nearly twice the expense of two years ago, to support the San Francisco Police Department's special narcotics enforcement effort, much of it spent to fight crack.

➪ The bill to California taxpayers for each criminal's day in Superior Court has risen to $2,877, a 32 percent increase in five years.

➪ The daily expense of a stay at San Francisco's Youth Guidance Center, where increasing numbers of crack offenders wind up, is equivalent to a night in one of the city's better hotels: $115.

These direct costs to the community do not capture the full economic wrath of crack and cocaine abuse. Research has indicated that the annual cost of fighting drug abuse in the United States would keep the government of Oregon running for 15 years. A recent congressional report estimated that Americans spent about $140 billion in 1987 (as compared to $110 – $120 billion in 1986) to buy 178 tons of cocaine, 12 tons of heroin and about 60,000 tons of marijuana. The proposed fiscal 1989 budget contains $6.6 billion to fight drugs, an increase of 91 percent over the current year. The amount includes an addition by the Senate of $2.6 billion over what President Reagan had requested.

No social crisis has burdened so many inner-city services and other government agencies as this "appalling drug abuse," as syndicated columnist Jack Anderson termed it. Like a gigantic malevolent octopus, its tentacles have gripped millions of ad-

25. "Bay Cities Can't Cope with Crack Onslaught," by David Dietz, May 9, 1988.

dicts and countless families in a slow strangle. The following facts and statistics reveal the extent of substance abuse today; it remains to be seen what the long term social impact will be.

⇨ Some 20 million Americans use marijuana at least once a month. One of every 18 high school seniors — more than 5 percent — uses marijuana daily. Some 4 million people, half of them between the ages of 18 and 24, use cocaine. Approximately a half million individuals in the U.S. are heroin addicts.[26]

⇨ Well over half the men arrested for serious crimes in a dozen U.S. cities tested positive for illegal drug use; in New York the drug-use rate hits nearly 80 percent. In Washington, the rate is 77 percent and in San Diego, 75 percent.[27]

⇨ With the advent of crack, juvenile arrests in New York tripled, from 386 in 1983 to 1,052 in 1987. Detroit area police busted 647 youths in 1987, almost twice as many as in 1986. In Washington, from 483 in 1983 to 1,894 in 1987.[28]

⇨ There are 2,000 dope arrests every single day in the nation.[29]

⇨ Drug use rates have risen from 1,000 percent to 3,000 percent during the last 20 years.[30]

⇨ Our teens have been the most drug-pervaded youth in the world. A 1985-86 drug-use survey of some 40,000 youngsters revealed that more than one in 10 high school seniors and one in 13 juniors use cocaine occasionally to daily; one in 20 seniors uses marijuana daily.[31]

⇨ Every five seconds a teen has a drug- or alcohol-related traffic accident. More than half of teenage deaths are the result of drug or alcohol abuse. The average age to begin using marijuana is 13 years. 15 million teenagers risk damage

26. *Comment*, Columbia magazine, December 1986.
27. Test sponsored by the National Institute of Justice, in *San Francisco Chronicle*, January 22, 1988.
28. "Kids Who Sell Crack," op. cit.
29. "American Vice: The Doping of a Nation," KTVU, Channel 2, Geraldo Rivera, December 2, 1986.
30. Robert L. DuPont Jr., M.D., former Director, National Institute on Drug Abuse (NIDA).
31. Survey by Parent Resource Institute for Drug Education (PRIDE).

to their lungs, brain, and reproductive systems by smoking marijuana everyday.[32]

⇨ It is estimated by the National Institute on Drug Abuse (NIDA) that there are now between five and six million regular cocaine users in the U.S., consuming more than 45 metric tons of the drug annually.

⇨ Emergency-room admissions due to cocaine have increased 500 percent over the past three years. In the same period the number of deaths by cocaine intoxication has tripled in the U.S.[33]

⇨ Studies show that alcohol and drug abuse is a major problem among physicians, afflicting nearly one-fifth of all of them in the United States.[34]

⇨ Fifty-nine percent of doctors and 78 percent of medical students say they have used mind-altering drugs at least once for self-treatment, to get high or to help them stay awake.[35]

⇨ In the last 10 years, the number of babies born to drug addicts is up 1,000 percent. Overdoses have increased 300 percent and deaths from cocaine alone rose 1,000 percent.[36]

⇨ 800-Cocaine, the first and largest phone bank hotline center, reports young people calling with greater frequency. Twenty-nine percent are addicted to crack; 18 percent have tried suicide.

⇨ The Drug Hotline estimates that one million Americans have tried crack, while as many as 20 million have used cocaine in some form at least once.[37]

⇨ Five million Americans are regular users of cocaine. Each day 5,000 more tempt self-destruction by trying the drug for the first time.[38]

---

32. Fact sheet from The National Federation of Parents for Drug-Free Youth.
33. *Sports Illustrated*, July 14, 1986.
34. Editorial, *San Francisco Chronicle*, June 11, 1987.
35. *USA Today*, September 25, 1986.
36. "Drugs: A Plague On The Land," op. cit.
37. "Cocaine Country — A National Forum," NBC News Special Report, September 5, 1986, Tom Brokaw.
38. "They Dared Cocaine — And Lost," by Henry Hurt, *Reader's Digest*, May 1988.

⇨ In New York City, 55 percent of all cocaine arrests involve crack. Large organizations back 20,000 to 30,000 small-time dealers. Seizures are actually small.[39]

⇨ It is estimated that 60 percent of the world's output of illegal drugs is consumed in the U.S.A. Over 500 tons of illegal drugs — cocaine, marijuana and heroin — were seized in this country through the first half of 1986. By the government's count, that means 2,000 tons of illegal drugs still made it through and onto the streets.[40]

⇨ Officials estimate that only 10 to 20 percent of illegal shipments of marijuana are seized. The *San Francisco Chronicle* headlined Federal agents' seizing 37½ tons of hash and 15 tons of marijuana from a barge entering San Francisco Bay on May 23, 1988, at that time considered the largest bust in U.S. history.

⇨ The California roadway shootings that killed five and injured more than 20 during the summer of 1987 drew intensive publicity. But seven of the 12 people who die each day in accidents on California freeways die because of motorists who drive under the influence of abused substances. "Drivers impaired by alcohol or drugs," says CHP Sgt. Mark Lunn, "cause 100 times more violence, death and destruction than do motorists with guns."[41]

⇨ With so much drug-related horror in the inner cities, it is easy to assume that crack is an exclusively underprivileged-class problem. Not so. There is a terrible symbiosis between the wealthy addicts and the inner city dealers. Privileged kids who venture into the ghetto to spend hundreds and thousands of dollars on crack are largely responsible for the booming drug business.[42]

Illegal drug use leads too easily to violence — to brutal crimes, murders and suicides — committed by young addicts virtually deranged by the drugs. A news report in New York featured a 26-year old who stabbed and killed his mother and afterward had

39. "Cocaine Country — A National Forum," op. cit.
40. "48 Hours On Crack Street," CBS News Special, September 19, 1986, with Dan Rather.
41. *San Francisco Examiner*, August 28, 1987.
42. "Kids Who Sell Crack," op. cit.

no memory of the grisly episode. In Baltimore a 25-year old college student, believing he had seen something too horrible to bear, gouged his eyes out. In California a 15-year old youngster troubled by terrifying visions later hanged himself.

It is undeniable that illicit drugs are victimizing us all. What began in the 1960's as a local problem affecting only relatively few towns and cities has now spread to every geographic area and economic level. The social problems associated with illegal drug use have made us realize that we are all vulnerable. Illicit drugs like cocaine and heroin which declined in their use for the last 20 years have made a comeback deadlier than ever before in their new forms and derivatives.

What the statistics will never show, as John Cardinal O'Connor of New York wrote, are the broken pieces of lives, of whole families destroyed by what is essentially a flourishing, profitable business: the drug business.

2

THE DRUG ARSENAL

Let us, unprovoked, set a trap for the innocent; Let us swallow them up ... alive, in the prime of life. All kinds of precious wealth shall we gain, we shall fill our houses with booty.

— Proverbs 1:11-13

— The Hazards of Drug Use —

Drugs interfere with memory, sensation, and perception. They distort experiences and cause a loss of self-control that can lead users to harm themselves and others.

Drugs interfere with the brain's ability to take in, sort, and synthesize information. As a result, sensory information runs together, providing new sensations while blocking normal ability to understand the information received.

Drugs can have an insidious effect on perception, for example, cocaine and amphetamines often give users a false sense of functioning at their best while on the drug.

Drug suppliers have responded to the increasing demand for drugs by developing new strains, producing reprocessed, purified drugs, and using underground laboratories to create more powerful forms of illegal drugs. Consequently, users are exposed to heightened or unknown levels of risk.[1]

The marijuana produced today is 5 to 20 times stronger than that available as recently as 10 years ago. Regular use by adolescents has been associated with an "amotivational syndrome," characterized by apathy and loss of goals. Research

---

1. *What Works: Schools Without Drugs*, published by the U.S. Department of Education, 1986.

has shown that severe psychological damage, including paranoia and psychosis, can occur when marijuana contains 2 percent THC,[2] its major psychoactive ingredient. Since the early
1980s, most marijuana has contained from 4 to 6 percent THC
— two to three times the amount capable of causing serious
damage.

Phencyclidine (PCP), first developed as an animal tranquil-
izer, has unpredictable and often violent effects; also known
as "angel dust" it can cause wild hallucinations, schizophre-
nia-like psychosis, violence, convulsions, coma and death.
Often children do not even know that they are using this drug
when PCP-laced parsley in cigarette form is sold as lysergic
acid (LSD), itself a substance that can cause irreparable brain
damage.

Popular among the young are methaqualone and Quaaludes,
a powerful depressant, which figures constantly in injuries and
deaths, overdoses, accidents and suicides. One pill is equivalent to eight ounces of 100-proof whiskey and young adolescents usually take two. Within half an hour of ingesting the drug,
the users lose their balance and bump on chairs, tables and
walls.

Heroin is a nightmare. An addict risks coma and death from
an overdose which depresses the brain's control of breathing,
slowing respiration to the point where the body simply does not
get the oxygen it needs.

These drugs and many others can cause irreversible damage
to users. Appendix A contains more detailed information, published by the United States Department of Education, about
abused drugs and their effects on the mind and body, listing
their street names or other names, what they look like and how
they are used. Also at the end of this Appendix is a table
presenting the common effects of excessive alcohol consumption.

Let's take a closer look, now, at one of the most potent and
fascinating drugs to capture American youth and adults alike:
cocaine, a drug unprecedented in its myriad and widespread
effects on both mind and body, on the individual and the society
as a whole.

---

2. THC (delta-9-tetrahydrocannabinol).

— The Perils of Cocaine —

After nearly a decade of being America's drug of choice, evidence is emerging that cocaine is a very addictive substance. Actor Stacy Keach who spent six months in jail in England for cocaine possession admitted: "Cocaine is a drug which initially entices the user as a pleasurable, recreational diversion. Because of its seductive nature, it lures its victim into greater demands for constant companionship, finally forcing its prey into total submission, making itself the exclusive and singular priority of a person's existence. I know because I was a victim of this very phenomenon."

That cocaine could cripple and end an athlete's promising career had already been witnessed to by Don Reese, a professional football player who said in a *Sports Illustrated* story that his career had been ruined by cocaine. Steve Howe, once the dazzling pitcher of the Los Angeles Dodgers and the National League's 1980 rookie of the year, was also a career casualty of this drug. Then came sudden, shocking proof that it could kill too — even the young, seemingly invincible players. Len Bias, superstar at the University of Maryland, was signed up by the world-champion Boston Celtics — two days later, he was dead of heart failure triggered by cocaine use. Eight days later, the Cleveland Brown's defensive back Don Rogers took the same route. Jeep Jackson of Texas University at El Paso never knew which NBA team would pick him in the pro draft — he too flirted with drugs and died.

Well-known athletes who courted death but lived are basketball players John Lucas and Michael Ray Richardson, baseball pitcher Vida Blue, and professional boxer Aaron Pryor. Some who shook the cocaine habit eventually became productive players again: Keith Hernandez, Dave Parker, Dwight Gooden and Jeffrey Leonard. Delvin Williams also broke his drug dependence and organized an excellent drug-preventive program known as Pros For Kids.

Because they were young and strong they thought they were immortal and indestructible. It is now a fact that cocaine is a killer drug. Let's take a look at its effects on the vital organs of the body. *American Health* magazine reported cocaine's chain reaction and how this drug of the 80s takes its user from high to low — and sometimes beyond:[3]

> Whether taken by nose ("snorted") or inhaled into the lungs like crack, coke is immediately absorbed into the bloodstream where it travels to the heart, then the brain. There, it produces a euphoric high that lasts about 30 minutes if snorted, 15 minutes if smoked. During this "high" period, coke jams the mechanism that conserves dopamine, a neurotransmitter, possibly causing severe depression.
>
> Coke has many effects on the heart. In addition to constricting the blood vessels that feed it, calcium is released, causing an irregular heartbeat. Recent research from Stanford University has linked cocaine usage to permanent heart damage. Researchers found microscopic streaks of permanently contracted tissue known as myocardial contraction bands in the hearts of people whose deaths were linked to coke. These cells may block normal electrical conduction, causing arrhythmia and sometimes sudden death. Chronic use may cause an enlarged heart.
>
> Cocaine travels to the adrenal glands where it stimulates adrenaline production. Blood vessels constrict and heartbeat accelerates in a classic "fight or flight" reaction. Coke also reduces the body's ability to remove adrenalin, causing an even greater stimulant surge. "With cocaine, someone is basically administering a stress test to himself," says Dr. Jeffrey M. Isner of Tufts University School of Medicine.

This report parallels the findings of Dr. John E. Smialek, Chief Medical Examiner for the State of Maryland, who confirmed that the death of Len Bias was caused by heart failure. Cocaine caused the athlete's heart to beat wildly. This irregular beating is known as fibrillation. When the heart beats irregularly, it is unable to contract and push blood throughout the body. With less blood flowing to the brain, brain cells are damaged. The brain then sends signals that cause the body to shake uncontrollably.

Since cocaine is addictive, strong cravings follow after the euphoric high of 5 to 20 minutes is over. The sudden crash and depressed feelings trigger the intense desire to have another high and another and on and on. Potential serious problems related to cocaine use include these facts: Users have been known to develop paranoia after long term daily use and hallucinations similar to LSD reactions. Repeated use, as reported by

3. *American Health*, June 1987.

the *New York Times* can also result in extreme restlessness, anxiety, hyperactivity, weight loss, sleep loss, nasal injury, impotence, orgasmic failure, stomach problems and perhaps liver and lung damage.[4]

Other effects of cocaine include physical changes such as: insomnia, pale skin color, uncontrolled tremors, aggressive behavior, nausea and vomiting, racing heartbeat, vitamin depletion, fatigue, cold sweats, headaches, dilated pupils, hoarseness and loss of consciousness.[5]

Among the psychological effects are arrogance or over-confidence, poor concentration, confusion, loss of drive and ambition, change in personality, a strong tendency to lie, withdrawal from normal daily activities, irritability, and high risk for mental illness due to brain chemistry changes. Personal and social problems include participation in illegal activities to obtain the drug, stealing from family and friends to support the addiction, job and career problems, deterioration of personal relationships and involvement in traffic accidents.

Findings by researchers in a review of records at San Francisco General Hospital going back seven years on 1,212 cocaine users — who went to the hospital for a variety of reasons — disclosed that 145 patients reported neurological problems such as seizures and 92 displayed psychiatric impairment.[6] The study was conducted by Dr. Daniel Lowenstein, chief resident in neurology at San Francisco General, who presented the results in 1987 at a meeting of the American Academy of Neurology. Observations showed psychological derangements among patients judged from behavior that was highly anxious, agitated, or assaultive. Some patients were fully deluded, or psychotic, or were hallucinating, and others were deeply depressed. Neurological impairment includes epileptic-like seizures, stroke, severe headaches and blurred or faded vision.

In a related development, Dr. Nancy M. Newman, ophthalmologist at Pacific Presbyterian Medical Center in San Francisco, and four colleagues, Drs. David A. DiLoreto, James T. Ho, James C. Klein and Neal S. Birnbaum, reported to the American Medical

4. Reprinted in the *San Francisco Chronicle*, May 31, 1984.
5. *Cocaine, The Great Addicter*, a pamphlet published by Committees of Correspondence, Inc., rev. edition, January 1986.
6. "San Francisco Doctors Find Brain Damage in 2 of 10 Cocaine Users," *San Francisco Chronicle*, April 9, 1987.

Association the newly noted optical hazard of heavy cocaine sniffing. Their report appeared in the *Journal* of the American Medical Association. In an interview, Newman explained that the optic nerves pass through the two cavities called ethmoid sinuses that are located deep behind the nose, where cocaine tightly constricts the tiny blood vessels. The drug dries up mucus secretions in the region and the constriction of the blood vessels causes the equivalent of a series of "little strokes." Repeated "little strokes" cutting off blood supply in the bony sinuses had inflamed and actually dissolved the bone in her 43-year-old patient who snorted cocaine every day for 15 years straight. It also destroyed the cartilage known as the septum that separates his nostrils. The result is destruction of the optic nerve and potential blindness. The physicians feel that even far less heavy use of the drug can lead to serious vision problems.[7]

The lure of white lines and smooth mirrors has led many on the path to nothingness. Andy Gibb, superstar at age 19, blew his fortune on cocaine and died; Quaaludes helped cause the death of Freddie Prinze, a promising young actor. "No one is immune to this savage infection," writes Henry Hurt, "not the strong, not the wealthy, not the gifted. Even when cocaine does not kill the body, it devours the spirit, sucking every morsel of dignity and self-respect, often bringing an agony much worse than death." Peggy Mann, a regular writer on the drug scene has this to say: "Today's $50-billion-a-year cocaine traffic leaves behind thousands of ruined lives, medical problems ranging from heart damage to pulmonary disorders to scrambled genes and severe psychosis, and countless deaths." Her statement is reaffirmed by Kathleen R. O'Connell, an experienced drug counselor who writes: "Too many people are dying from cocaine addiction ... too many people are suffering disabilities including brain hemorrhages and strokes."[8]

As a final note on the devastating effects of cocaine addiction, let's listen to John Kelly, a recovering cocaine addict, writing on the lure of the drug culture.[9]

7. "Cocaine Can Cause Blindness, San Francisco Doctors Warn," David Perlman, Science Editor, *San Francisco Chronicle*, January 1, 1988.
8. *End of the Line: Quitting Cocaine*, Kathleen R. O'Connell, 1985.
9. "Who's cool today — and who isn't," *U.S. News & World Report*, April 20, 1987. John Kelly works as a drug-abuse counselor at Raritan Bay Medical Center in Perth Amboy, N.J.

Who's Cool Today — And Who Isn't

First, let me mention a few names: There was David Kennedy, the son of Bobby. And Len Bias, the great basketball player from the University of Maryland. And John Belushi, the actor and comedian. And famous musicians such as Jimi Hendrix and Janis Joplin. And let's not forget Ronald Roberts, the son of TV evangelist Oral Roberts.

By now, I guess you know what these people had in common. What a waste! God only knows what their accomplishments and contributions would have been if they had lived. Drugs aren't prejudiced; they will kill anyone regardless of race, color, religion or social status.

A few years ago I thought I was pretty cool. I had a thriving business, plenty of cash and a nice big car. I went to a lot of clubs, and I bought a lot of drinks for a lot of people. I enjoyed acting like a big shot. But I hung around with a wild crowd, and I started using drugs. The upshot is that I lost everything and almost died.

Today I'm a cocaine addict in recovery. "Recovery" means that I don't use drugs any more. But if I am around drugs or if I associate with people who use them, there's a damn good chance I will start using again — and this time I'll die. I was lucky, but I wasn't very cool or very smart.

Do you know who's cool today? The people who don't use drugs or hang around with those who do. It's more than just saying "No" to drugs; it's staying away from those who use them. I believe that Kennedy, Bias, Belushi, Joplin and all the rest would be alive today if they had not been hanging around people who thought they were cool because they did drugs. Let's face it: They didn't wake up one morning to find the tooth fairy had left a bag of drugs under their pillows.

What I'm trying to say is: Don't think that drug-using friends are cool just because they've got hot cars and loads of money. These people are very smart and very sneaky. They'll try to make you feel important. And I'm sure you understand why: If they can get you hooked on drugs that will help them support their own habits, they'll deal to you in a minute.

The people who are cool today are those who live in the here and now, facing up to life with its good times and its bad. And remember that when the bad times come — and they will — it's O.K. to ask for advice or help. Ask your parents or someone in your family. And if no one in your family can help, go to a church and ask for help from the clergy or counselors. Go anywhere to get your answers, but please don't go to drugs. Because when you get to the end of the road and quit using, your problems will still be there. And they'll be a thousand times worse. Take my word for that!

— Pharmaceutical Frankenstein —

"What about the new drugs coming," asks Bill Moyers, "those cheap but stronger synthetic drugs that loom in our future like a pharmaceutical Frankenstein? Which one of us can be sure we're not the next monster or victim?"[10] Moyers is referring to illegal drugs that underground chemists have manufactured, producing analogs known as "designer drugs" by modifying and altering the molecular structure of organic chemicals. One such drug — and one of the most powerful and addictive — is crack, the street name given to tiny chunks or rocks of freebase cocaine, a "designer" coke, a purified, highly potent cocaine distillate. It is a smokeable form of the drug extracted from cocaine hydrochloride powder in a simple chemical procedure using baking soda, heat and water. Crack, because of the way it is taken, is more insidious and more toxic than cocaine and highly addictive. And, because it is cheap, dealers prefer to sell crack rather than cocaine powder. Crack's unit cost is between $5 and $20 for a vial versus $50 to $100 for a gram of powder. The affordability of this drug intensifies its already grave danger to young people who can get hooked easily because of its highly addictive nature, and can stay easily supplied because of its low cost.

With the advent of crack and its enormous profits reaped by drug dealers and pushers, underground labs have fast become a multi-billion-dollar business — and hence the unstoppable proliferation of more designer drugs in the future. We don't know for sure what is being concocted in those laboratories or even where they are — these illegal operations may be closer to our own streets than we might think, in our neighbor's yacht, motorhome, in the back of a van or pickup truck, in a basement or backyard shed.

Nationwide, state and Federal authorities raided 647 clandestine drug labs during 1987, an increase from 479 during 1986. Three-quarters of those labs were located in Southern California. "We're dealing with a situation here that's not Colombia or

---

10. "48 Hours On Crack Street," op. cit.

the Golden Triangle," says Gilbert Bruce of the U.S. Drug Enforcement Administration's drug-lab task force. "It's right here.
We should be able to control it, but we're having a hell of a time.
The number of labs we're taking off [raiding] is growing by 50
percent a year."[11] Laboratories are springing up everywhere
and are inventing synthetics and derivatives faster than they
can be outlawed. The drugs mentioned in this chapter and
throughout the book are presented in table form in Appendix A,
with information regarding their substance and effects. We'll
take a quick look here at the more spectacular ones.

— Known Designer Drugs —

China White. It first hit the street in 1979 in Southern California,
where a pack of this white powdered substance was discovered
to be an analog of Fentanyl, a narcotic painkiller and believed
to be the first synthetic heroin to appear on the scene. Hal
Straus, a freelance writer specializing in medicine and science,
wrote:

"The appearance and euphoric effects of heroin and de-
signer-fentanyl were almost identical but there was a difference: Fentanyl packed from 20 to 2,000 times the wallop of
heroin. Novice or low-grade users who unknowingly shot
their normal doses soon discovered that the designer-fen-
tanyl was completely lethal."[12]

MPTP. In 1982 another synthetic heroin appeared in Northern
California. This one didn't kill, it crippled. Users arrived at a San
Jose hospital paralyzed, twisted, unable to speak — victims of
brain damage similar to advanced-stage Parkinson's disease.
After exhaustive laboratory investigation, neurologists ana-
lyzed the culprit as MPTP, an analog of meperidine, another
narcotic painkiller commonly known under the trade name
Demerol — it had turned seven people into living mannequins.

Black Beauties and Pink Hearts. Beautiful names and deadly as
their companions known as christmas trees, white crosses and
purple pyramids. They are analogs of amphetamines, stimulant
drugs that are manufactured legally and illegally in laboratories.
One type of amphetamine called "crank" (methamphetamine)

11. "National Affairs," *Newsweek*, April 25, 1988.
12. "From Crack to Ecstasy," Hal Straus, *American Health*, June 1987.

DON'T WRECK IT WITH DRUGS

Your body is one of the most finely-tuned machines in existence. But tinker with drugs and it may never run the same again. So don't let drugs wreck your future. A message of concern from the United States Marine Corps. **Stay in shape. Stay off drugs.**

MARINES

has achieved widespread popularity and is sold for $50-$80 a gram. Crank is often sold in ⅛, ¹⁄₁₆ and ¹⁄₃₂ of a gram and thus is affordable to teenagers. The present street quality of amphetamines ranges from 5 to 10 percent pure; the remainder may contain substances such as caffeine, ephedrine, and PPA (phenylpropanolamine, a nasal decongestant), which are over-the-counter stimulants.

A user taking a small dose of amphetamines (about 10-30 mg.) feels wakeful and alert, while his/her concentration level and ability to physically perform simple tasks may be increased. One may also experience euphoria and an increase of initiative, confidence and psychomotor activity. Others may feel nervous, jittery and become easily agitated. Its side effects: Amphetamines raise blood pressure and pulse, enlarge or irritate nasal and bronchial passages when inhaled, slightly increase body temperature, decrease sleep including REM — rapid eye movement — sleep. They can cause painful urination and constipation, nausea and diarrhea. Those using large doses, generally over ½ gram per day, over two weeks ("speed runs") may suffer from weight loss, malnutrition, lack of sleep, paranoia and may experience a psychotic episode. Oftentimes these speed runs are followed by a day or two of deep sleep, depression and craving for the drug. Association has been made between high dose use and violent behavior. Amphetamines or any other psychoactive drug used intravenously present a serious medical threat, especially to the heart.[13] Another analog of amphetamines is called MDMA, better known by its street name "ecstasy". It is a mild psychedelic, similar in effect to mescaline and LSD yet reportedly without visual hallucinations.

Two years ago, in what became a nationwide drug scare, a typewritten letter was sent to parents which came from schools and church groups across the nation. It was a warning guaranteed to strike fear in their hearts concerning "Blue Star," LSD-soaked blue stars affixed to strips of white paper. Some of the letters described Blue Star as a kind of tattoo, so that the LSD would be absorbed through the skin; others were designed with comic-book characters which would make them appealing to young children.

---

13. "Amphetamines," *New Connections* newsletter, Drug Education Program and Counselling, October 1985.

It turned out to be a hoax, although nobody was able to pinpoint the original source of the documents. Whether it is true or not, the potential for designer drugs or analog possibilities in a variety of forms is virtually limitless. "Blue Star" or whatever exotic ideas that could appear may have been on the drawing boards of underground labs a long time ago. Blue Star furor may have been the idea of some concerned citizens or could have been the schemes of the marketing strategists in the underground labs. With the event dissipated and totally forgotten now — then the hoax could become a reality. The boy who cried wolf may serve as a lesson to all so we may not be caught off guard when it happens for real.

As Hal Straus observed: "The same natural laws that provide the molecular backdrop for medicine create the context for thousands of drugs of medical use and for thousands of drugs of recreational abuse."

— The Myth of a "Harmless" Drug —

Marijuana is the common name for a crude drug made from the plant *cannabis sativa*. Many "experts" from the drug culture have been advising parents and children that it's a relatively "harmless" drug and its use is a normal part of adolescence. "These twin ideas," says Dr. Robert L. DuPont, Jr., "are among the most dangerous pieces of information in our society."

Is marijuana a "soft" and "harmless" drug, as pro-pot lobbyists have been advocating for decades? Is it just a "harmless giggle" to many of the young users? Where does the truth really lie? Upon closer examination, in the light of what we know now, its myth of harmlessness disappears into smoke.

To date, there are "over 8,000 published scientific papers," says Peggy Mann, "that clearly show that marijuana damages brain cells, the lungs, the immune system, has impairing effects on the reproductive system, the fetus and newborn of a pot-smoking pregnant woman, has serious psychological effects, impairs driving, etc."[14]

14. "Reasons to Oppose Legalizing Illegal Drugs," Peggy Mann, Committees of Correspondence Newsletter, September, 1988. Also see other effects of Marijuana or Cannabis in the Appendices.

Dr. Carlton Turner, former director of the National Institute on Drug Abuse (NIDA) Marijuana Research Project at the University of Mississippi once said: "There is no other drug used or abused by man that has the staying power and broad cellular actions on the body that cannabis does."[15] Zig Ziglar expressed his disappointment on the lack of knowledge of many parents and youngsters on the dangers of marijuana: "The incredible damage done by marijuana and the appalling, almost total, ignorance of kids and their parents about the devastating, irreversible damage caused by smoking pot are shocking to me. I challenge you, even plead with you, to become informed on the subject. There is far more misinformation about pot than about any other drug in America."

What is marijuana? It is not a simple or single chemical drug like PCP, LSD, cocaine or alcohol. Its wide range of effects on body and mind is caused by the complex chemicals unique to the marijuana plant. It is a *chemical factory* by itself. In its unburned state, it contains over 400 chemicals, especially the 60 or so that are unique to it — the *cannabinoids*. "As the dried plant is burned to make smoke," says Dr. DuPont, "it produces more than 2,000 chemicals which, with every puff, are brought into the smoker's body and distributed to every cell" — and he challenges everyone to give this sobering fact a thought:

> Pause and think for a moment about what 2,000 uniquely different chemicals may possibly do to the human body. Imagine, if you can, the prodigious research task required to identify and understand the far-reaching effects of such an intake. Think especially about the problem of understanding the *long-term* effects of prolonged use of this multi-chemical drug. Weigh also the challenge of understanding the combined effects of multiple drug use, since most marijuana users also use other drugs in combination with cannabis. Any thinking we may do about the hazardous effects of marijuana on humans is complicated by another worrisome fact: Over the last decade, we have had tremendous increases in the potency of marijuana.[16]

15. Ibid.
16. *Getting Tough on Gateway Drugs*, Robert L. DuPont, Jr., 1984, p. 67.

Some facts on the findings about marijuana's strength and potency:

⇨ The tar content in a marijuana joint is anywhere from 7 to 20 times the tar content of an ordinary cigarette. Think about what it does to the trachea and the bronchi — the tubes leading into the lungs — and the eventual damage to the lungs. Dr. David L. Ohlms, medical consultant to the Missouri Division of Alcoholism and Drug Abuse, wrote: "In the 1980s we're seeing young people in their 20s or 30s — even kids in their teens ... come in breathing like old men and women. They have severe emphysema. When I measure lung capacity, I'll find that 50-60-70% of the lung tissue is gone — that is, irreparably destroyed which means that the patient will have to live whatever life he's got left as an invalid ... I think we're also going to see a lot more lung cancer in pot smokers since we're talking about the same process, tars and irritation of lung tissue."[17]

⇨ The carcinogens benzanthracene and benzopyrene are present in marijuana smoke in amounts 50 to 70 percent greater than in the smoke of cigarettes. Both smokes — a typical unfiltered U.S. tobacco cigarette and a marijuana joint — contain roughly equal amounts of such irritants and gaseous toxic agents as carbon monoxide, ammonia, acetone and benzene.[18] (Note: The study comparison was done in 1971-74. In the early 1970s, the THC potency of street pot was much lower than it is today.)

⇨ A noted researcher, Dr. Sidney Cohen, points out: "We should not forget that it takes 20 to 30 years of consistent heavy use of tobacco to produce a lung cancer. We have been smoking marijuana heavily in the U.S. for a decade or less ... There is real reason for concern that marijuana alone, or marijuana smoked with tobacco, will bring forth a new wave of lung cancer in another 10 to 20 years."[19]

17. *Pot*, David L. Ohlms, M.D., 1983, p. 5.
18. "Marijuana Alert II: More of the Grim Story," Peggy Mann, *Reader's Digest*, November 1980.
19. "Marijuana: The Myth of Harmlessness Goes Up in Smoke," Peggy Mann, reprint from *The Saturday Evening Post*, 1980.

➪ In studies published in February 1980, [20] Dr. Gary Huber, director of the Smoking and Health Research Program of Harvard University, showed that marijuana activates — by some 200 percent — enzymes which contribute to the "eating" or digesting of the lung tissue.

➪ The average strength of marijuana has increased by 500 percent over the last 20 years as reported by the American Council for Drug Education.[21]

➪ THC (delta-9-tetrahydrocannabinol), marijuana's main ingredient, produces most of the mind-altering and psychoactive effects. Street pot contains 60 other toxic molecules which have not been sufficiently studied. The average concentration of THC by weight has increased from about 1 percent or less in the 1960s and 1970s to anywhere from 4 percent to 10 percent in the 1980s. "The delta-9-THC content of sinsemilla marijuana grown in California was assayed at 11 to 14 percent,"[22] writes Dr. Robert G. Heath, a noted neurologist, and Chairman of the Scientific Advisory Board of the American Council on Marijuana.

➪ The Marijuana Research Project at the University of Mississippi grows cannabis for use by researchers. "But all the sobering results," wrote Peggy Mann, "which accrue from this research were formulated using cannabis with a THC potency of 2 percent or less. Any higher potency, says the government (NIDA), would be too dangerous for experimentation with human subjects."[23]

➪ Marijuana differs in one important aspect from all other psycho-active drugs. All the others are water soluble and excreted from the body rather rapidly because "our bodies," says Dr. DuPont, "have a water-based waste disposal system of blood, urine, sweat, and feces. When we take in chemicals that do not dissolve in water, they remain trapped in our bodies." By contrast, THC is strongly fat

---

20. Ibid.
21. *Marijuana and You — Myth and Fact*, by the American Council for Drug Education, 1982.
22. "Marijuana and the Brain," Robert G. Heath, M.D., D.M. Sci., reprint from Committees of Correspondence, Inc. newsletter.
23. "Reasons to Oppose Legalizing Illegal Drugs," Ibid.

soluble and is stored in the fatty tissues of the body. It is called lipophilic, meaning "fat-loving." The most fatty tissues are the lungs, the liver, adrenal glands, kidneys, bone marrow, testicles, ovaries, and the brain.

⇨ By 1982, 57 million Americans had used marijuana at least once.[24] "According to government surveys," reported Dr. Heath, "15 million people in the United States now use marijuana regularly. Moreover, as the pursuit of pleasure has intensified, most smokers have sought increasingly stronger marijuana. And some smokers, still not satisfied, are using other pleasure-inducing drugs as well. In addition to the psychological factors, the drive for stronger pleasure-inducing drugs results from the fact that stimulation of the brain mechanisms for pleasure is, in time, depleting."[25]

⇨ There is a concern that a drug-induced loss of brain cells of 20-30 percent, combined with a similar loss through normal aging, might cause a rise in conditions similar to Parkinson's disease at an earlier age, wrote Dr. Marvin Snyder of the National Institute on Drug Abuse.[26] "There was abundant evidence of diminished academic performance among users," observes Dr. Heath, "and acute psychotic behavior resembling schizophrenic psychosis was being reported, in addition to disturbances in motivation and impairment of memory. Finally, there were reports of gross brain aberrations."

How does this happen, especially the impairment of our cognitive functions (including learning and memory)? To understand this, let's look at some known facts about how THC affects the brain cells. Dr. Robert C. Gilkeson, adolescent neuropsychiatrist and brain researcher, explains:[27]

No chemical can alter your mood, your feelings, your coordination, or your behavior unless it has altered the cells in your brain and disrupted their normal chemical function. Before using a drug of any kind, one should know what chemicals it contains,

24. *Getting Tough on Gateway Drugs*, op. cit., p. 64.
25. "Marijuana and the Brain," op. cit.
26. "THC in Pot Eats Away at Brain Cells," *San Francisco Examiner*, September 25, 1987.
27. "Marijuana: Myths and Misconceptions," Robert C. Gilkeson, M.D., reprint from Committees of Correspondence, Inc., newsletter.

which cells in your brain it most affects, and what brain cell chemistry it changes.

The wall — or the membrane — that surrounds every cell is composed of fat (lipid) molecules and complex protein molecules. These molecules form an intricate membrane around each cell arranged in patterns specific to each cell type, according to its functions and its specific needs.

All the chemicals providing the energy necessary to keep each cell alive must somehow pass through this membrane into the cell, and the waste products from its metabolism must exit through these membrane molecules back into the circulation.

This constant movement of chemicals in and out of the membrane occurs through submicroscopic channels between the lipid or the protein molecules specifically assigned for them. Marijuana contains 421 bioactive chemical molecules. Sixty-one are called cannabinoids, which are extremely soluble in fat, or lipid, molecules. When inhaled or ingested, these cannabinoids become absorbed by, and remain imbedded in, the lipids in the membrane of every cell in the body. Since they are of no chemical use to the cell and are hidden from the water-soluble enzymes outside the cell membrane, the cannabinoids are not broken down, but remain imbedded there for months at a time.

Whenever you smoke marijuana at a rate faster than the cannabinoid molecules can be eliminated, they accumulate in the membrane, leaving it in a chronic state of saturation. As they accumulate one after the other in the membrane, they increasingly prevent the passage of those chemicals which must enter and leave the cell. Progressively robbed of such nutrients, cells become starved and slowly lose their energy.

Saturated membranes may not lose the cannabinoids for nine months or more. Smoking marijuana faster than your cells can eliminate the cannabinoids leads to the saturation of the cell membrane. As they accumulate, cannabinoids interfere more and more with the cell's metabolism, decrease its energy and growth, and retard the development of every cellular system.

The most important, the most specialized, the most complex, and the most fragile cells in the body are the 100 billion cells of the human brain, called *neurons*. These cells make 100 trillion connections or *synapses* along which chemical messages are passed.

The purpose of these messages is to keep track of all the other cells in the body, to keep them functioning properly, and to keep them alive. Internal messages relate the needs of the cells in the body. External messages tell us everything going on in the "outside world." The brain "reads" these messages, analyzes them, then plans and initiates the correct movements, the glandular secretions, and the other functions to meet those needs.

To pass accurate messages, sodium, potassium, calcium, chlorides, and the complex messenger chemicals called *neurotransmitters* must all go in and out through their membrane channels in the correct amounts, in 0.4-1.0 thousandth of a second. Because of their chemical complexity, their constant activity, and the speed at which they must operate, *substances which block membranes affect neurons more than any other cells in the body.*

The center of the brain coordinating the interaction of all the other brain centers and controlling the amount of brain energy is called the *Reticular Activating System* or the RAS. Since it makes the most connections and is always in operation, it is the most saturated and affected of all the centers. This center controls how alert we are and the level of our "consciousness." When the energy of the RAS is decreased, the energy of the entire cortex is lowered. This activating system turns *on* and increases, or turns *off* and decreases, the chemical messages between areas of the brain that regulate the very level and complexity of human thought and behavior. It regulates the intensity of messages between the centers for memory, the center for feelings, and the center for analyzing all the messages from inside and outside the body. This information in turn triggers necessary motor behavior or glandular activity. The less energy flowing in the neuronal circuits, the less rich and sensitive our feelings will become and the less clear our imagination, plans, and ideas will be.

More simply, *the less energy available to run our brains, the more stupid we become.*

"Today's pot smoker," says Dr. Nahas, "may not only be damaging his own mind and body, but may be playing genetic roulette and casting a shadow across children and grandchildren yet unborn."[28] And from the findings of the scientific community, there is no question that marijuana wreaks a havoc in the human mind and body that is difficult to reverse. And "the research which is still going on," writes Otto Moulton, "shows far more serious effects, effects which could make the next generations of Americans not only the listless ones, but the last ones."[29]

28. "Marijuana Alert: Brain and Sex Damage," Peggy Mann, *Reader's Digest*, 1979.
29. *Papers on Drug Abuse*, Otto Moulton, 1983, p.2.

— A Continuing Challenge —

"The condition upon which God has given liberty to man [and woman] is eternal vigilance," wrote John Philpot Curran, the great Irish statesman.

To be vigilant is timely advice and a challenge to each and every American to be constantly aware of outright lies emanating from pro-pot organizations and their representatives. The drug information, for years, has been industriously filled with misinformation, distortion and twisting of facts and the discrediting of available scientific findings. The objective is to make marijuana seem the harmless ingredient of the "now" way of life.

"The 20 year 'partisan politicization' of marijuana has led to the dangerous, wholly illogical, but still widely accepted misconception that marijuana is the least harmful of all the 'recreational' neurotoxic drugs," observes Dr. Gilkeson. And the same thinking pervades the drug culture regarding the use of drugs. As a challenge, especially to us parents, we have to be alert for contradictory messages that writers in the pro-drug culture are bombarding us with. One common ploy used by these writers is to give pro-drug messages and then cover their tracks by including "cautions" about using drugs or about how to use them. Another is by glamorizing drug use by describing wonderful feelings associated with the drug use while minimizing its harmful effects.

We should watch out for "warning flag" phrases they commonly use in their talks and writings. There is no such thing as "responsible" use of drugs. The use of illegal drugs is irresponsible and harmful to health. There is no such thing as "the child's own decision" to experiment in drugs. Children have yet to learn the meaning of responsibility and it's the parents' responsibility to provide them with correct and updated information, to teach children to make decisions for which they are responsible and accountable. Children do not "experiment" with drugs, nor do adults, as scientists experiment with substances. The only place for experimentation is a laboratory. There is no such thing as "recreational" or "social" use of drugs. Using illegal drugs is not an acceptable form of recreation and they are anti-social and destroy families, friendships and the society in general. There are no "soft" or "harmless" drugs. They are all toxic which means they are all poisons to the human body. Any illegal drug that is inhaled, injected or ingested in the body is poison — plain and simple. Use of illegal drugs is never okay and any use is abuse. Who can control the contents of illegal drugs and their addictive qualities? There is no such thing as a "meaningful" or "intelligent" or "good" relationship with drugs. Meaningful, intelligent and good relationships do not end up in the loss of drive and ambition nor in depression, addiction and sometimes self-destruction.

Another ploy used by the drug culture is to compare medications like aspirin, caffeine or even chocolate with illegal mind-altering drugs. There are vast differences here and this approach gives a message that dangerous drugs have a benign quality like the substances they are compared with. The expression that "there are no good or bad drugs, just improper use," is often found in pro-drug literature, which serves to confuse the reader and minimize the very distinct chemical differences among substances. Another scheme that the pro-drug culture uses is to disseminate information that scientific findings on the dangers of drugs are scare tactics. The truth is: *Scientific research results are not scare tactics. Facts are facts and children, as well as adults, need to know the truth.*

What's the "hidden agenda" behind this drive to "poison" the minds of our youth with lies and misinformation, and the equally strong drive to legalize marijuana and other illegal drugs?

Consider the following facts about why "there is a movement of people out there," according to Beverly Kinnard, "who truly want to get our kids involved in illegal drugs."[30]

⇨ Thousands of professional farmers, many of them in Northern California, have transformed American "homegrown" from a cottage industry into a multi-billion-dollar-a-year agribusiness. These knowledgeable farmers use sophisticated techniques like hydroponics (rooting plants in chemical solutions instead of soil) to cultivate pot powerful enough to command high prices — more than $100 an ounce in big cities.[31]

---

30. From an address at Marijuana Dependence: A National Conference, October 3-4, 1986, San Francisco, Calif.
31. "Marijuana: Should We Worry About It?" Winifred Gallagher, *This World*, July 17, 1988, *San Francisco Chronicle & Examiner.*

⇨ Gross misinformation has come from organizations whose funding derives from those who are intent on either decriminalizing or legalizing marijuana use in the country. The majority, and in many cases, the entire selection of books on marijuana to be found in most of our school libraries today originates from organizations such as STASH, Do It Now Foundation, The National Organization for the Reform of Marijuana Laws (NORML), and others who consistently ignore the research done by hundreds of scientists all over the country who have shown by one study after another just how dangerous a substance marijuana really is.[32]

⇨ The marijuana advocates admit decriminalization of the marijuana laws is just one step in their attempt to legalize marijuana completely. Their next goal is to throw out laws against possession altogether, to remove penalties for cultivation ... and they are beginning to ask why it is a crime to sell marijuana if it is not a crime to possess bought marijuana. The more widespread the use of marijuana, the easier it is to convince society of the need to soften the laws.[33]

⇨ There is a decided attempt by pro-pot advocates to discredit and virtually censor the real facts about marijuana. The first scientist to study the effects of THC on the human immune system was Dr. Gabriel G. Nahas. His first book, *Marijuana: Deceptive Weed*, published in 1972, by the prestigious *New England Journal of Medicine* was, for reasons best known to the editors, given to NORML advisory board member Dr. Lester Grinspoon for review; Grinspoon wrote that the book was filled with "half-truths, innuendos and unverifiable assertions ... psychopharmacological McCarthyism." Another book, *Keep Off the Grass*, on the health hazards of marijuana published in 1976 and intended for the general public, was reviewed by another NORML advisory board member, Dr. Norman Zinberg, who gave the usual unfair review, reflecting his lack of knowledge about the dangers of drugs. Nahas' latest book, *Marijuana in Science and Medicine*, (1984) was again given by the *New England Journal of Medicine* to Dr. Andrew Weil, another

32. *Papers on Drug Abuse*, op. cit.
33. *Sensual Drugs*, op. cit., p. 277.

NORML spokesman who gave it a particularly unprofessional review. It is sad when a major medical journal acts as spokesman for the commercialized, criminal drug culture.[34]

⇨ A man named Arthur Lesberg, from the state of Massachusetts, and head of a drug counselling program, testified at the State Capitol that making the sale of drug paraphernalia illegal would not stop drug abuse. Yet this same individual *runs* a Drug Rehabilitation Center and also *owns* two headshops in Boston, where this paraphernalia is sold![35]

We see clearly from these random facts that the bottom line in the hidden agenda of the drug culture is economics — money. The illegal drug industry is a big, bad, merciless business. It is a multi-billion dollar empire.

The interests of those who deliberately sow confusion in the minds of our young people, and the public in general, are threatened by the hard facts of scientific findings. As a result, we see among these pro-drug advocates the prevalent attitude known as the "flat earth syndrome." They spread the same attitude to affect the lives of marijuana "customers" who are led to believe what they ought not to believe despite the availability of scientific evidence.

We have a big job to do. We must all face the same direction and share the burden of social responsibility and discipline. That's what "We the People" means. When crisis descends upon us, as the drug plague in our midst, that phrase offers both inspiration and challenge to take that kind of responsibility and concern for today's young people and the future of Americans yet to be born.

"We are at war," says President George Bush. "Drugs are a terrifying, insidious enemy ... Defeatism and despair about drugs will not do."

Drugs are a dead-end street. We cannot allow drugs to wreck our lives and the future of our children. We cannot let America down.

This is our continuing challenge.

34. *A Man of our Time,* Thomas Gleaton, Ed.D., The National Parents' Resource Institute for Drug Education, Inc., distributed by the Committees of Correspondence, Inc.
35. *Papers on Drug Abuse*, op. cit.

3

THE MERCENARY AGGRESSORS

*Drug pushers have one thing going for them: they can
dream — of wealth, of escape, of a different life. Not
so the unfortunates they prey upon — whose dreams
have long since disintegrated into nightmares.*

— *New York Times*

— The Rogues' Gallery —

The underworld of the illicit drug business is crowded with
criminals ranging from novices, unskilled amateurs and vicious
gangs to well-entrenched, powerful organizations such as the
Mexican and Colombian cartels. The only motive is sheer greed
without regard to the harm done to the individual or society.
Operating inside and outside the continental United States, they
are responsible for the outflow of staggering amounts of money
which causes a massive drain on the American economy. There
can be no doubt that this mindless spending on drugs by our
fellow Americans leads to worse social conditions and endless
suffering for those who are caught in the crossfire of the drug
wars.

The vast cocaine, heroin and marijuana distribution machin-
ery in the U.S. is growing at an alarming rate. There is not a single
community which is not besieged by one or more of these
mercenary factions. In New York alone, 20,000 to 30,000 small-
time dealers operate efficiently, backed by the resources of
large organizations. Drug fighters are convinced that as long as
this distribution network remains intact, our war against drugs
is doomed to failure.

Who are the people who deal in this deadly commodity and,
to a great extent, do so unmolested? In some places they operate
almost hassle-free. They have made drugs so available without

problem that a recent magazine article noted: "In the typical heartland city, there is nothing dramatic about the drug problem. It has simply proved insoluble."[1]

They operate like legitimate capitalists but with little or no capital outlay or risk. They are bold and arrogant, contemptuous of the law. They are intelligent, smart and cunning — using young people to peddle their poisons knowing in most cases that when arrested, these young runners and lookouts frequently will be released on their own recognizance. They know that jails are overcrowded and the criminal court system is so overloaded it has no ability to prosecute the hordes of young offenders that are caught daily. Their business doesn't need advertising budgets — their products sell themselves. Customers usually go out of their way to find them — a back alley, a streetcorner, a clammy tenement, an abandoned building or a garbage-strewn lot. The customers, mostly middle and upper income earners, are not picky about the place to get their "goods." Most of the transactions are done openly and unabashedly. Dealers know they have a perfect product on hand and a captive clientele to sell to on a daily basis.

Those chiefly responsible for the vast distribution of illicit drugs in the U.S. comprise the following individuals, groups and organizations:

The Amateur. The lure of fast and enormous profits has enticed a number of professionals into the drug trafficking business: diplomats, servicemen, lawyers, doctors, pharmacists, airline pilots, investment bankers and businessmen, as well as students and sales clerks — for one simple reason: greed. Some have abandoned their practices or professions and are dealing full-time, realizing a 500 percent return on their money in two to three months, simply from financing a little coke or heroin deal. Most are young and aggressive, in their early thirties; their clients belong to the upper middle income groups, mostly their peers in business. It's not unusual to see a real estate agent selling to the members of his or her profession, or a stock-broker drug dealer selling where the action is — Wall Street or other trading centers. Clientele are sophisticated and affluent, preferring cocaine. The age range of users, according to government

---

1. "Drugs on Main Street: The Enemy Up Close," *U.S. News & World Report*, June 27, 1988.

studies, is the late 20s to 30s. They are influential citizens and ultimately make up a wide range of buyers from the computer programmer who snorts with his pal the dentist, to a contractor who shoots up with his friendly grocerman. The clientele is vast — those tuned into the "high life" and the swaggering attitude of non-stop go-getters.

Street Peddlers and Dealers. He's male, young, 12 years to 20 years old, poor, a minority, Black or Hispanic, independent of authority, unskilled and uneducated with little if any hope for the future. His instincts for self-preservation are good. He is protective of his turf and could be predatory. He does not see his conduct as "wrong," is generally selling to make money and to support his own addiction, does not discriminate in his dealings among customers and has no regard for the effect his dealing has on others.

Human life, other than his own, is cheap and expendable. Addict customers cross both race and community lines, as most dealers peddle in middleclass suburbs. The cornerstone of their operation is supply — and lots of it. They are in touch constantly with wholesalers or sub-contractors whenever inventory diminishes and these wholesalers in turn are in close contact with the tight-knit U.S. distribution systems which comprise the numerous large organizations behind illegal trafficking. Aside from street hustling and selling, pushers maintain "dope houses" fully equipped with electronic surveillance equipment, gates, case-hardened locks and even lookouts who earn more than $100 a day. Dope houses are like hot-dog stands, springing up every other day on a different corner or section of town. They're evident in areas heavily infested by drug peddlers and dealers. You close one guy down, two days later he's back in operation again. It's called "being back in the box." The dealer just goes to court and he's back on the street the next day. Sometimes, even the same night.

They are leeches and hangers-on, especially to celebrities and superstar athletes whom they supply with drugs. They dress flashily, drive expensive cars and are frequently idolized by youngsters who crave the glamorous clothes, the fancy gold chains and jewelry that drug dealers have. Even in death the hero-worship continues, as in the funeral of Felix Mitchell, a reputed drug dealer in the city of Oakland. His funeral resembled a pageantry, replete with all the trimmings fit for royalty.

He seemed larger than life to kids who worked as lookouts for him and made him their hero, more grieved in death than Martin Luther King.

"Lookout" is the entry-level position for nine- and ten-year-olds who are lured into drug dealing to make money the quickest way. As *Time* reported:

> They make $100 a day warning dealers when police are in the area. Sometimes the pint-size apprentice is rewarded with the most fashionable sneakers, bomber jacket or bicycle. The next step up the ladder is runner, a job that can pay more than $300 a day. This is the youngster who transports the drugs to the dealers on the street from the makeshift factories. Finally, an enterprising young man graduates to the status of dealer, king of the street. In a hot market like New York City, an aggressive teenage dealer can make up to $3,000 a day.[2]

The Drug Gangs. Spurred on by the flourishing narcotics trade, they are transforming some of the country's toughest streets into ghetto-based drug trafficking organizations. Equally alarming is the fact that a number of these gangs have now established direct connections to major Colombian smugglers, resulting in more violent competition among gangs already infamous for violence. Consider the various gangs spread across the country as reported by *Newsweek* in a cover story:[3]

⇨ An estimated 70,000 gang members live in Los Angeles County. Despite years of experience combating street crime, few LA cops will deny that their war against the groups has taken a decisive turn for the worse. The gangs are better armed and more violent and more adept at evading the law. The two most notorious are the "Bloods" and the "Crips."

⇨ In Chicago, gang membership has now reached an estimated 13,000 after a lull in the 1970s. The infamous "El Rukns" are under active investigation for drug trafficking. Other gangs are the Cobras, Disciples, Latin Kings and Vice Lords.

⇨ In New York, where a rookie cop was assassinated by a cocaine kingpin's hit man, police are struggling to contain an explosion of drug-related violence that has left more than

2. "Kids Who Sell Crack," *Time*, May 9, 1988.
3. "The Drug Gangs, Waging War in American Cities," *Newsweek*, March 28, 1988.

500 persons dead in upper Manhattan during the past five years.

⇨ A Miami-based gang called the "Untouchables" is pushing crack northward to Atlanta, Savannah and other cities of the Southeast where the group is known and feared as the "Miami Boys." Another gang is called 34th Street Players.

⇨ Police from Boston to Houston are alarmed by the emergence of Jamaican gangs known as "posses." According to federal sources, there are 30 to 40 posses with a total of about 5,000 members now operating in the United States. In Kansas City, one posse at one time was operating 75 crack houses that grossed $400,000 a day. Clannish, cunning and extraordinarily violent, the Jamaicans are dominating the drug trade from Texas to Alaska. Well-known gangs are the Montego Bay, Reema, Riverton City, Shower, Spangler, Spanish Town, Tivoli Gardens and Waterhouse.

There are also other gangs, Black, Hispanic and Asian. The ghetto gangs' entry into drug trafficking on a major scale may be creating the nation's biggest crime problem in the coming decade. The extra level of violence in gang warfare, likened to a form of urban guerilla warfare over drug trafficking, can be attributed to the availability of military and paramilitary weapons. Guns like Uzis, AK-47 assault rifles and AR-15 semi-automatics are widely bought by gang members who finance their high-tech arsenals with profits from the drug trade. It is known that some of these gangs have sales totalling up to $1 million a week.

The proliferation of gangs, as in the case of Los Angeles with 600 known gangs, has resulted in a division of territories and an increase in violence. An ABC News special presented these facts: Gangs have carved up parts of Los Angeles into exclusive sales territories, often using graffiti on walls to mark their domain and warn others to stay away. But like successful businesses, they still compete for market share, often with violent consequences. Some 387 people died in Los Angeles in gang-related violence in 1987. The death toll is running even higher in 1988. They've pushed eastward, past the Rocky Mountains and as far as New Jersey, tripling, quadrupling their profits. In Kansas City, LA's "Crips" are competing with Jamaican gangs for drug dollars. They have appeared in Portland, Oregon with as many as 500 "Bloods" and "Crips," bringing with them fear and violence. They also have surfaced in Minneapolis. The Chicago gangs growing in numbers have shown up in Minneapolis and Milwaukee and even smaller towns like Racine, Wisconsin. The Miami Boys from Florida are moving their crack business through the Deep South and up the eastern seaboard. They have carved up Atlanta into five drug territories, each pulling in as much as $300,000 a day. The Jamaicans, an infamous group believed to be responsible for more than 800 homicides in the past three years, sell crack in 15 U.S. cities. And there is the Chambers gang of Detroit who run a multimillion dollar cocaine business; with that kind of money to be made, membership in such gangs is exploding, especially in the inner cities.[4]

It is evident that some gangs have quietly emerged as organized crime families. The Jamaican gangs, for example, have supplanted the Mafia as crime lords in Kansas City. Ronald Koziol, a reporter for the *Chicago Tribune*, wrote: "The Mafia family that once controlled the lucrative drug, sex and gambling rackets here is a shadow of its once powerful self since a series of federal convictions five years ago ... The Jamaicans are just one of several emerging groups moving into the crime vacuum created by the imprisonment and deaths of numerous longtime Mafia leaders and their trusted lieutenants. Other aspiring newcomers include Japanese, Chinese and Colombian crime organizations."[5]

There is every indication that the gang/drug problem will get worse. The emergence of drug gangs from coast to coast is very similar to what occurred during the early years of the Prohibition era when the Cosa Nostra, the Mafia, consolidated its status as an underworld cartel by building on the profits of illicit alcohol. Assessing the current problem *Newsweek* pointed out: "If the analogy to Prohibition is accurate, the gangs have only begun to consolidate their hold on drug trafficking — and given their growth so far, it seems reasonable to expect that they, like the Mafia before them, will become even more skillful in evading law enforcement."

The Mexican Mafiosos. During the past decades, complex crime organizations have been operating the illicit drug distribution

---

4. "Drugs: A Plague On The Land," op. cit.
5. In the *San Francisco Examiner*, March 28, 1988.

and for heroin in particular, which was typically "cooked" in Europe by highly skilled rogue chemists, then shipped across the Atlantic as a finished product, terminating at the "shooting galleries" of New York and other American cities. They have done business comparable to major conglomerates with unlimited financial resources, operating through legitimate business fronts, using warehouses and properties to further their illegitimate enterprises. For a long time they muscled their way as "bosses and kingpins" of the drug trafficking business, especially the vast heroin networks. New York, for example, has been the home of such infamous networks as those run by the French Connection, Auguste Ricord, Joseph Valachi, the Citroen and Jaguar cases and Vito Genovese — to name a few of the celebrated cases that have been broken one by one. Police victory in the 1970s however, in the case of the French Connection mob, proved to be temporary. Within a decade, members of the original gang were back on the heroin trail but the connection was severed once again in 1986 when drug agents broke up the $225 million heroin "deal of the decade." In human terms, as *Newsweek* reported: "That was enough to sell the city's 200,000 addicts more than one million fixes."[6]

In recent years, however, along U.S. borders guarded by DEA agents in what is known as the South Central Region, smuggling is a growth industry.[7] It is through these borders that Mexican heroin and marijuana find their way into the streets of the United States. Because of law enforcement pressure exerted in Florida and elsewhere on the East Coast, some traffickers of Colombian cocaine and marijuana also find their way in along the Texas Gulf Coast. The seizure of a cocaine cache at an international bridge (Ysleta) in El Paso was the largest ever on the U.S./Mexican border with an estimated street value of nearly $1 billion.[8] The seized cargo was hidden in a truck trailer compartment which contained 63 white plastic bales weighing 55 pounds each, and stacked about 10 feet high.

The Rio Grande in Starr County, Texas, has emerged as the hot corridor for drug runners and often the site of armed encounters between lawmen and well-organized, well-financed

6. "The Return of the French Connection," *Newsweek*, April 13, 1987.
7. *Drug Enforcement*, October 1979.
8. *San Francisco Examiner*, September 10, 1987.

narcotics rings. *Time* reported: "Nowhere is the traffic heavier than in Starr County, a remote, Rhode Island-sized expanse of gentle hills that flanks the Rio Grande southeast of Laredo. From heavily armed safe houses in tiny riverfront hamlets, smugglers oversee the packaging and shipment of drugs by truck and plane into the U.S. interior. By one federal estimate, 40 percent of all the drugs crossing South Texas move through Starr, sometimes amounting to 15 tons of marijuana and 1,000 pounds of coke a week ... Starr County's 92 miles of riverbank affords myriad landing points for rubber rafts and the human 'mules' who wade across with backpacks ... The drug trade is controlled by a dozen Mexican 'mafiosos,' some of whom live south of the border. The mafiosos are assuming new muscle as Mexico's economy declines and illegal aliens pour into Texas. Drug gangs have enlisted wetbacks as couriers, paying them $150 or more to float sacks of pot across the Rio Grande. Many illegals stay on to become full-time drug runners ... U.S. officials say rogue Mexican cops sometimes provide armed escorts for truckloads of dope moving north to the U.S."[9]

Corruption in the law enforcement establishment in Mexico was disclosed in an interview with *Time's* correspondent Elaine Shannon by a former consultant for Mexico's internal security police, the Direccion Federal de Seguridad (DFS).[10] He revealed stories of gunrunning, bribery, violence and death, much of it perpetrated by his old agency. One of the informant's intriguing disclosures concerns La Pipa (the Pipe), a smuggling operation carried on by the DFS. The revelation pointed to the agency's late 1970s activity where it acquired about 600 tanker trucks ferrying natural gas from the U.S. for sale in Mexico. On the northbound leg of the trip, DFS men packed the empty trucks with marijuana provided by Mexican dealers and ran ten to twelve trucks a day into Phoenix and Los Angeles. At the border, several Mexican officials and U.S. Customs personnel were bribed $50,000 a load to let the trucks pass.

Traffickers in Mexico cannot operate without the assistance of Mexican officials. As a result of DEA and Customs probes in Mexico, several senior officials have been linked to drug traffick-

9. "The Rio Grande's Drug Corridor," Richard Woodbury, *Time*, November 17, 1986.
10. "Police on the Take," *Time*, March 7, 1988.

ers. One cabinet-rank official is known to have accepted payoffs from dealers. Corruption appears rampant at the state level. One DEA investigation tied a large drug operator both socially and financially to five former state governors and at least one current governor. "Corruption has penetrated all levels of Mexican government," says a ranking U.S. law enforcement official. "It's vertical, it's horizontal and it's total." One of the biggest drug operators in Mexico is Caro Quintero who has been identified as the head of one of Mexico's five largest drug families, shepherding a narcotics empire that employs over 5,000 workers and is believed to have netted him more than $434 million in 1985 alone. Quintero, along with three former Mexican police officials, a commandante with the Mexican Federal Judicial Police and a police officer, were indicted in the murder of Enrique Camarena, a DEA agent.[11]

Elsewhere in Central America, a safe haven for traffickers is Honduras, whose officials also bear the taint of corruption. As one Honduran official charged: "The upper echelon of our military has been corrupted." But nowhere is corruption more complete than in Panama, about which *Time* has reported: "If Colombia's political leaders are being challenged by the drug dealers, some of Panama's leaders are the drug dealers." Panamanian military ruler General Manuel Antonio Noriega was indicted by a U.S. grand jury for drug smuggling and racketeering. A sealed indictment was returned after a one-year investigation. Floyd Carlton, Noriega's former personal pilot, who was convicted of drug trafficking charges, revealed that he flew more than $1 million in bribes to Noriega from Colombia's Medellin cocaine cartel. He also said Noriega had skimmed profits from cartel cocaine shipments as they passed through Panama. Jose Blandon, another former Noriega associate, has said members of the Medellin cartel had paid a $5 million bribe to Panama's top military leaders to open a drug-processing plant in Panama's Darien province. Witnesses who testified before Senator Kerry's subcommittee charged that Noriega and his cronies institutionalized corruption, putting the country's military services, corporations, banks and airfields at the disposal of the traffickers in exchange for hundreds of millions of dollars.

11. "Mexican Drug Lord Indicted," *San Francisco Chronicle*, January 7, 1988.

The International Mafia. International drug trafficking, especially of heroin, has come a long way since the French Connection case of the 1960s, the story of transoceanic narcotics smuggling which caught public attention in a hit movie about the Frenchman Jean Jehan. Celebrated in movies and books, the daring conspiracy shipped heroin from Marseilles to Manhattan until the police cut the link in the early 1970s. But the French Connection paled by comparison with the so-called Pizza Connection two decades later, when 22 persons were accused of masterminding a huge Sicilian-based heroin operation. The case earned its nickname from pizzerias in four states used as distribution points in the drug network. In five years, investigators estimated, the defendants smuggled into the U.S. 1,650 pounds of heroin, with a street value of $1.6 billion. Such was the well-organized network known as Pizza Connection One.

It was Pizza Connection Two that gave a severe blow to the Sicilian Mafia, one that practically decimated their ranks. FBI and DEA agents called the arrest of more than two hundred traffickers the "largest arrest ever to take place in the history of mankind."[12] It took three years of demanding undercover work from 1985 to 1988. With the help of local police, other federal agencies and most significantly, the authorities in Italy, the FBI did what it does best: It bypassed the street-corner pusher to reach the organizations that import and distribute drugs. Field agents for both the FBI and DEA got to the highest rungs of the ladder by working back up to get to the kingpins. The suspects were charged with importing heroin into the United States from Europe and distributing it through a network stretching from coast to coast. Court documents in the case described in detail Sicilian Mafia involvement in the distribution of cocaine in the United States and revealed an unusual barter system that included the export of cocaine from the United States to Italy, where it was exchanged for heroin that was smuggled into this country.

After many decades, evidence shows that the Sicilian Mafia are still the biggest players in the U.S. heroin trade. With its high-priced legal and financial help, the mob moved in the 1980s into worldwide drug distribution networks that reached South

12. "Big International Heroin Bust," *San Francisco Chronicle*, April 1, 1988.

America, Italy and France, employing secret bank accounts in Switzerland and Bermuda. But an alarming trend now is the partnership of the Colombian dealers with these older organized crime families. Italian Mafia chieftains, once content to distribute heroin to Black and Puerto Rican ghetto residents, decided to "marry up" with the Colombians upon seeing the enormous profits to be made from cocaine. The Mafia, in turn, has provided the Colombians with larger distribution networks and more sophisticated money-laundering schemes, such as real estate investments, limited partnerships and blind trusts in foreign banks, safe from confiscation.[13]

The Medellin Cartel. Medellin has been called the biggest cocaine-producing region in the world. Cocaine is behind everything — from murder sprees in Bogota to bank fraud in Florida. And the people who deal with it make the Cosa Nostra look like choirboys.

For years, the Latin American drug business was dominated by Mexican marijuana and heroin dealers. Mexican organized crime, though still flourishing, has been surpassed in wealth and political influence by Colombians. In little more than a decade, the Medellin cartel, which supplies 80 percent of the world's cocaine and is also responsible for up to 80 percent of the illicit cocaine that reaches the U.S., has come to be recognized as a law unto itself.

Its vast financial resources and revenues, which run into the billions, have enabled the cocaine lords to wield immense political power. The cartel itself is comprised of a small group of men who operate out of Colombia's second largest city, Medellin, and who have come to dominate the cocaine business as well as the economies and governments of several countries. The cartel operates through a wide network of associates, and controls a tightly organized enterprise. Colombia's dubious distinction as a principal drug source country — estimated at producing 75 tons of cocaine worth $6 billion a year[14] — may be attributed to its strategic location and the ruthless tactics of an experienced, well-ordered trafficking community.

Assassination for profit and political influence has become a way of life in what used to be a model democracy. Over the past

13. *U.S. News & World Report*, February 25, 1985.
14. Ibid., February 8, 1988.

five years, 50 Colombian judges have been murdered including 12 Supreme Court justices. Hundreds of politicians, informants, some 300 policemen and a score of journalists have died. And the latest victim early in 1988 was Carlos Mauro Hoyos, the country's Attorney General. Most of the 3,000 murders in 1987 in Medellin, as *Time* noted, "had something to do with drugs."[15] The corruption and violence that have made a mockery of Colombia's judicial system and are now tearing apart the country's social fabric are directed by the Medellin cocaine cartel. "They are," *Fortune* magazine writes, "billionaires who live outside the law, the most notorious [of whom] are three Colombians: Pablo Escobar, Jorge Ochoa and Carlos Lehder Rivas. The infamous trio allegedly got rich by smuggling up to 15 tons of cocaine into the U.S. and Europe each month."[16] *Forbes* magazine's cover story on "The World's Billionaires," dated July 25, 1988, features a new entry in its 192 listings: another Colombian named Gonzalo Rodriguez Gacha. He is known as "The Mexican" for his fondness for Mexican culture. According to a U.S. indictment, he is in charge of all Medellin cocaine distribution to the U.S. West Coast.

Together they have turned into powerful cocaine overlords — almost as rich and powerful as the Colombian government itself. They remain so powerful that in 1984 they were able to approach the country's attorney general with a startling offer: if the government agreed not to extradite them to the U.S., they would help pay off the country's $13 billion foreign debt. They take advantage of a justice system that is riddled with loopholes and vulnerable to bribery — local residents were heard to say that the cartel "owns" many of the officials, judges and policemen in the Medellin area. The cartel has also corrupted foreign police agencies, customs officials and entire governments. This corruption, if not stopped, threatens the law enforcement agencies of the United States.

The arrest, extradition and conviction of billionaire Carlos Lehder, sentenced for two consecutive life terms plus 150 years, may prove to be but a slight blow to the ever-growing cocaine cartel. Surely he will languish in jail but others are already filling the void left by him — new as well as familiar faces like Gonzalo

15. *Time*, March 7, 1988.
16. *Fortune*, October 12, 1987.

Rodriguez Gacha, Gilberto Rodriguez, Hugo Anez and Hernan Botero, who together with the two original members of the cartel, Pablo Escobar and Jorge Ochoa, all remain the "Kings of Coke."

Lately, Federal drug agents citing intelligence reports say major Colombian drug traffickers, squeezed by plummeting cocaine prices, are turning to heroin as a new source of profits. Heroin is much more expensive than cocaine and law enforcement officials agree that more heroin would mean more addicts and drug deaths and sharply increased street crimes. The heroin reports came amid a continuing downward spiral in the wholesale price of cocaine that began in 1982 with the appearance of crack.[17] The average wholesale price of a kilogram of heroin in 1987 was $200,000, about 20 times the cost of a kilo of cocaine, according to DEA estimates. The particularly frightening possibility that looms on the horizon is the likely increase in AIDS cases among drug addicts when Colombian drug lords finally launch their all-out effort to flood the U.S. with heroin as they have done with cocaine. With more than 500,000 heroin addicts, an already captive market, we could only expect that number to swell within the next few years into a "river of misery" that will engulf millions of people. The cartel has the means and a more powerful network than the Mafia to wreak havoc on the lives of many.

The cartel poses a formidable challenge for law enforcers. They own a mammoth fleet of sophisticated seacrafts and private airplanes that carry their deadly cargoes into the U.S. and Europe. They own regiments of smugglers and runners who carry the drugs to the wholesalers and local drug kingpins and dealers who can be found in virtually every city of the nation coast to coast. They have partnerships with organized crime and an established connection with drug gangs in every major city in the country.

— A Nation Besieged —

The cartel has remained unstoppable and seemingly invulnerable to prosecution. A concerned citizen, voicing the feelings of a majority of Americans, articulated the sense of hopelessness we feel: "All across America, people are gripped by fear that killer drugs will soon appear in their communities in the person

17. *San Francisco Chronicle*, January 7, 1988.

of young, ruthless drug dealers in the employ of the cartel, indifferent to pleas to stop the madness and the callous disregard to the taking of human life." That fear is intensified by the knowledge and perception, unfortunately all too accurate, that law enforcement agents and the criminal justice system seem powerless to combat them.

Even numerous arrests and seizures could mean just a brief moment of exultation for the law enforcement agents. They know that there will be other groups to pick up the slack and satisfy America's appetite for drugs and that they may be in a battle they can never win. Another reason is that drug cartels are known to be well-equipped with the latest advanced arsenals in their fight against law enforcement agencies. A picture illustration that appeared in a local newspaper spoke louder than many words can convey this one-sided battle: It shows law enforcement agents equipped with bows and arrows against the formidable tanks, rocket launchers and sophisticated surveillance equipment of the drug pushers. In a way, the federal crackdown on drug dealing, as one agent observes, may be likened "to one cop writing tickets while everybody in town is running the stop sign. How can police stop them?"

The presence of the criminal elements spawned by drug dealing in our society has radically changed the social reality of mainstream America. We are indeed a country under siege. For the first time in our history Americans are afraid of strangers, and for good reason. Burglar alarm sales are booming. People living in suburbia have attack dogs to guard their houses. In the cities, nobody answers doorbells anymore. Everywhere mothers herd their youngsters away in a hurry upon sight of a stranger. Trust and the time honored virtues of friendliness and hospitality have nearly disappeared today.

People are cautious, terrified by daily news headlines featuring stories of appalling savagery perpetrated by addicts and pushers on innocent victims. There seems to be no depths to which those involved in illegal drug trafficking will not sink. Meanwhile, outside our doors roam the mercenary predators ready to intimidate, kill and maim. Motivated by both the drugs themselves and the lure of enormous profits, the pushers and dealers have thrown away human dignity and the respect for life in the pursuit of power and pleasure. Nobody is safe.

The truth rings loud and clear in this statement by William James, 19th century philosopher and psychologist: "Man, biologically considered, is the most formidable of all beasts of prey, and, indeed, the only one that preys systematically on his own species."

— No Let Up in World Supplies —

Where are the principal sources of supply that feed America's expensive habit? And how do those deadly cargoes arrive here? Some are located in faraway parts of the world, shipping the drugs to the U.S. in the most ingenious ways that drug smugglers can think of. Other sources are right here, grown or processed in our own backyard — enough to supply the world's demand. A brief look at the known suppliers of drugs will reveal the incredible "natural" resources we are fighting.

Golden Triangle. Known as the world's opium heartland, this 60,000 square miles of jungle-clad mountains straddles the borders of Northeastern Burma, Northern Thailand and Northwest Laos. It is a wild place inhabited by rugged hill tribes, irregular troops, organized insurgents, local warlords and large-scale smugglers. Here the poppies bloom abundantly in the region's vast and fertile fields. The delicate flowers, like flimsy tulips, sway on their long stems in the mountain breeze. When the petals drop, the central bulb remains with claw-like razors. The bulb oozes white sap that dries and is scraped off carefully with a knife. It's opium, the base of the world's heroin supply. The region supplies 70 percent of the world's demand — a multibillion dollar business that claims thousand of lives and causes untold numbers of crimes each year.

In the line-up of world-class criminals, Khun Sa, 54, a Burmese separatist, reigns as the "father" of narco-terrorism.[18] He rules his remote domain in the rugged Golden Triangle area with feudal brutality. Deserters from his army are tracked down and shot, informants buried alive. He built a narcotics empire that today makes him the world's foremost heroin trafficker. The U.S. Drug Enforcement Administration believes that Khun Sa controls 80 percent of the 90 or more tons of heroin that is produced in the Golden Triangle. He also has some 15,000

18. "Reign of an Opium Warlord," *U.S. News & World Report*, May 4, 1987.

well-equipped, highly disciplined men at arms. Both Burmese and Thai military forces make periodic attempts to dislodge him — all have failed.

Golden Crescent. Mexico was the world's supplier of heroin in the early 1970s until its government, pressured by the U.S., instituted a program of spraying its fields with paraquat, a herbicide, significantly reducing the country's contribution to the world market. Turkey was also at one time the major source of heroin that entered the U.S. but like Mexico agreed to halt all opium growing in the 1970s. Middle Eastern nations — the Golden Crescent region of Afghanistan, Pakistan, Iran and India — picked up the slack. Of this region, Pakistan became the newest center of heroin production.

Pakistan, in the past, supplied enormous amounts of opium to Iran according to U.S. narcotics agents, but that market dried up after the Iranian revolution in 1979. It was then that Pakistan began making heroin from opium, sending it to markets in Europe and the United States. By the end of 1981, Pakistan had become the major supplier of heroin for American users in New York, Miami, Los Angeles and other cities.

The lifting of martial law in late 1985 by Pakistan's dictator, Gen. Mohammed Zia ul-Haq, resulted in a staggering increase in the production of opium in the country and the export of its by-product, heroin, to the U.S. No one foresaw the malignant side of the apparent progress toward democracy, as Jack Anderson wrote: "The unexpected development is attributed to the rule of civilian politicians, who are apparently even more corrupt and incompetent than the military officers they replaced. This is the inescapable conclusion," he added, "to be drawn from an unpublished report on global dope traffic prepared by the House Foreign Affairs Committee staff after months of on-the-spot investigation."[19] The study notes that more than half the heroin reaching the U.S. comes from Southwest Asia, and Pakistan's share of this deadly traffic has grown like a weed since Zia ended martial law. In 1986, the study points out that opium production exploded to 140 tons, making Pakistan one of the largest opium producers in the world. The figure represents a 350 percent increase in Pakistan's opium production from the previous level of about 40 tons.

19. "Drug Trade in Pakistan," *San Francisco Chronicle*, March 10, 1987.

Mexico's Hinterland. Mexico today has become the major stop on Latin America's cocaine trail. Until the mid-70s, it was by far the major supplier of heroin to the U.S. and exported huge quantities of marijuana as well. But in 1974, the government launched an extensive eradication program by spraying growing areas with herbicides. By 1978, the Mexican share of the U.S. heroin market had dropped from 80 percent to 30 percent. The Mexican traffickers later turned to cocaine to fill the void — accounting for as much as a third of all U.S. cocaine smuggled in from south of the border.

The vast area of Texas, Mexico and Arizona is primarily the trans-shipment point for cocaine and other illicit drugs reaching the U.S. daily.

Marijuana is grown in Mexico and once more is the principal contraband for the traffickers. Because air smugglers can haul bigger payloads more often, it is the ideal illicit drug for such operations. The smuggling organizations are controlled solely by Mexicans with strong family ties to local residents. The most well-known group is the Guadalajara cartel headed by Caro Quintero and four other drug families.

Pot supplied by Mexico is still America's most popular illicit drug, with 18 million Americans using it regularly.[20] Mexican heroin, after the eradication effort in the 1970s, is making a comeback in the street today as "Black Tar." It is an expensive variety which is as much as 80 percent pure, costing $500 per gram or more. Its bargain brown-powder heroin sells for $120 to $150 per gram.

South America: Cocaine Empire. The evil empire of cocaine extends from the coca fields of Peru, Bolivia and Ecuador to the jungle refineries of Colombia and Brazil. The cultivation of coca is divided primarily between Bolivia with its 86,000 acres and Peru's 123,000 acres. As *Newsweek* reported: "Peasant farmers abetted by corrupt generals and politicians on the right and rural guerillas on the left, cultivate a total of 300,000 acres of coca fields in Peru, Bolivia, Colombia and Ecuador. In 1984 alone, farmers harvested an estimated 135,000 tons of the raw coca leaf which sold for about $4 a pound."[21] After the farmers

20. "A Street-Side Pharmacopeia," *U.S. News & World Report*, March 28, 1988.
21. "Along the Cocaine Trail: Money, Murder and Politics," *Newsweek*, February 25, 1985.

process the coca leaf into a dry paste, jungle labs in Colombia use ether, acetone and hydrochloric acid to refine the paste into cocaine. The drug cartel ships the powder north by air and sea. From refining labs in South America, drug runners have developed many refueling and trans-shipping stops for small ships and planes, particularly in Mexico and the Bahamas. Drug traffickers smuggle a king's ransom of cocaine into the U.S. every day. They penetrate the borders through major airports, deserted airstrips and sleepy ports.

Despite the effort of guarding our borders or striking at its source, illicit drugs are increasingly flooding the streets of the U.S. The supply of smuggled drugs — Asian and Middle Eastern heroin, Mexican heroin and marijuana, and cocaine in particular — seems limitless. As a drug enforcement agent laments: "Illegal drugs are coming in at an alarming and ever-increasing rate and anti-drug apparatus has so far not been able to cope with the tremendous influx — we are being overwhelmed."

The U.S. "Golden Triangle". The law enforcement agencies' problem of halting the steady supply of drugs is compounded by the growth of marijuana domestically — considered now as the second biggest cash-crop in the nation, second only to corn. It's growing like weeds in the vast region of the combined counties of Del Norte, Humboldt, Mendocino and Sonoma in California — in what has come to be known as the "Golden Triangle" in this part of the world. All the marijuana grown in the U.S., plus the designer drugs manufactured here by underground labs, are enough to meet the world's demand.

Since 1983, the state's Campaign Against Marijuana Planting (CAMP) has seized three million pounds of dope worth $1.6 billion from vast outdoor operations, dislodging California as the nation's No. 1 pot producer. The leader now is believed to be Oregon. The eradication effort and devastating raids by CAMP, however, have only forced many big-time rural growers back into the cities where they have set up high-tech indoor pot farms. A *San Francisco Chronicle* staff writer, Ray Tessler, reports: "The operations in warehouses and ordinary urban and suburban neighborhoods are producing tons of highgrade grass hidden from police aerial surveillance."[22]

22. "Pot Growers Going Indoors and High-Tech," *San Francisco Chronicle*, July 11, 1988.

Tom Alexander, publisher of Sinsemilla Tips, a 20,000-circulation magazine for gourmand dopers, gloats, "All CAMP has done is shifted production from a hillside in Humboldt to a warehouse in San Francisco. They can brag all they want but production is greater than ever." Alexander asserts that San Francisco, Los Angeles and San Diego are now the major producing areas in California.

4

A MASTER PLAN?

*It's almost impossible to believe that Americans con-
sume sixty percent of the world's production of illegal
drugs. We are the marketplace coveted by every
criminal drug grower, processor, manufacturer, pack-
ager, distributor, and pusher.*[1]

— Buck Rodgers, *The IBM Way*

So great a demand for illicit drugs has created an overflowing
supply. The profits are easy, abetted by laws so unenforceable
that they invite contempt, corruption and open market transactions. The drug scene is reminiscent of John Bunyan's description of Vanity Fair in his *Pilgrim's Progress*:

> When they were got out of the wilderness, they presently saw
> a town before them, and the name of that town is Vanity; and at
> the town there is a fair kept, called Vanity Fair. At this fair are all
> such merchandise sold as houses, lands, trades, places, honors,
> preferments, titles, countries, kingdoms, lusts, pleasures and
> delights of all sorts, as whores, bawds, wives, husbands, chil-
> dren, masters, servants, lives, blood, bodies, souls, silver, gold,
> pearls, precious stones and what not.

Today's modern version of the fair covers an even wider
spectrum of merchandise for sale. Souls are for sale too — with
no discrimination as to age, color or creed. Titles, honor, integrity, professions, offices and governments are available to the
highest bidders. Deadly weapons and arms are bartered openly
for drugs. Children and mothers bear signs "for sale" by addicts
to support their craving for drugs. All imaginable pleasures are
available — enjoyed by kingpins and drug lords. Murderers,

1. *Getting the Best Out of Yourself and Others*, Buck Rodgers, 1987.

hitmen, terrorists, spies, informants, double agents command high prices.

Here you can buy all sorts of drugs in a variety of prices, shapes and sizes, colors, makes and designs, psychedelic and nonpsychedelic alike. They can paralyze or kill instantly depending on what drugs you choose, usually the hard-drug variety. At least, here you can have a choice (it's a free country after all and you can do whatever you want) to die young or prolong your misery for a while or acquire a lifelong, chronic and relapsing illness.

There are cemeteries inside the fair crowded with tombstones of thousands who died young. Some headstones bear darkly humorous signs: "Rest in peace — until we shoot and snort again"; "In memory of John Hero who accidentally snorted too much coke"; "Here lies the body of Jim Nutty who thought his brain was in his head. But gosh, it was in his nose." Other epitaphs are serious and offer advice as does this one: "Real strong was I, athletic in frame. But felled by heroin and cocaine. Reader, take warning of my fate. And if you haven't tried yet, Good — don't ever do it."

Shoppers are allowed to play Russian roulette, waiting in line for days to get a chance to try the stronger variety and the newly-packaged designer drugs. They are deadly. But who cares? The names are attractive: Ecstasy, Angel Dust, Loveboat, China White, Snowbirds, Climax and Blue Heaven — inviting death and misery. Fun seekers who want to remain junkies for years are assured of places in the shooting and snorting galleries, places that provide dizzying experiences to the land beyond — from which the majority never come back. They sell drug paraphernalia in these places called headshops — pipes, tubes, needles and syringes, smooth mirrors, tourniquets, razor blades, spoons and glass tooters, freebase kits and much more.

Drug users, pushers and dealers also come in varying descriptions and nationalities — an interesting mix of haves and have nots, short, tall, thin, fat, junkie and non-junkie, menacing and less menacing, strong, able-bodied and semi-handicapped, young and old, atheists, Christians, Moslems and with party or non-party affiliations.

From the street-side pharmacopeia comes the ultimate choice of the smorgasbord — the desserts of all drugs. They are top grade and command the highest prices and profits.

Their street names: coke, pot, and smack. Their true identity: cocaine, marijuana and heroin. One addict loved coke so much that she admitted: "Coke made me absolutely insane. I'd steal silver and gold jewelry from my family and friends. That would be my motivation for going to people's houses. I was like a vampire needing blood." That's an honest revelation from an addict.

The fair is notoriously a polydrug marketplace. It's allowed to sell legal, prescribed and over-the-counter drugs that are frequently abused by users who run out of money to buy their more expensive illegal counterparts. Pharmaceutical narcotics such as Dilaudid, Talwin, Seconal and Valium are the most salable and are causing a wave of abuse. There are over 20,000 psychoactive drugs available and more than 20 billion doses of them are distributed legally each year everywhere.[2] They are often available to anyone and the choice is to abuse or not to abuse. One hard fact: they are all habit-forming and deadly as *any* drug can be.

This is the Vanity Fair of the 1980s. All are looking forward to bigger and better attractions for the extravaganza of the 1990s!

— Destination: U.S.A. —

High-Tech Smuggling. As we discovered in the previous chapter, drugs of all kinds come from many sources throughout the world (in addition to the U.S. itself), and although heroin and cocaine addiction is a problem in many countries, the U.S. is a special target, partly due to the affluence that can afford such things, and that also initiates the desire for drugs. But how does such an incredible quantity get by the watchful eyes of Customs officials, x-ray equipment, and police dogs specially trained to "sniff things out"?

Smugglers are very resourceful people: their methods are often close to ingenious. Consider the following ways of importing drugs: Customs agents have discovered packs of cocaine inside watermelons, teddy bears and cans of spray deodorant. Some are stacked neatly inside frozen food containers, others in canned goods and some cocaine in condoms sewn skillfully in the bellies of cod and goldfishes. Some were hidden in hollow

2. *800-Cocaine*, Mark S. Gold, M.D., 1984.

legs of furniture or taped behind frames of paintings. The common method of entry is through small boats that ply the numerous inlets and coves of our rugged coastlines. They come in the bags of merchant seamen, carried by some airline personnel, taped to tourists' bodies or wrapped as colorful candies. The smuggler's most foolhardy practice is called body-packing, described here by one correspondent:

> They swallow cocaine-filled rubber packets, usually made of fingers snipped from surgical gloves. The carriers, known as "mules," gulp down the packets in Colombia with the intention of excreting them in the U.S. The danger to the mule is that a packet may rupture, causing a massive drug overdose. The technique is becoming either safer or less popular. Since late 1980, the Dade County coroner has not come across any body-packing fatalities after an earlier spate of such deaths. A mule commonly ingests upwards of a pound of coke inside 100 packets or more.

With billions of dollars at their disposal, smugglers are becoming more and more sophisticated with the employment of high technology. Federal agents, for example, uncovered a transport operation which used spotter planes, infrared beacons and decoy plane passengers called "cover girls."[3] The ring, based in Florida, was the largest transportation network used by the Medellin cartel between 1982 and 1986. Investigators calculate that it may have smuggled 60,000 pounds of cocaine over the four-year period and was paid about $90 million by the cartel. The ring contracted to build radio infrared beacons to be attached to cocaine loads dumped at sea, which are then retrieved by spotters with radio receivers or infrared goggles. The ring owned aircraft and vessels with elaborate covers of women posing as vacationers on charter flights.

Drug traffickers are continuously exploiting the use of new technology. A report by Jack Anderson was conclusive. Referring to a panel of Pentagon analysts' study on the means and methods used to detect and neutralize traffickers and terrorists, he wrote: "Their secret report states: 'Without question, there

---

3. "High-Tech Ring Smashed in Florida," *San Francisco Chronicle*, November 5, 1987.

is a dynamic technology race underway between the drug traffickers — as well as other criminal elements — and the law
enforcement agencies. It is by no means clear which side is
better funded or better equipped."[4] According to the report,
drug traffickers are resorting to such countermeasures as tape
recorder detections, metal detectors, radar detectors and electronic alarm systems. Law enforcement tactical communications frequencies are being monitored through the use of scanners. On a regular basis, scanners tuned to DEA, FBI, Customs,
Coast Guard as well as state and local law enforcement agencies
are seized during interdiction operations.

Anderson's news report also covered the trafficker's use of
cellular telephones and new, high-tech techniques to thwart
interception of their conversations. They are using sophisticated paging and electronic mail systems, personal computers
for accounting, record keeping and the transmission of data. He
also cited the experts' prediction of the total involvement of the
drug traffickers in the cellular telephone technology that is
turning toward a worldwide market. What this means is the link
of this new technology via satellite to the U.S. telecommunica-
tions systems. The traffickers will have an instant communication network that extends from the coca plantations to the
consumer. Analysts believe that it's only a matter of time before
various organizations begin to utilize the same networking systems used by financial institutions and large corporations. They
also may use more remotely piloted boats and planes. And who
knows, soon they may buy and own their own satellite systems!

— Global Conspiracy: The Indisputable Evidence —

The allegation that there is a conspiracy behind the largely
inner-city drug scene "to destroy the black folks," as believed
by some well-meaning leaders in the black community, deserves
serious thought and consideration. But the fact is: illegal drugs
don't discriminate against color of skin, one's nationality, or
religious belief, or anybody's status in life, whatever it may be.
In fact, the indisputable evidence points to this sobering reality:
there is a global conspiracy to destroy all Americans. That's you
and I, all of us. The evidence strongly shows the complicity

4. "Sophisticated Drug Trading," *San Francisco Chronicle*, January 7, 1988.

among twisted minds and leaders of some nations bent on destabilizing Western nations, particularly the U.S. Here are some compelling facts to confirm this diabolical plot:

⇨ Carlos Lehder Rivas,[5] the Colombian drug lord, declared that illegal drugs are the Third World's "Atomic Bomb." He further boasted that "Coca has been transformed into a revolutionary weapon for the struggle against American imperialism. The Achilles' heel of imperialism are the *estimulantes* [drugs] of Colombia."

⇨ Soviet surrogate countries — Bulgaria, Nicaragua and Cuba — are involved in drug trafficking, usually taking a nod-and-wink attitude when narcotics bound for the U.S. or Western Europe pass through their territories. "The directions of the flow are ideologically attractive," says Michael Ledeen, Georgetown University terrorism expert and former consultant to the National Security Council. "Drugs," he adds, "go to the bourgeois countries where they corrupt and where they kill, while the arms go the pro-communist terror groups in the Third World."[6]

⇨ Intelligence sources believe that officials in Syria and Iran are deeply involved in the drug trade, and divert profits to support revolutionary activities as well as to shore up their shaky economies.[7]

⇨ The government of Laos is promoting cultivation and export of marijuana as a means to earn foreign exchange. Crime syndicates are behind the expanding marijuana trade in the region.[8]

⇨ In 1983, former Nicaraguan diplomat Antonio Farach defected to the U.S. He testified on Capitol Hill on the complicity of Sandinista officials in shipping cocaine to the U.S. at Cuba's instigation. Farach explained that using drugs as a political weapon directly benefits their revolutionary cause and provides food for their people.[9] The payoff: Millions of dollars for them and suffering and death for the youth of the U.S.

5. "Narcotics: Terror's New Ally," *U.S. News & World Report*, May 4, 1987.
6. Ibid.
7. Ibid.
8. "Laos Drug Trade Role Growing," *San Francisco Chronicle*, July 13, 1987.
9. "Narcotics: Terror's New Ally," op. cit.

⇨ Fidel Castro was quoted by former Sandinista leader, Eden Pastora, as saying: "We are going to make the people up there white, white with cocaine."[10] The growing ties between Cuban officials and Colombian drug lords are well-documented. The proof is undeniable: In return for massive payoffs like a fee of $800,000 for a boatload of cocaine and illicit drugs, Cuba not only allows and escorts drug vessels through its territorial waters but also provides refueling and repair services at its ports. The boats are allowed to fly Cuban flags, and gunboats escort these "mother ships" to rendezvous with small Florida or Bahamas-based boats that sneak the drugs into the U.S. The smuggling has pumped millions of dollars into Cuba's cash-starved economy and provided weapons for insurgents in Nicaragua, Guatemala, El Salvador and Colombia.[11]

⇨ General Jan Sejna, former Secretary of the Czechoslovakian Defense Council and Chief of Staff at the Ministry of Defense, sought political asylum in the West in 1968. He recalls attending a secret meeting of top Warsaw Pact leaders chaired by former Soviet Premier, Nikita Khrushchev, who urged these leaders to exploit drugs to destabilize Western societies while generating foreign exchange. Sejna quotes the Soviet leader as saying: "There were some who were concerned that this operation might be immoral. But we must state categorically that anything that speeds the destruction of capitalism is moral."[12] When Khrushchev came to the U.S. and said, "We will bury you," we took it as a joke.

⇨ Five years after that meeting in Moscow, a document was drafted by the heads of Warsaw Pact Security services, and some 500 secret documents were brought to the West in 1971 by defector Stefan Sverdlev, a Colonel in the KDS, the Bulgarian Committee for Security (the counterpart of the Soviet KGB). One of the document's subjects: Destabilization of Western society through various methods, including drugs.[13]

---

10. "Narcotics: Terror's New Ally," op. cit.
11. "Havana's Drug-Smuggling Connection," Nathan M. Adams, *Reader's Digest*, July 1982.
12. Ibid.
13. Ibid.

⇨ U.S. renegade Robert Vesco, living in Havana under Castro's protection, directs his own drug conspiracy in Costa Rica. He was also a pivotal figure in a Colombia-Nicaragua-Cuba axis that shipped cocaine to Europe and the U.S.[14]

⇨ Timothy Leary, the "high priest of pot," convicted for smuggling marijuana from Mexico into the U.S. in the 1960s, and held without bond, was subsequently arrested 14 times on drug charges, escaped from jail and reached Libya safely where he announced his intention to destroy the U.S. He admitted his close relationships with militant organizations, specifically communists. This episode started the drug abuse epidemic.[15]

⇨ For decades on end, throughout the 1920s, the 1930s, the 1940s and 1950s, the Soviet press kept writing: "Western capitalism, your end is near. We will destroy you." In his many critical essays and speeches Alexander Solzhenitsyn, Russian writer of the well known *Gulag Archipelago*, spoke: "The most frightening aspect of the world communist system is its unity, its cohesion ... all the apparent differences among the Communist Parties of the world are imaginary, all are united on one point: your social order must be destroyed ... this has been their aim for 125 years and it has never changed ... a concentration of hatred, a continual repetition of the oath to destroy the Western world."[16]

Without knowing these facts we're tempted to ask the same question posed by Dr. Boris Sokoloff in his book, *The Permissive Society*, "What is the origin of the drug epidemic? Why [has] this country ... suddenly became ill with drug abuse? Was this epidemic spontaneous? Autonomous and self-propelling?"

The unquestionable evidence shows otherwise pointing strongly to the culpability of those leaders of nations bent on weakening the resolve and will of the West with the help of illegal drugs. Dr. Sokoloff's insight was to the point when he answered his questions: "We must reject this assumption without hesitation and doubt. The close relationship of drug promotion with the anti-war organizations, some of which are spon-

14. Ibid.
15. *The Permissive Society*, Dr. Boris Sokoloff, Arlington House, 1971.
16. *Warning To The West*, Alexander Solzhenitsyn, Farrar, Straus & Giroux, New York, 1984.

sored by communists, and the fact that it is directed toward the youth of our country and even more so toward the army indicates, in my opinion, that a powerful organization, probably communistic, is behind this drug promotion. Soviet Russia attempts to demoralize its enemies by various ways and means." His indictment of the Kremlin's role was documented by *U.S. News & World Report* regarding Moscow's history of fostering terrorism and its role in the plague of heroin and marijuana that enervated many GIs during the Vietnam War.[17] The evidence cited a damaging report in the involvement of the Soviet Union in the growing drug trade and terrorism.

We were lulled before by *detente* and played catch-up as we were overtaken by Soviet Russia. Solzhenitsyn warned us before: "Today, they don't say, 'We are going to bury you,' now they say 'Detente.' Nothing has changed in Communist ideology, the goals are the same as they were." At the moment, however, some good feeling that seems to be pervasive among our policy makers could lead to disaster, according to Howard Phillips, who wrote: "The center of the administration's policy is the president's unfounded assertion that Mikhail S. Gorbachev is a 'new kind of Soviet leader' who no longer seeks world conquests. The summit meetings and so-called arms control treaties are a cover for the treasonous greed of those who manipulate the administration. Reagan is no longer in any way accountable to the millions who recognize that we are in a deadly, strategic end-game with the Soviet Union ... by removing American Pershing and ground-launched cruise missiles from the European theatre, we surrender military and political domination of Western Europe to our enemy ... If this treaty is ratified by the Senate, a major battle of World War III will have been lost by default, without a shot having been fired."[18]

Paraphrasing Solzhenitsyn, we warn against Russia's real intention: "Today they don't say, 'We are going to bury you,' now they say *glasnost* [openness] and *perestroika* [restructuring of the economy]." The goal of this new "giant experimentation" is to revive the lagging economy and to compete in an era of rapidly changing technology — even if this means stealing and paying spies to get vital documents and technological data from

17. "Narcotics: Terror's New Ally," op. cit.
18. "Open Forum," the *San Francisco Chronicle*, December 15, 1987.

the U.S. Former Secretary of State Henry Kissinger fears the Soviets will succeed and become more competitive, stronger economically and a more formidable rival to the U.S. If on the other hand, Gorbachev fails, Kissinger fears a renewed regimentation of Soviet society, a more militant, tough-minded foreign policy and increased hostility toward the U.S. Mortimer B. Zuckerman, chairman and editor-in-chief of *U.S. News & World Report*, asked: "Do the changes mean the Soviet Union has altered its view of its international role? We cannot swallow that. Soviet aspirations to be a decisive player in the international arena have not changed." In his editorial commentary he also cited the clear thrust of Soviet foreign policy: relentless expansionism. He added that the U.S.S.R. has taken advantage of friendly gestures in the past and will do so in the future. Consider the following facts written in 1983 by Jonathan Steele in his book, *Soviet Power:*

⇨ The size of the Soviet arsenal, conventional and nuclear, has grown dramatically. The Soviet Navy is no longer a coastal force, but has acquired a global reach, as Kissinger puts it, "an unprecedented Soviet geopolitical offensive all over the globe." Does the rest of the world face a Soviet threat? Its battleships maneuver in every ocean of the world.

⇨ In the United States the number of graduate students in Russian studies has dropped to its lowest point since World War II, leading to an estimate that in 1982 the Soviet Union had three times as many specialists on American policy as the U.S. had on Soviet foreign policy.

⇨ The Soviet view of the United States is inherently ambiguous. The U.S. is the object of envy and scorn; the enemy to fight, expose and pillory — and the model to emulate, catch up with, and overtake.

⇨ A communist Western Europe seems to be the Soviet leader's fondest dream — to look forward with satisfaction and relief to the prospect of cooperative comrades at the helm of government in Paris, Rome, Bonn and London.

In an unusual move, a Moscow proposal was presented to the United States Drug Enforcement Administration that would set up a formal agreement outlining cooperation between the two nations in an all-out effort to control international drug trafficking.[19] The Russian overture was spurred by the report of a more serious drug problem within Soviet borders than was formerly acknowledged, namely, that the number of Soviet addicts has increased to nearly 200,000 from 46,000. According to the Soviet report, 45 percent of the addicts used marijuana. As a result, the Soviet officials want the latest U.S. scientific studies on the use of marijuana, a drug now being grown with increasing frequency within the Soviet Union.

The U.S. State Department has the Soviet proposal under study. Our government should approach this overture with extreme caution and examine thoroughly the motive behind the Soviet proposal. We are seeing the far-reaching effect of *glasnost* and we cannot afford to be naive anymore. If Russia has a drug problem, it could be short-lived and under an iron-fist regime it wouldn't flourish for long. Japan licked its drug problem by being tough with the pusher and especially with the users who were subjected to "cold turkey" treatment. Russia could easily do the same.

Maybe we could make an educated guess about the extraordinary appeal for help by Russia. Perhaps some questions are appropriate to raise: If verifiable, are there really that great a number of addicts in Soviet Russia? Why are they growing marijuana in the Soviet Union? Is it grown by underground entrepreneurs or state-backed farming? Is it for domestic consumption or intended for "export" to the United States and Western nations? Why the request for the voluminous scientific studies on marijuana from us? Is the latter aimed at studying marijuana's chemical properties in order to increase its potency to 50, 100 times or more? They know that marijuana is still the No. 1 illicit drug preferred by millions in the U.S. Instead of the Communist pledge to "bury and give a rope for the Bourgeoisie to hang itself," the new rope becomes the drug of choice in the U.S.

If for 42 years, between 1917 and 1959, the Soviet Union had no qualms about snuffing the lives of more than 110 millions of its citizens[20] — then it follows that this kind of ruthlessness

19. Editorial, *San Francisco Chronicle*, July 25, 1988.
20. Interview with Alexander Solzhenitsyn, BBC Radio Network, March 24, 1976.

applies to others to be exterminated without mercy and discrimination by whatever means. In this case, the means for over two decades now is the illicit drugs that flood the Western world.

The drug problem, viewed by some legislators as a more major threat to our national security than Communism, must be seen in the context that it was brought about by a global conspiracy which is communistic in origin. It's clear by now that to invade, sabotage and sap the strength and might of the U.S. need not involve the launching of missiles, ships and airplanes — the only thing that the communist countries need is to inundate this country with illicit drugs. We are not only deluged with them but as Mayor Ed Koch of New York declared at the 56th Annual Conference of Mayors: "This country today is swimming in drugs."

If America's enormous drug appetite continues toward its destructive course, we can only surmise about the possible outcome to a nation already reeling from its many social problems. The scenario below — mostly conjecture — *could* actually happen as tomorrow's facts, news and headlines. It can be averted if we know the difference between sanity and depravity in our "romance" with illicit drugs; if we know the difference between voluntary acquiescence and the organized plot to destroy all of us. We also have to be reminded by that famous remark by George Santayana: "Those who cannot remember the past are condemned to repeat it." The great Roman Empire self-destructed from within; *glasnost* is another version of *detente*.

A Scenario

Disinformation orchestrated by KGB spies permeates all media, especially the printed media. Books are tainted with misinformation promoting the use of illicit drugs as good for the health and good for certain kinds of ailments. Illegal drugs have been legalized and are sold on every corner of the U.S. Mental hospitals are crowded with lunacy cases, living mannequins who wander aimlessly in the corridors. There are 10 million cases and the numbers are increasing rapidly. There are human zombies everywhere.

The situation was exacerbated with the coming of "The Great Depression of 1990", as predicted by Dr. Ravi Batra in his book of the same title.

The U.S. deficit has risen to an unprecedented level of over one trillion dollars. For the first time the country's debt also has gone to $400 billion from $250 billion in 1986. Americans spent a staggering $500 billion on drugs since legalization in 1993. By that time recession was severe — ushering the collapse of more than one thousand banks and financial institutions. Drug dealing is rampant — the only means of livelihood for most people. Unemployment is at the 35 percent level — the highest in the nation's history. Stocks have crashed worse than the Black Monday of October 1987 and the Depression of the 1930s.

There is total anarchy in the land. Crime has quadrupled since 1988 and law enforcement agencies are helpless to stop it.

Since legalization, almost all secret and classified documents have been up "for sale" by greedy employees to double agents and spies from the Communist countries.

Every level of the government is infiltrated by KGB agents. Assassinations are rampant. Corruption pervades state and local levels. Gangs have taken over the helms of government in some major cities.

A scenario of such magnitude could really happen. Given time, the evil machinations, long underway, will surely succeed — with the bitterest irony of all, that is, with our help, naivete and complacency. This is a planned — hardly noticeable — but subtle and silent takeover of all democratic societies. Is it so easy to sit enjoying the good life and prosperity all around us until it's too late to prevent the fate that will surely befall us?

There was a time when Russia planned to sow widespread murder and mayhem *in peacetime* as reported by *Reader's Digest*.[21] The plan was aborted by the defection of four former KGB agents to the West. The plot called for assassinations of politicians, journalists, academicians and businessmen in Western Europe and the U.S.; agent networks posing as messengers, deliverymen or tourists would enter government buildings and litter the corridors with tiny, colorless capsules which when crushed underfoot would emit vapors fatal to anyone breathing them; KGB were to infiltrate by planes and submarines, squads of Soviet saboteurs to blow up power stations, bridges and rail junctions and to poison municipal water supplies; to put into

21. "Double Agents in a Secret War," John Barron, *Reader's Digest*, May 1985.

operation *Spetsnaz*, a secret, elite element of Soviet military intelligence consisting of about 27,000 men and women whose mission was to destroy the "brains and nerve centers" of Western nations by killing political, military and scientific leaders, and by sabotaging critical installations.

Because of the former Soviet agents' revelations, Russia can no longer count upon those schemes to surprise the West. But they found and recognized that the most lethal political weapon of all is illicit drugs. Lehder is right to call those drugs the "atomic bomb" that will kill or subdue the Western world. If this happens, the words of Abraham Lincoln will be prophetic: "If this country fell, it would fall from within without a shot being fired."

Part Two
The Enemy Within

5

THE INNER DRUG WAR

The deadliest enemies of nations are not their foreign foes; they always dwell within their own borders.

— William James[1]

— The Real Enemy —

We can put wall to wall AWACS, seal the borders and coastlines, enact the toughest criminal sanctions, employ the full might of the military — and still the flow of illicit drugs won't be stopped. As long as there is a demand, the supply will continue to overwhelm us — either coming from outside or springing up from within. As some laws and principles are unchangeable, so is the law of supply and demand. There's nothing we can do about it. We have to realize that the drug plague was not brought upon us by the drug pushers — we brought it *upon ourselves*. We created the drug shopping centers and we help build the clandestine operations found in every little street corner and alley of urban places.

We are all naked prey, vulnerable to the onslaught of the greatest enemy of all — the enemy that lurks within the dark recesses of our souls. This is the enemy within all of us — by far the most formidable enemy to overcome. The national failure to turn back from our gates the enemies among us testifies to one simple reality: *More than anything, we need the courage of self-control and discipline to fight vice — our own and others.* As Aristotle stated simply: "I count him braver who overcomes his desires than he who conquers his ene-

---

1. Late 19th century American psychologist and philosopher, brother of the novelist Henry James.

mies; for the hardest victory is the victory over self."[2] More than two thousand years later, a celebrated convict, Edgar H. Smith, Jr., the author of *Brief Against Death*, said it another way: "For the first time in my life, I recognized that the devil I had been looking at in the mirror for forty-three years was me."

The real drug war, therefore, is the one fought inside the individual. There's no retreating to self-righteousness, or an "It's not my problem" attitude. Winning the battles and surviving the war requires us to know more than what drugs are and what they can do to us; it requires more than what we know about drug trafficking; and because this is a unique war, it requires, above all, a discovery of the real enemy we have to overcome — *us*. "To a nation that espouses self-reliance," as *Time* reported, "drug dependence has emerged as the dark side of the American character, the price of the freedom to fail. It is as if America, so vain and self-consciously fit, has looked upon itself and suddenly seen the hideously consumptive portrait of Dorian Gray."[3]

We are a drug society. Beyond the illicit ones and those manufactured in underground labs faster than they can be outlawed, we have prescription and over-the-counter drugs. Together, they present a difficult challenge to everyone, especially the faint-hearted. The temptation is great and "the impulse to shun collides with the impulse to embrace," says Roger Rosenblatt, senior writer for *Time*. And as a result the war to be fought becomes all-encompassing. Rosenblatt noted: "The war that is being called for is a civil war, to be fought in the schoolyard or kitchen, in which the casualties may range from a thug in Miami to the dearest of civil liberties; a wild war in the house."[4] Everyone is a potential victim and everybody is a potential drug pusher. But what prevents us from becoming either one of these? Who is vulnerable and who is not? The thin line that separates those who do drugs and those who don't lies in the ageless question of "Who am I?" It spells the constant search for one's identity — someone slowly emerging and sol-

2. From *The Great Thoughts*, edited by George Seldes, Ballantine Books, New York, 1985.
3. "America's Crusade," *Time*, September 15, 1986.
4. *Time*, September 15, 1986.

idly building, but never giving up, a defense against the encroachment of the enemies from outside. And for those cold and timid souls afraid to ask such a simple question, the absence of meaning in their lives can be overwhelming, and defeat is inevitable when the enemy appears to mask the emptiness with drugs and alcohol and other illusions.

The Greeks, knowing the value and significance of this Delphic admonition, "Know thyself," inscribed it permanently in the timeless marble of the 2,500-year-old temple of Apollo at Delphi which stands at the foot of a sheer cliff on Mt. Parnassus. Philosophers, writers and thinkers since then have written many words on this theme. One such writer was British author Arnold Bennett whose book *How To Live On Twenty-Four Hours A Day*, a little classic on the science of self-direction, offers an antidote to mental flabbiness, a technique which assures added zest to one's daily activity. To govern one's life wisely, he admonished:

> Man, know thyself. These words are so hackneyed that I blush to write them, yet only the most sagacious put them into practice. I don't know why. I am convinced that what is more than anything else lacking in the life of the average well-intentioned man of today is the reflective mood ... we do not reflect upon genuinely important things; upon the problem of our happiness, upon the main direction in which we are going, upon what life is giving to us, upon the share which reason has (or has not) in determining our actions, and upon the relation between our principles and our conduct.

Another thinker, Matthew Arnold, summed it this way: "Resolve to be thyself; and know that he who finds himself loses his misery."[5] Knowing ourselves, we can live life to the fullest without chemical assistance. Those who lack personal purpose in life show us who is vulnerable.

Given to us, as we search our true selves, is the awesome realization that we live in this world making constant choices. Everyday we are confronted by the need to choose between many things and always, in a cumulative way, between what is good and what is bad for us. This is not an easy thing to do, especially when we are faced by the reality that we are in control

---

5. From *The Dictionary of Quotations*, edited by Bergen Evans, Avenel Books, New York, 1968.

of ourselves; our acts are our own and we have full responsibility for every moment of every day — the success and failure of our lives rests squarely on our shoulders. Individual choice gives us the freedom to buy drugs or not, to try them and stop using them, to be enslaved by them, to make our lives a blessing or a curse. We have the choice. One thing is certain though in this matter of choice: the path trodden by those who choose chemical dependency may be a momentary experience of delight, but it is guaranteed to be pure hell on earth.

— To Know Oneself —

Very often we undervalue ourselves and never really take the time to give serious thought to the many gifts we have. We are all special people, unique in every way, and we support each other in our strengths and weaknesses. It is especially through the latter, and not in our virtues and strengths, that we touch one another, identify with each other and share sympathy. We can be helped in our self-search by seeing ourselves in the imperfections and shortcomings of others. A Latin saying attests to this: When he sees the faults of others, a wise man corrects his own (*ex vitio alterius sapiens emendat suum*).

We have collected a lot of baggage along our way and our closets are full of skeletons that we don't want to get rid of. But it's all right. We can all relate to that: unresolved feelings, resentments, hatreds, jealousies, loneliness, fits of depression and more. But this should not give us a reason to turn to alcohol or drugs to prop us up and keep us moving. They paralyze and immobilize, and, more often than not, we only find bitterness at the bottom of the bottle or heartache and even death from a fast and slippery downhill chemical dependency.

To know oneself is a life-long process but the discovery, even if it takes a bit-by-bit effort, is worth it. As we gain insight into who we are, we begin to understand our surroundings, our problems and even those around us. We become more open to life and more understanding of what the human condition means, in realizing how we are a part of it. We learn to associate with all types of individuals — the honest and the corrupt, the rational and the irrational, the understanding and the obstinate, the greedy and the generous. We can identify with all of them because we *were* all of them at one time or at least, we have the potential to be anyone of them. We learn to give more of ourselves because we have something to give. As a community lacking in peace within ourselves, we see this lack projected in the violence of the drug epidemic. We hate others because we hate inside ourselves first. Most hearts rot because of this lack of peace, and we find instead the collective hatreds in these violent times.

As we grow in self-knowledge, we begin to understand life's contrasting events and paradoxes: slavery and freedom, success and failure, ease and suffering and even life and death. We learn that without life's seeming contradictions, life would be a dreary monotony of emptiness. Where would there be room for joy if there were no sorrows to hollow our hearts? How could we appreciate the miracle of a sunrise had we not waited in the dark?

As we learn to understand ourselves, we take life seriously — fully aware of the alternatives it offers us, thinking about them with all the intensity we can gather in full recognition that every choice is a great risk with its accompanying consequences. These consequences are sometimes hard to bear — disapproval from our peers, being branded as a crackpot, ostracized from our circle of friends, finding people cynical to our point of view. Or we find ourselves caught between Scylla and Charybdis[6] and this could be one of the most painful choices. It is inevitable that we face in life such dreadful alternatives and we must be ready to make a choice even if that means pain or loss on our part — because these are the situations which forge our character like tempered steel. An ancient Chinese proverb affirms this truth: "No gem can be polished without friction, nor man perfected without trials."

As we discover who we are we become self-assured and confident and all the frightening possibilities that assail us become a challenge and an opportunity for greater growth. We learn that there are only two choices: *to break down* by refusing to grow or *to break through* in order to continue moving on and grow. The choice is ours.

6. Scylla was a loathsome and dangerous monster, inhabiting an inaccessible cave in an unscalable rock. Charybdis was a fatal whirlpool. The two names have come to stand for dreadful alternatives between which a man or a woman must make a choice.

We give away our power when we let others control our lives — or when we let drugs dictate our destiny. We become powerless, as Stacey Keach found out: "By far the worst form of incarceration is to be trapped within one's own powerlessness to help oneself."[7] Keach knew that the place to start was within himself. He knew what was happening inside him and acted upon it with a firm determination to conquer his drug dependence. And he came clean and sober — using his experience to warn others about the evils of cocaine dependency. Too often we find people finding solutions to their problems in what others call "the attitude adjustment time" in the happy hour of bar rooms. And long before they realize it, they are permanently adjusted to a life of alcoholism. Similarly, what starts in the case of illicit drugs as a "recreational and responsible use" also becomes a permanent road to drug addiction.

Know thyself. Its promise is rich to one who wants to put order in his or her private world. It's a continuous struggle and one of the greatest challenges we will ever face because our most dangerous battle in life is against the enemy within the gate, the blind, unreasoning desires deep within each of us. It is in knowing ourselves that self-esteem is forged and where basic decisions about values, commitment and loyalty to principles are made. It is only from within that real and lasting help can come in our fight against the deadly menace of drugs. The great historian, Will Durant, wrote as a reminder: "A great civilization is not conquered from without until it has destroyed itself from within."[8]

— With Eagles' Wings —

We are all caged like birds, only our cages are invisible. We are held captives as slaves of our passions and sometimes, we don't realize it. Why live in a prison when we could be set free? Life is simply too tremendous to waste! Why let imagined possibilities disturb our peace of mind, especially if they are negative? Why let fatigue, disillusionment, failure and defeat overcome us? There is no reason to when there are so many wonderful things

7. "TV Star Keach Calls Cocaine a 'Prison'," *San Francisco Chronicle*, July 17, 1985.
8. From *The Great Thoughts*, op. cit.

life is unceasingly giving us. And they are all free. Why choose things that imprison and lead us to harrowing adventures in a land of no return? We are given the tremendous power to discern what could be good and what could be dangerous to the health of our minds and bodies. Again we only have to choose.

We find many upper and middle-class Americans who are impoverished in spirit, which is why they turn to drugs for temporary or permanent solutions. Who then is rich? I believe he or she is rich who knows the moment, openly receiving it with its so many blessings unencumbered by many desires which destroy body and spirit. Who is rich? And how do we enrich our spirits? One simple way is to avail ourselves of the timeless messages and insights given to us for free from the wisdom of great thinkers of the past. We need only to listen and quiet our minds and hearts to receive their thoughts. Here are some "sparks of wisdom" that might ignite our hearts in our search for the elusive self:

❏ The unexamined life is not worth living. *Socrates*

❏ The wise man in the storm prays to God, not for safety from danger, but for deliverance from fear. It is the storm within which endangers him, not the storm without. *Ralph Waldo Emerson*

❏ The fault, dear Brutus, is not in our stars, but in ourselves, that we are underlings. *Shakespeare*

❏ The easiest thing of all is to deceive oneself; for what one wishes he generally believes to be true. *Demosthenes*

❏ Self-reverence, self-knowledge, self-control — these three alone lead life to sovereign power. *Alfred Lord Tennyson*

❏ The virtue of all achievements is victory over oneself. Those who know this victory can never know defeat. *A.J. Cronin*

❏ One must know oneself. If this does not serve to discover truth, it at least serves as a rule of life, and there is nothing better. *Blaise Pascal*

❏ Alone of all creatures on earth, man can change his destiny simply by changing his attitude. *Norman Vincent Peale*

❏ The only tyrant I accept in this world is the "still small voice" within me. *Mahatma Gandhi*

❏ He who is unable to live in society, or who has no need because he is sufficient for himself, must be either a beast or a god. *Aristotle*

❏ The worst ruler is one who cannot rule himself. *Plato, The Republic*

❏ The true value of a human being is determined by the measure and the sense in which he has attained liberation from self. *Albert Einstein*

❏ The greatest thing in the world is for a man to know how to be himself. *Michel Montaigne*

❏ Most powerful is he who has himself in his own power. *Seneca*

❏ Not till we have lost the world, do we begin to find ourselves. *Henry David Thoreau*

❏ Without knowing what I am and why I am here, life is impossible. *Leo Tolstoy*

❏ I must say to myself that I ruined myself, and that nobody great or small can be ruined except by his own hand. *Oscar Wilde*

❏ You are not in charge of the universe: you are in charge of yourself. *Arnold Bennett*

❏ The first and worst of all frauds is to cheat oneself. *James Bailey*

❏ To believe that if only we had this or that we would be happy, or to pursue any excessive desire, diverts us from seeing that happiness depends on an adequate self. *Eric Hoffer*

❏ A false conscience is a false god — a god which says nothing because it is dumb and which does nothing because it has no power. It is a mask through which we utter oracles to ourselves, telling ourselves false prophecies, giving ourselves whatever answer we want to hear. *Thomas Merton*

❏ The unfortunate thing about this world is that good habits are so much easier to give up than bad ones. *W. Somerset Maugham*

❏ The only reason you are not the person you should be is you don't dare to be. Once you dare, once you stop drifting with the crowd and face life courageously, life takes on a new significance. New forces take shape within you. *William Danforth*

The task of discovering who we are is the only way to conquer the enemy within. The drug pushers would be out of business if we took care of the "demand" side. The reality is: *There is nothing so distasteful to many of us as to go the way which leads us to ourselves.* That's the reason we can be full of maxims or creeds but never really understanding and applying them to ourselves and consequently, we build a character that may remain entirely unaffected and unchanged for the better. It's too easy to justify and rationalize our thinking and behavior that keeps us from taking action and making a commitment to things of enduring value. Allan Bloom, in his book *The Closing of the American Mind*, cites the reason: "We have [an] easy-going lack of concern about what that means for our lives." We can always daydream about our hopes but "the great thing in the world," says Oliver Wendell Holmes, "is not so much where we stand as in what direction we are moving."

One sad thing is how we go through life with ears too dull to listen to the friendly counsel within us. Jacques Barzun offers this advice: "Pascal once said that all the trouble in the world was due to the fact that man could not sit still in a room. He must hunt, flirt, gamble, chatter ... but the educated man has through the ages found a way to convert passionate activity into a silent, motionless pleasure. He can sit in a room and not perish."[9] We are bound to be disappointed if we expect such an ability to quiet ourselves to come as a gift. It does not happen overnight. But it *can* happen.

Know thyself — its profound significance gives meaning to our lives. To know oneself is not an objective that begins and ends. It's a gradual process that demands inner change and the conversion of hardened hearts which can then absorb the wisdom of the ages. It is only then that strength and courage will be ready at hand in time of trial. The prophet Isaiah described the blessings given to steadfast hearts: "They will soar as with eagles' wings; they will run and not grow weary, walk and not grow faint."[10]

9. "The Educated Man," Jacques Barzun, *Life*, October 16, 1950.
10. Isaiah 40:31, *The New American Bible*, Good Counsel Publishers, Chicago, Illinois.

Facta, non verba. Deeds, not words make things possible. We all know that the road to hell is paved with good intentions and nothing will happen unless we make the first step in our journey to discover who we are. Kahlil Gibran, a Lebanese mystic, was direct in addressing this problem of passivity: "Learn the words of wisdom uttered by the wise and apply them in your own life. Live them — but do not make a show of reciting them, for he who repeats what he does not understand is no better than an ass that is loaded with books." The Letter of James also provides this admonition: "Act on this word. If all you do is listen to it, you are deceiving yourselves."[11]

In retrospect, we have to realize that we don't have a drug problem — we have a people problem.

11. The Letter of James 1:22, ibid.

6

WHY?

The things that will destroy America are prosperity at any price ... and love of soft living and the get-rich-quick theory of life.

— Theodore Roosevelt

— A Historical Overview —

History offers ample evidence of drug use dating back to ancient civilizations — to Greece and Cyprus as early as 2000 B.C. and to the Indians of the Andes region on the western rim of South America, as far back as 5,000 years ago.

In a special report, *Time* wrote about the growth of drug use in the United States: "The fortunes of early New World merchants were amassed by trading opium. After the Civil War, opium use was widely tolerated in the U.S. and even extolled by some leading thinkers ... Cocaine first became popular in America in the late 19th century ... at the time an estimated 1 in 400 Americans used opiates regularly ... Chinese immigrants were blamed for importing the opium-smoking habit to the U.S."[1] In 1909, the U.S. banned the import of opium and by the 1920's public revulsion against drugs verged on the hysterical.

The ban drove cocaine and opium underground. After a brief lull, marijuana began arriving in large quantities in the 1920's and 1930's. It too was regarded with horror evidenced by a film called "Reefer Madness" which warned the nation's youth that smoking pot was a direct road to hell.

Despite warnings, bans and crusades conducted by the government, drug abuse and addiction continued in the decades of the 50's with the "Beat Generation" and the rebellion of the

---

1. "America's Crusade," *Time*, op. cit.

youth in the 60's. We saw the second coming of cocaine in the mid-70's — the perfect drug for the "Me Generation" of that decade. And we have seen the magnitude of the drug problem in the 80's, which has covered the full spectrum of mind-altering chemicals.

Drawing from historical data, writers today on the drug culture find ways to justify their assertions that drug use is a normal part of life, a means of satisfying the inner need for experiencing other modes of consciousness, a need to respond to tensions over foreign wars and domestic crimes, as a means of promoting and enhancing social interactions, a means of aiding religious practices and a number of other reasons.

One prolific writer in the drug culture scene is Andrew Weil who claims that our use of drugs such as caffeine, nicotine and alcohol is no different from that of illegal drugs. In his book, *The Natural Mind: A New Way of Looking at Drugs and the Higher Consciousness* he wrote: "In South America I hope to live with Indians ... In particular, I want to understand the specifics of their methods of introducing children to the ritual uses of drugs."[2] In the same book, he described what he would like "to see come about as steps in the right direction ... to see all people interested in the drug problem begin to seek out people who actually use drugs to learn from them about their experiences ... to see social programs aimed against drug abuse begin to make use of persons who have learned how to use drugs intelligently."

He further hoped that users of illegal drugs would come forward to volunteer information about states of consciousness and techniques for using drugs to best advantage. Musician David Crosby of Crosby, Stills & Nash, had this response:

> Most people who go as far as I did with drugs are dead. Hard drugs will hook anyone. I don't care who you are ... I know better. I have a Ph.D. on drugs. Fool with them and you'll get strung out. Then there are about four ways it can go: You can go crazy; you can go to prison; you can die; or you can kick. That's it. Anything else anybody says is bull.[3]

2. *The Natural Mind: A New Way of Looking at Drugs and the Higher Consciousness*, Andrew Weil, Houghton Mifflin, Boston, 1972.
3. "The Confessions of a Coke Addict," David Crosby, *People Weekly*, April 27, 1987, p.54.

What came to pass as a result of drug experimentation happened as expressed by Rosenblatt: "Suddenly the whole system feels poisoned by a world in which millions of one's countrymen eagerly dream themselves to death."[4]

Why? In a society as complex as we are living in today, we are confronted with more questions to ask and fewer answers being found. Why are people hooked on drugs? Why are they inflicting pain that is almost self-administered? I found reasons different from those advocated by the drug culture.

— Pathway to Drug Abuse —

Lack of Information. There is a lot of ignorance among us. Writers and anti-drug crusaders, sometimes, are branded as exaggerating the situation, overstating the risks and damages, and frightening people by facts and statistics. Most, however, shrug it off, or even worse, deny the existence of the drug problem even in their own homes when children or loved ones are involved in drugs.

Not knowing the hard facts about drugs is the hardest price to pay. In the largest treatment center in the nation in New York City, the Phoenix House, a recovering addict found out: "I didn't start using drugs to destroy my life. That wasn't my intention. But out of the ignorance of not knowing, I did it anyway."

How many lives are destroyed by not knowing? R.G. Ingersoll puts this lack of effort in a rather harsh statement: "There is no slavery but ignorance."[5] Two hundred years ago Samuel Johnson said: "He that voluntarily continues in ignorance is guilty of all the crimes which ignorance produces."[6] To many, as we all have observed, this business of not knowing becomes nothing less than voluntary misfortune. The drug problem is so unique and so tragic that, according to the Media-Advertising Partnership for a Drug-Free America, it is "totally self-inflicted."

The lack of insight into the potential consequences of drug use and the lack of correct and up-to-date information prove to

4. *Time*, September 15, 1986.
5. From "Liberty of Man, Woman and Child," quoted in *The Great Thoughts*, op. cit. Robert G. Ingersoll was an American lawyer and orator in the late 1800's.
6. From "Popular Quotations," *Webster Encyclopedic Dictionary of the English Language*, The English Language Institute of America, Inc., 1971.

be beyond reasonable doubt the major reason why people are hooked on drugs. It's extremely difficult, and sometimes impossible, from what we have seen, to change the attitude of an already hooked generation. Tom Brokaw described the reality of the current drug situation as a way of life for many unfortunate souls:

> Whoever the users, the road between use and addiction is often short, a frantic race to dependence and often death. Addiction means drug binges for days on end, hundreds of thousands of dollars lost. People fall deeper and deeper into the pit. Some will never recover. Others will learn from their hard experiences.[7]

Peer Pressure. The teenage years can be considered the most difficult stage in our young children's lives. This is a period of personal struggle often marked by rebellion and the search for identity. It is a painful, challenging, complicated, and often confusing and chaotic time of life involving the confrontation of peer pressure and risk-taking. This is also a most trying time in the lives of parents who often resort to excessive discipline which is viewed by adolescents as a "lack of love" on their parents' part. The other extreme is found among parents who are lax and tolerant of their children's use of drugs as part of growing up and a normal "phase" of the teenager's life.

Both are extreme approaches in our dealing with our children. Nothing can substitute giving them lots of attention and affection, giving them quality time instead of quantity time, to teach them how to become responsible at an early age, to learn honesty, to love life and to have a healthy self-image. Young children, especially adolescents, are cast into a limbo between the safe reality of belonging and acceptance and the reality of adult life which seems both rigid and too complex for them to grasp. But it is a reality that they long for — this belonging and acceptance and recognition and above all, the desire to be loved by their families. Love alone can accomplish what nothing else can.

Adolescents use drugs for a number of reasons, often because they are readily available and because they provide a quick, cheap way to feel good. But there is no more powerful motivation than doing drugs to gain acceptance among peers. This

---

7. "Cocaine Country: A National Forum" transcript of NBC News Special, September 5, 1986, p.3.

happens among alienated adolescents who cannot find support and encouragement in a home setting. Peer pressure is one reality that most teenagers fear most: they don't want to be rejected. The need to be accepted by others of the same age is very strong, making it extremely difficult for a child to refuse drugs and still "save face."

Some years ago, I found some inspirational verses that I thought might help young people deal with peer pressure:

> Don't let your parents down. They brought you up. Be humble enough to obey. You may give orders someday. Choose companions with care — you become what they are. Don't let the crowd pressure you. Stand for something or you'll fall for anything.

My mother left me a legacy that helped me resist peer pressure when I was young: "Son, there's no more pitiful sight in this world than someone who has relinquished to others his power to decide for himself, and consequently, cannot make a decision for himself anymore. Stand up for what you believe is right and fight for it and if need be, die for it."

As family unity and ties disintegrate, kids come to rely more and more on their peers, which often results in misadventure and slipping into a "fog of drugs." We parents *must* learn to listen and communicate more with our "young folks" who cannot wait to be adults.

Stress and Isolation. Stress is not always what it connotes, that is, a negative force. Simply to live is to undergo a certain amount of stress which pushes us to perform at our very best. What we are talking about here, however, is the kind of stress that debilitates and becomes a harmful force in our lives — a by-product of this modern age where the sole motivation is the relentless drive for success. This is shown by the remarkable willingness of many to sacrifice their personal lives, including time spent with family and friends in their pursuit of their goals. In one of his many writings, Martin Luther King, Jr. noted: "Success, recognition, and conformity are the bywords of the modern world where everyone seems to crave the anesthetizing security of being identified with the majority."

Success and the constant desire to have more things can be very demanding and many young workaholics find it difficult to cope when stress sets in. Many turn to alcohol and drugs to anesthetize the stress produced by emotionally upsetting events and the great demand of work they place upon themselves. The drug taking which develops into addiction causes a host of other problems and in turn creates more stress. It becomes a vicious and harmful cycle in one's life.

This inability to cope with the stress and pressure of work and other problems results in a frantic search for drugs — tranquilizers, barbiturates, amphetamines, hallucinogens, and other stimulants — in order "to feel good" and stimulate performance. The same holds true in the ferocious competition of amateur and professional sports motivated by the drive to win, to be number one, where more and more pills of all kinds are being popped to enhance skills and overcome the stress of competition.

What is the effect of this pathological obsession with "getting ahead?" One of the biggest problems with this kind of drive is that its effects, aside from stress, are obvious: nervous breakdown, depression (in case of job loss, etc.) and isolation. Taking drugs to overcome these feelings gives a false sense of relief to the user who experiences momentary exhilaration, and then goes back again to where he was before once the "high" recedes. Because drugs feed on the ego, it makes one think he is in the groove when he's actually in a rut. It makes one feel masterful, relaxed and confident. It creates a false sensation of rewards. It makes one accept that the only solution to the problem is more chemical solution.

There are people out there, self-styled saviors of those who feel trapped by a boring existence, always ready to make our lives a paradise on earth by proclaiming the good news of "getting high," because "it's cool and the right thing to do." They are enterprising people, out to dig in our pockets and as we get hooked we find their promise of paradise doesn't exist at all.

In the end, what do we really hunger for? "Our souls," wrote Rabbi Harold Kushner, author of *When All You've Ever Wanted Isn't Enough: The Search For a Life That Matters*, "are not hungry for fame, comfort, wealth, or power. The rewards create almost as many problems as they solve. Our souls are hungry for meaning, for the sense that we have figured out how to live so that our lives matter."[8]

8. Quoted in "They're Rich and Miserable," Joan Frawley, *Catholic Digest*, December 1986.

Escapism and Low Self-Esteem. Many of us are seeking to dull the pain of facing life's challenges by using mood-altering chemicals to induce altered states of awareness as a routine means of escaping reality. "Drugs used to anesthetize feelings and anxiety further remove the individual from what he feels and who he is. They block important pathways to true and real feelings and destroy the possibility of discovery and growth ... Drugs are temporary escapes," says Dr. Theodore Isaac Rubin.[9] And the road to escapism has, for many, been a trail straight to the hell of addiction and dependence.

Research and studies made by NIDA in 1983 which examined the relationship between self-concept and drug use revealed that alcohol and drug addicts are consistently reported as being associated with an insidiously low level of self acceptance. This kind of acceptance is in fact the outgrowth of poor self-image. Drugs are a cop-out and an escape that threaten one's self-esteem. Teaching people how to accept themselves and to like themselves is the first step before drug education will ever work, many experts believe. Educators are calling it the new direction in teaching: Education through enhanced self-esteem with peer involvement. Direction Sports, Inc., calls it: Give a Kid a Way To Be Somebody.

All these ideas are empowering young people and adults as well to gain control over their lives, that is, if they are willing to be motivated to enhance their own capabilities and performance. They then discover there's no limit to what they can achieve once they stop being preoccupied with self-pity and negative thoughts.

Fr. Christopher Cartwright, S.J., executive director, Campus Ministry, University of San Francisco, describes the drug problem and too much obsession with one's self as "a misdirected attention and a fear more than anything else to take responsibility for oneself and missing the opportunity to truly fulfill one's life by not taking responsibility for others as well." And too many have this feeling of ambivalence regarding the attitude they take toward themselves and others. But too often, the root of the problem lies in the "alienated self" that has to be confronted first before the needs of others can be met.

9. *The Angry Book*, Theodore Isaac Rubin, M.D., MacMillan Publishing Co., 1969, p.150.

From Thomas Merton, we can learn that "the world itself is no problem, but we are a problem to ourselves because we are alienated from ourselves, and this alienation is due precisely to an inveterate habit of division by which we break reality into pieces and then wonder why, after we have manipulated the pieces until they fall apart, we find ourselves out of touch with life, with reality, with the world and most of all with ourselves."[10] And having alienated ourselves we find it hard to accept ourselves, we short-sell our abilities and undermine the flowering of our full potential.

Dr. Carl Jung's insight on the problem of self-acceptance which is associated with low self-esteem is timely advice for all to meditate upon:

> To accept oneself as one is may sound like a simple thing, but simple things are always the most difficult things to do. In actual life to be simple and straightforward is an art in itself requiring the greatest discipline, while the question of self-acceptance lies at the root of the moral problem and at the heart of a whole philosophy of life.
>
> Is there ever a doubt in my mind that it is virtuous for me to give alms to the beggar, to forgive him who offends me, yes, even to love my enemy in the name of Christ? No, not once does such a doubt cross my mind, certain as I am that what I have done unto the least of my brethren, I have done unto Christ.
>
> But what if I should discover that the least of all brethren, the poorest of all beggars, the most insolent of all offenders, yes, even the very enemy himself — that these live within me; that I myself stand in need of the alms of my own kindness, that I am to myself the enemy who is to be loved — what then?
>
> Then the whole Christian truth is turned upside down; then there is no longer any question of love and patience; then we say "Raca" to the brother within us; then we condemn and rage against ourselves! For sure, we hide this attitude from the outside world, but this does not alter the fact that we refuse to receive the least among the lowly in ourselves with open arms. And if it had been Christ himself to appear within ourselves in such a contemptible form, we would have denied him a thousand times before the cock crowed even once.[11]

10. *Contemplation in a World of Action*, Thomas Merton, Image Books, 1973, p.171.
11. *Healing the Unaffirmed*, Drs. Conrad W. Baars and Anna Terruwe, Alba House, New York, 1976, p.38.

One of the most regrettable facts in life is the realization that we are not using our full potential. It is inspiring to know that many handicapped individuals, despite seemingly insurmountable odds, rose to become great men and women who never bowed down to discouragement and defeat. Beethoven produced the world's greatest music when he was deaf. Mozart lived in dire poverty all his life, and close to our time, Helen Keller fought hard against impossible obstacles in her life and became one of the most educated women in history despite being deaf, mute and blind. What is their secret to overcome hardships and frustrations and not wallow in self-pity and lack of hope? Earl Nightingale in his gold record that sold over a million copies, *The Strangest Secret*, said this: "If you really understand, it will alter your life immediately ... your life will never be the same again. Here's the key to success and the key to failure. *We become what we think about.* Throughout our history the great wise men and teachers, philosophers and prophets had disagreed with one another in many different things; it's only in this one point that they are in complete and unanimous agreement." William James spoke of this "secret" in a similar way: "The greatest discovery of my generation is that human beings can alter their lives by altering their attitude of mind." A member of a San Francisco Toastmaster Club called her winning speech, "The Altitude of Your Attitude." She described how we could be a thermostat that controls the temperature from inside rather than being a thermometer which changes with the temperature from outside. She spoke of the potential and difference we can make if we take time to establish the kind of attitude that we must have. The problem of low self-esteem or poor self-image is mainly an attitudinal problem.

The story of "The Golden Eagle" by the late Anthony de Mello, author of *The Song of the Bird*, best illustrates in story form the problem of low self-esteem. De Mello told about a man who found an eagle's egg and put it in the nest of a backyard hen. The eaglet hatched and grew up with the chickens *thinking* he was one of them. He did what the chickens did — scratched for worms and insects. He clucked and cackled. Once in a while he would thrash his wings and would fly a few feet into the air. He soon grew old and one day saw a magnificent bird gliding gracefully above him in the cloudless sky with its strong golden wings. He looked up in awe and asked: "Who's that?" His neighbor answered that it was the eagle, the king of the birds and added rather matter-of-factly: "He belongs to the sky, we belong to the earth, we're chickens." And finally, the eagle who lived as a chicken died like a chicken for that's what he believed he was and what others told him he was.

We hear the often-repeated phrase: "Never settle for less than you can be." It sounds trite but it's good food for thought. We have to dare to be different. We are all unique and special people with special gifts and talents. Limits exist only in the mind and we can make the difference in a world turned upside down by those who conform, not knowing why they do things, because they don't think anymore. Eleanor Roosevelt once remarked: "No one can make us feel inferior without our consent." Truly, nobody can dictate to us to be a drug addict or to be an alcoholic unless we allow it to happen or we try to conform.

We are born to be great because "we live in a country where the best and the finest can be brought up," says astronaut John Glenn. We live in a land with abundant blessings and a lot of opportunity to be great. That is God's big plan for all of us. Never settle for less than you can be!

The Business of Pleasure. Why do people take the plunge into drugs? One reason is to find pleasure. It doesn't matter how hard the fall back into reality is after the experience. All that matters is the instant gratification that drugs provide. Freudian psychology has had great influence in producing this way of thinking which declares that all is permitted and should not be suppressed or even controlled.

"Our entire psychical activity is bent upon procuring pleasure and avoiding pain, is automatically regulated by the pleasure-principle," says Sigmund Freud.[12] According to him, the human race is motivated chiefly by pleasure. The pleasure-principle is the most essential if not the only essential force in our lives. And this principle demands sexual gratification. "The problem of sex was an obsession with Freud," wrote Dr. Sokoloff, "everything started with sex and ended with it. The motivating force of man's behavior, man's pleasure, his gratification, his happiness was in sex."[13]

---

12. *The Permissive Society*, op. cit.
13. *The Permissive Society*, Boris Sokoloff, M.D., Arlington House, New York, 1971.

The considerable influx of Freudian fellows, psychoanalysts who emigrated from Europe to the United States, sowed the seeds of the sexual revolution. Dr. Sokoloff cited the tremendous influence of liberal intellectuals "who applauded, promoted and fully approved the permissive movement ... as the beginning of a New America." He also mentioned in his book how Freud saw in the properties of cocaine a chance to make his name known by using it first on himself and declaring that the drug increased his energy. With enthusiasm, he advised everyone to take cocaine, including even his fiancee, his sister, and his colleagues. He suggested cocaine as an aphrodisiac and promoted and declared it as the "magical drug." After using it for a considerable time on a patient whose condition deteriorated with attacks of fainting, convulsions, severe insomnia and uncontrollable behavior, Freud realized that cocaine was a dangerous drug. "The cocaine episode, as well as many others of Freud's publications and statements," Dr. Sokoloff noted, "indicates the extreme egocentrism of his character. Almost every self-observation, every fact which he experienced himself, he tended to consider as a general phenomenon, applicable to other men."[14]

The influence of Freud's teaching has changed the face of America and was adopted by many but according to William F. Buckley, Jr., nowhere was it implemented "more prodigiously than [by] Hugh Hefner, the founder of *Playboy* magazine and godfather of the sexual revolution. His formula was as straightforward as the advertisements in *Playboy* for sexually stimulating paraphernalia: make a lot of money by pandering to the sexual appetite, elevating it to primacy — then spend part of that money co-seducing critics or potential critics."[15] He pointed out what *Playboy* is essentially about: "an organ that seeks to justify the superordination of sex over all other considerations — loyalty to family, any principle of self-discipline, any respect for privacy, or for chastity or modesty: *sex omnia vincit.*"[16] Sex conquers all brought sexually explicit magazines, in every conceivable format, and flooded America to the core.

14. Ibid.
15. *Right Reason*, William F. Buckley, Jr., Little, Brown & Co., 1985, p.42.
16. Ibid.

We need not be social scientists to see the connection of sex and drugs in the current drug plague. Sex is aimed at experiencing pleasurable sensation and nothing offers this stimulation more potently than taking stimulants like cocaine. In their book, *The White Stuff*, authors B.J. Plasket and Ed Quillen wrote: "The idea was to think about yourself, to fill your own space, and to share your experience with anyone you could corner ... much of the space being shared was in the bedroom. Singles bars, Plato's Retreat Clones, and freewheeling discotheques spread almost as fast as venereal diseases. Sexual performance became yet another anxiety ... men in resort towns began to complain that the only way to get laid was to produce cocaine; a new creature, the coke whore, evolved. Cocaine heightened sensations if snorted ... cocaine seemed to elevate mundane writhings into sustained sensual performances." [17] It's touted as the all American tonic and symbolizes what the American Dream is: power, money, and pleasure.

A culture inwardly drained of the spirit, where the main obsession is material pursuit and the maximizing of pleasure and minimizing or avoidance of pain, offers a sad paradox for those who are hooked on drugs. Dr. DuPont observes: "Drug dependence which begins as a search for pleasure progresses to an increasingly unsuccessful effort to avoid the pain of withdrawal ... few chronic drug-dependent people seem to be happy. In fact, most of them look miserable as their brain-reward systems fail as a result of unnatural excessive stimulation."[18]

We have today a neo-pagan society in our midst. We have seen the factors that influenced its creation. We are experiencing daily the constant bombardment of messages that offer the "good life" and "the glimpse of heaven on earth," a spell-binding goal toward the ever consuming and endless pursuit for pleasure. An associate and former product manager of Smith, Kline & French Overseas Company, Gualbert R. Gabriel, expressed this *new culture* as "the weakening of our resolve against the vicious onslaught of that euphoric life style that everyone

17. *The White Stuff*, B.J. Plasket and Ed Quillen, Dell Publishing Co., Inc., 1985.
18. "Getting Tough on Gateway Drugs," op. cit., p.40.

seems to worship — a return to hedonistic living that is so pervasive today."

We find a strong expression of distaste for the course we have led our society into — one that is "distinctly regressive ... immature ... primitive," as Dr. Keith Yonge of the Canadian Psychiatric Association puts it — in the words of Lord Byron:

> Think'st thou there is tyranny but
> that of blood and chains?
> The despotism of vice —
> The weakness and the wickedness of luxury —
> The negligence — the apathy — the evils
> Of sensual sloth — produce ten thousand tyrants,
> Whose delegated cruelty surpasses
> The worst acts of one energetic master,
> However harsh and hard in his own bearing.

Excusitis.[19] Never heard it before? The search is on for treatment but there is no known medical cure and there *never* will be. This kind of "disease" is so pervasive that it precludes any attempt to stay away from drugs. All the phrases such as: *I had no choice, I can't stop, I'm hooked, They made me do it, I was forced to act, My urge is so strong, I can take it, I want to quit but I can't, Everybody is doing it, If drugs were not around I would have no temptation for this horror* — are examples of a number of excuses people resort to in order to rationalize their behavior and justify their taking of drugs. It's easy to make an excuse and there's millions to choose from. "The price of freedom is responsibility," writes Hugh Downs, TV anchorman, "but it's a bargain because freedom is priceless. All [such] phrases become hypocritical nonsense," he adds.

Excusitis takes on many disguises. One is imitation. Children especially look for role models and a youngster will already have said "yes" to drugs by observing permissive behavior long before opportunity presents itself to him. The message is clear: "If a major league baseball or football player does drugs, why can't I? My Mom and Dad and my favorite rock stars are doing it, why can't I?" And other celebrities, jet setters, trend setters provide the examples for emulation, not only by the young but adults as well. They feel that they too are entitled to be like

---

19. *Excusitis*, Tom J. Ilao, book in progress for Fall 1989, Light Publishing House, San Francisco.

somebody else, to act like somebody else. The desire for success is deeply-rooted in the psyche of many that it is a "must" to identify with successful people. Why do you think people are buying jackets or shirts with the name and logo of a major league winning team?

Another of excusitis' forms of disguise is what we call "the myth of immortality syndrome." Many people get involved in drugs, especially celebrities and superstars who think they are exceptionally blessed and therefore extraordinary beings — invincible and immortal. Cocaine becomes the ideal drug for this type of person because cocaine feeds their ego and creates feelings of euphoria and power and energy. It reinforces their belief that nothing can harm them.

Similar to imitation is the "fad syndrome" that is prevalent today. It is akin to the old saying, "When in Rome, do as the Romans do," or "If you can't lick them, join them." This excusitis is as trendy as the latest brand craze in blue jeans. It's the latest thing, the rage, the *dernier cri* as the French call it. "If everybody is wearing it, buy one," seems to be the message which finds a parallel in the world of drugs because it is the current fad and the fashionable thing to do.

Some excuses border on self-delusion as some people boast, "We can handle it." But the odds say they can't and drugs will handle them. We doubt if they ever get a time to stop and think. Chances are, they don't and that's the problem for many who wonder why they do drugs. Earl Nightingale told how the late Nobel prize winning scientist, Dr. Albert Schweitzer, answered when he was asked in an interview in London: "What's wrong with men today?" He responded, "Men simply don't think!" For no other time in history is his response more applicable than today.

Family Factors. "The severity of the adolescent drug abuse problem has been found to be significantly related to such family factors as the religious and educational level of parents, the disruption and dissolution of family structure, certain family constellation factors, and the number and type of problems perceived to be present in the families."[20] Parents, particularly the mother, are a powerful modeling influence for their children, either encouraging or discouraging drug use. Studies reveal that

20. *Contemporary Drug Problems*, by A.S. Friedman, et al., Fall 1980.

the examples set by mothers and older brothers and sisters often influence decisions of teenagers to use or not use drugs. For example, when mothers are cigarette smokers and/or moderate drinkers, teenage children are more likely to use a variety of drugs. Other factors like absence of parents, lack of parental closeness, unconventional parents, excessively passive mothers and drinking patterns of parents have been positively correlated with drug use.

Marijuana use, for example, was seen as serving a variety of functions to "help" adolescents cope with family problems:[21]

❏ As a defiant or provocative act directed against parents in particular, and, by extension, to other authority figures
❏ As a self-destructive act
❏ As a modifier of disturbing emotions such as anger
❏ As a reinforcer of fantasies of effortless, grandiose success
❏ As a help in withdrawing from conflicts concerning competition and achievement

Marijuana serves to detach adolescents from the problems of the real world — from their anger and unhappiness with their parents and from the need to work and compete to achieve success. It permits some to appear casual and lighthearted, while they feel miserable inside. In an unrealistic way and with self-destructive effects, marijuana helps sustain the desire for power, control, achievement and emotional fullness. "The same psychodynamic patterns," wrote E. Farley *et al*, "often are seen among abusers of other drugs, i.e., drugs that have a higher risk level than marijuana. Thus the same psychodynamic purposes or functions may be served by abuse of any one of a variety of drugs or of alcohol, or in fact by multi-drug abuse. The typical drug-using pattern of adolescents who get into treatment is to use a number of different types of drugs rather than only one drug. In a national sample of adolescent drug abusers in treatment, they reportedly had used, on the average, six different types of drugs."[22]

21. *Treatment Services for Adolescent Substance Abusers*, U.S. Department of Health and Human Services, 1985.
22. *Youth Drug Abuse: Problems, Issues and Treatment*, by E. Farley et al., Lexington Books, Massachusetts, 1979.

— Kindling An Epidemic —

Glorification of Drug Use. When President Reagan assailed the movie and music industries for "glorifying drug use," Hollywood struck back at him and said he had been watching too many old movies. Some critics insisted that Reagan's comments might have been true in the past, but not now. A recording executive echoed the sentiment of the entertainment industry by saying that the President's concept came from the late 60's when all segments of society were romanticizing drugs. The drug culture classic film *Easy Rider* of that decade glamorized dope routinely in many scenes.

However, the President cited a *Parade* magazine report from 1985 that named 60 movies in the preceding five years, including some Academy Award winners, that portray drug use in a "positive, upbeat way." He pointed out that artists who claim First Amendment rights in portraying drugs as acceptable "are really more concerned with their profits."[23]

Tom Dodge, a teacher at Mountain View College in Dallas, wrote in *U.S. News & World Report* about the story of a young undercover police officer who infiltrated the local high-school drug culture posing as a student. Suspicious students, always a step ahead of the authorities, were not duped. Behind his back they called him "21 Jump Street" referring to the popular TV show about undercover police work. The young cop was killed and police found his body outside of town, shot twice in the head. Three students and a 23-year old woman were charged in the case. The tragedy which happened in Dodge's hometown of Midlothian, Texas, sent the whole place into virtual shock. Recalling the incident, he posed this question, "Is the drug obsession among the young a result of the television networks using profits as their only motive in feeding trend-setting shows like 'Miami Vice' and '21 Jump Street,' to the young?"[24]

23. "Reagan Criticizes 'Glorifying' Drugs," *San Francisco Chronicle*, May 6, 1987.
24. "Is Their Town Like Your Town?" *U.S. News & World Report*, April 18, 1988.

Television is a ritualized or habitual activity. One writer called it a "plug-in drug" — both tend to be mindless, passive and ultimately lead to isolating experiences.

Television communicates values and interpretations of the world not only directly but implicitly in the kinds of programs and the attributes of the television performers and portrayals. The prominence of television in the thought processes of many seriously ill patients is one line of evidence that television is becoming like a religious institution. "Religiosity" is well known as a feature of schizophrenia, the most serious thought disorder.[25] Delusions about characters on entertainment television are now found in the reported thoughts of many schizophrenic patients. The portrayal of young children, in Midlothian, Texas, as "bad guys" is a triumph of character personification against the good guy who had to be eliminated.

"Television is also said to mold children's attitudes which later may be translated into behavior. Children who watch a lot of violence on television may come to accept violence as normal behavior."[26] Consequently, youngsters are constantly fed mixed messages, e.g., drugs are bad, but at the same time they receive a subtler message that "it's okay" to try drugs when they see their heroes wade through and overcome drug problems.

Not all television programs are bad. There are a number of them that are very informative and educational. But on average, what we see day in and day out is what television is all about, the selling of messages and programs that appeal to the mass market. "American television is essentially synonymous with commercial television ... As a matter of fact, it has been said that the true function of American television is not to entertain or to educate but to provide an audience for advertisers."[27]

The users of drugs like cocaine sound like a Who's Who in the entertainment industry, particularly the music industry, for instance: John Lennon, Eric Clapton, David Crosby, Mick Jagger, Andy Gibb, and many others. An Atlanta researcher, Dr. Fred Crawford, found that more than half of the current rock songs

25. "Do We Really Know Anything About the Long-Range Impact of Television?" G.Gerbner, presented at a meeting of the American Association of Public Opinion Research, Asheville, N.C., 1976.
26. *Televison and Behavior*, U.S. Department of Health and Human Services, 1982, p.6.
27. Ibid., pp.73-74.

have messages condoning or suggesting the use of drugs. One song with a strong "do drug" message is Clapton's "Cocaine."

Drug use shows up in soap operas and in magazines and American newspapers. Authors Plasket and Quillen provide an interesting revelation: "One reason for this favorable and judicial acceptance was that reporters, editors, and judges did try to avoid being hypocrites. Writers boasted that a sniff or two inspired great prose to emerge from their typewriters. Judges socialized with the same lawyers that accepted cocaine fees from their clients. It would be impossible to find a city room in the American Fourth Estate that doesn't have a cocaine user in it."[28]

One U.S. diplomat hit home about why the supply of drugs will never subside: "How do you tell some starving farmer in Peru that he has to give up the money he makes from growing coca, when back home the drug culture is glorified by glittering headshops on Hollywood Boulevard" and in movies, television, magazines, and other media that help this glorification. The romanticizing of drugs in movies of the past planted the "seeds" that are now popular television programs, so laced with violence and drug stories that writers seem unable to think up any better story lines and plots.

The Lure of the Fast Buck.   The proliferation of drug use means a staggering amount of money involved in drug dealing. It's the "New Gold Rush" of the century. Unlike the big rush to the West, "gold" today is within reach of every enterprising drug dealer and pusher. The bandwagon effect is still very much alive and everybody wants a piece of the action. There is no distant travel as in the past. One can strike a bonanza anywhere he chooses and anytime he decides to look for gold.

The rogue's gallery in the previous section lists the millionaires and billionaires who struck it rich. Many professionals who wanted a "share of the pie" also hopped in the bandwagon for one simple reason: greed. "Under the rule of the dollar human life falls to its lowest value," wrote former Congressman Charles A. Lindbergh, Sr., many years ago.

If there were no money in the illicit drug trade, it would vanish overnight. But the addiction to money becomes another problem

---

28. *The White Stuff,* op. cit.

that fuels the growth of illegal drugs. There's the hunger of the underprivileged to get rich the quickest way. And there's the privileged, whose insatiable drive to accumulate more knows no limit. In his book, *Wealth Addiction*, Philip Slater sees addiction to money as a national malaise, more prevalent than addiction to heroin or cigarettes. He wrote: "This servant has grown so powerful it has convinced us that we are empty and must find ways to fill ourselves up — that we are full of holes and must continuously plug our lacks and deficiencies with substances from outside ... This feeling of emptiness or incompleteness — this desperate dependence on external substances without which we feel incomplete — is the very essence of addiction."[29]

Thus, the creation of the symbiotic relationship between the pusher and the user is established. Soon the "have nots" become rich and it is not uncommon to see a reversal of fortune when the rich become the "have nots" later.

"The hoarder," says Erich Fromm, "who is anxiously worried about losing something is, psychologically speaking, the poor, impoverished man, regardless of how much he has."[30] He is an easy target to drug pushers to plug his "emptiness and holes" with illegal substances that offer the thrill and high he needs.

When greed is democratized and money-making is undertaken under compulsion, it is not surprising to see who is involved in drug dealing. *Time* reported: "Like most young American people, they are material girls and boys. They crave the glamorous clothes, cars, and jewelry they see advertised on TV, the beautiful things that only big money can buy."[31]

The lure of big bucks becomes so great a motivation for these young people that even their families are entirely dependent on their earnings in drug transactions. The question of working in menial jobs that give the minimum wage compensation becomes a sick joke for those who easily make a couple of thousand dollars a day. The lifestyle they enjoy is a way of identification with the rich and the famous and the realization of the American Dream.

In a highly technological society, amid prosperity, we still may find life flat, stale and meaningless. And though our gadgets

29. *Wealth Addiction*, Philip Slater, E.P. Dutton, New York, 1980.
30. "Best Strategy for Beating Stress," *The Plain Truth*, April 1985.
31. "Kids Who Sell Crack," *Time*, op. cit.

and appliances may not break, our hearts may. And we feel insecure. Others may feel otherwise — secure in the thought about what money can do for them. They wield immense power to dictate the course which the drug culture will take. Recently in his syndicated column, Jack Anderson wrote that "the drug-running Medellin cartel of Colombia is offering a $1 million bounty for the dead body of any American drug enforcement agent — the latest step in the cartel's barefaced campaign to eliminate anyone who gets in the way."[32]

It is now evident that the money we spend on illegal drugs is plowed back to create more demands on our part with the ever-increasing number of illegal drugs in the marketplace and the growing number of dealers and pushers in our society. In essence, we are providing "employment opportunities" for them and creating billionaires among those in the hierarchical organizations of the drug underworld in exchange for our miseries, and even the deaths of those who are sworn to uphold the law and the protection of all Americans and citizens of all democratic societies.

Corruption. It fuels the growth of the illegal drug business especially in the source countries where governments are literally overrun by the drug cartels. This reality vividly illustrates that the effort to stem the tide of illicit drugs coming from these places is an exercise in futility. The place of origin, tainted with corruption, spreads its contagion along the way, laying bare the vulnerability of all destinations. The power of drugs, if it corrupts, corrupts absolutely. Its influence has spared neither people in high places, nor many mediocre, self-seeking individuals (including law enforcement agents) motivated by an unmanageable greed for money. In a society that has brought about a meltdown of time-honored values, it is too easy to compromise one's integrity and submit to bribery and greed. "The dollar amounts are so great," one top law enforcement officer admitted, "that bribery threatens the very foundation of law and law enforcement." The following isolated facts attest to the truth of his statement:

32. "Colombian Cartel Tough on Drug Agents," Jack Anderson, *The Tribune*, September 26, 1988.

⇨ One cocaine ring, known as the grandma Mafia [three of its principals were grandmothers] banked more than $2 million a month. In the trial in Los Angeles, there had been at least four plausible allegations of corruption against DEA and IRS agents. A federal indictment in Georgia in December 1982 said that a state police sergeant and a local deputy sheriff were confederates in a 25-person smuggling ring. In one week in February 1983, a Los Angeles deputy sheriff, a California-based DEA agent and a San Jose policeman were charged with selling coke.[33]

⇨ In the last five years, 11 rural sheriffs in Tennessee were arrested. Most of the corruption charges are drug-related. In Miami, dozens of cops were arrested in what was probably the worst police scandal in Florida history, police officers splitting up millions of dollars in drug money. The police chief says a hundred cops may have been involved. In New York City, two dozen police officers were arrested in one drug scandal in just one precinct. One former cop, Henry Winter, said he not only stole the drugs, but turned into a drug dealer himself.[34]

⇨ Three U.S. soldiers and a Panamanian were intercepted by customs officials as they arrived aboard a Military Airlift Command, managed by the U.S. Air Force. They were arrested after 77 pounds of cocaine were found in the U.S. military plane they flew from Panama.[35]

The world moves on money and there's plenty in the illicit drug world. "We know the enormous wealth of the drug merchants," says former FBI Director William H. Webster, "which can alter the economy of an entire region, perhaps even the nation, and be used to corrupt or directly assault the criminal justice process."

And there's nothing so sad and tragic as the corruption of some of the best among us, the law enforcers and those charged with our national security. And indeed nothing helps fan the flame of the present drug epidemic faster than corruption in many places.

---

33. *Time*, April 11, 1983.
34. "Drugs: A Plague on the Land," op. cit.
35. "77 Pounds of Cocaine in U.S. Military Plane," *San Francisco Examiner*, February 4, 1988.

Misinformation. David Toma, former narcotics officer, author and lecturer on the subject of drug abuse, states in his book: "If the physicians don't know the truth about marijuana and the shrinks don't know, if the politicians don't know, and the educators don't know, then how in the hell can the children find out?"[36] This statement sums up the drug situation as it is today. Our lack of correct information and education on the health hazards of all drugs confounds the problem. And the drug culture proves to be one step ahead all the time.

To begin to understand the pervasiveness of drugs, particularly marijuana and cocaine, is to understand how the marketing strategy of the drug culture works. Any marketing plan to be effective and successful, after identifying its intended market or audience, sets a sizeable budget for its advertising promotion and hits the market real hard.

The multifarious propaganda machine of the drug culture has an unlimited budget for its promotion and like a deadly missile is aimed at our youth who are always eager to try something new, experiment on the forbidden and the glamorous. The intent and various methods of disseminating tainted information is best summed up by Suzanne Labin, a French writer, in her testimony before a Senate hearing: The so-called progressive intelligentsia has shed, through the mass media of communication, torrents of propaganda presenting the "hippie drug culture" with an interesting aura, as a pristine upsurge of our "advanced" youngsters, to enlarge human potentialities beyond the dull limits imposed by our ugly society. This propaganda, through the press, books, lectures, film, TV, magazines, songs, buttons, posters, mass rallies, and happenings, has reached much greater proportions than is commonly realized. The so-called underground hippie press has, in fact, an open circulation of millions of copies each week, most of which chant loudly the marvels of drugs. The record makers of the establishment have issued tens of millions of records alluding to the marvels of drugs.[37]

We have to remember that the drug culture industry is a multi-billion dollar business (the drug paraphernalia alone is a

---

36. *Toma Tells It Straight — With Love*, David Toma and Irv Levey, Dell Publishers, 1988.
37. *Papers on Drug Abuse*, Otto Moulton, 1983, p.14.

$3 billion enterprise).With such vast and unlimited resources at their disposal, there's no doubt that their well-orchestrated propaganda of misinformation is the greatest single factor that enkindled the "fire" of an epidemic more swift than all factors combined.[38]

Otto Moulton, the nation's foremost expert on information generated by the drug culture, stated in an international symposium in June 1980:

> The problem confronting us today is that the drug culture has controlled most of the information that has reached the general public ... Unfortunately, well-meaning and not so well-meaning organizations have been led to believe, in a lot of misinformation, brainwashing, etc. ... How the drug culture has accomplished this task in this country is by controlling and confusing Federal, State, and Local government agencies. The tragedy is that these agencies have had a great influence on the media, education, and medical profession, and citizens of our nation. Pressure from organizations like the so-called A.C.L.U., National Organization for the Reform of Marijuana Laws (NORML), The Drug Abuse Council, Do It Now Foundation, STASH, and young people misguided by the life, liberty, and pursuit of happiness theme generated by these same people have and are working against these same freedoms.[39]

And he asked: "How is it possible to have life through drugs? Liberty through drugs? And happiness through drugs? This could *never* be possible." And how many do we know who have died or are suffering addicts in our treatment and rehabilitation centers who fell into the trap of "Do Drug" messages for "recreational or social use." Recreational or social use usually does not take over one's life and destroy it. In 1984, a young kid in Cupertino, California, came out of the garage and called to his mother, "Mom, see this?" and blew his brains out. Recreational, responsible, intelligent use?

We see the prevalence of euphemisms and the deadly mass marketing of misinformation today that mislead and spread lies instead of enlightenment and correct information. Today, deadly drugs are given exotic and beautiful names, hiding what they really are — *deadly drugs*. It is part of the drug culture's

---

38. "Marijuana: The Myth of Harmlessness Goes Up In Smoke," Peggy Mann, reprinted article from *The Saturday Evening Post*.
39. *Papers on Drug Abuse*, op. cit., p.4.

marketing scheme that it is filled with distortion and manipula-
tion of facts. "They have flooded our bookstores and libraries
with their own misinformation," declared Otto Moulton in one
of his fact-finding tours.

Popular drug-culture magazines like *High Times*, *Hi Life*, *Rush*,
and *Head*, teach how to grow your own grass, how to smuggle
dope into the U.S., how to dress for pot parties, how to get
around the law. They are magazines extolling the joys of drug
taking that are to be found in newsstands throughout the country. The slick *High Times* boasts four million readers. Such
publications make illicit drugs seem as normal as popcorn and
apple pie. Comic books show how to smoke dope, how to cut
and snort cocaine. *McGrassey's Reader*, an easy-to-read primer,
explains how to roll a joint and comes with "practice grass"
(alfalfa), rolling papers and a "roach clip." Their advertisers
reach a market of young people with money to spend, and the
drug paraphernalia in their pages is available by mail — in effect,
portable head shops, accessible to young residents of even the
smallest, most remote communities. "The target for drug paraphernalia in the 1980's is ages 6 to 16," the operator of one of
Florida's largest head shop chains admitted, claiming it was "an
industry decision." Organized campaigns of this sort, added to
tremendous peer pressure, are misleading young people into
believing that pot smoking is a normal part of growing up.[40]

Books of drug misinformation that are commonly found in
school libraries today are *Chocolate to Morphine*, written by
Andrew Weil and Winifred Rosen, published by Houghton Mifflin, Boston, in 1983; *The Natural Mind*, also by Andrew Weil,
published in 1972 by the same publisher; *Licit & Illicit Drugs*, by
Edward M. Brecher and the editors of *Consumer Reports*, published by Little, Brown in 1972; *Understanding Psychology*, fourth
edition, a textbook, published by Random House, Inc., New
York, 1986.

The messages from these books are bound to pique the
curiosity of young people. "What adventurous youngster,"
Peggy Mann asked, "would *not* want to try mescaline or LSD, for
example, after reading in *Licit & Illicit Drugs* (page 337) that
mescaline users have found its most spectacular phase com-
prises the kaleidoscopic play of visual hallucinations in inde-

---

40. "Marijuana: The Myth of Harmlessness Goes Up In Smoke," op. cit.

scribably rich colors ... the 'seeing' of music in colors or the 'hearing' of a painting in music." Page 364 describes a 1960s study finding LSD valuable as "a therapeutic tool, a road to love and better relationships ... a door to religious experience ... a release from anxiety or troubles."[41] Charles Hiller Innes took LSD in his cell and quietly blinded himself by gouging out his eyes. "Anybody who looks into those dead eyes can see clearly that Charlie has been where nobody wants to go," reported *Reader's Digest*. Dr. Bruce W. Jafek, Chairman of the Department of Otolaryngology at the University of Colorado School of Medicine once saw a man in a state of cocaine-induced paranoia, who having shot himself, walked along the highway with blood dripping from what was left of his face. "It will take years of plastic surgery to rebuild that man's face. All I can do is wonder why people do that to themselves." Again, hardly a case of a beautiful out-of-body experience!

In his book, *The Natural Mind*, Weil talked about altered consciousness as having "great potential for strongly positive psychic development." And he added that "there is much logic in our being born with a drive to experiment and to attempt to thwart this drive would probably be impossible and might be dangerous." He admitted there are certain risks "but ultimately it can confer psychic superiority." He talked about his LSD trip and, as a result, his relationship with insects which, otherwise considered harmful and hostile, became his friends and a source of pleasure; he describes how, hearing about the power of mescaline to produce visions, it aroused his curiosity at once and he resolved to devote his ingenuity to getting and trying the drug himself; he writes of his experiment with Psilocybin, a hallucinogen, when he experienced "striking visual illusions that became more and more kaleidoscopic."

The popularity of *Chocolate to Morphine* by Weil and Rosen is no accident. The kind of advice they give to the young resembles a guru-follower relationship: "Grown-ups will give you so much misinformation ... Question your parents ... if you can convince them that your drug use is responsible, you may be able to allay their anxiety ... try to educate them ... Give them this book as a background to your discussion of drugs." (By the way, it's hard

41. "We're Teaching Our Kids to Use Drugs," Peggy Mann, *Reader's Digest*, November 1987.

to get a copy of this book. Librarians disclosed that most copies have never been returned. I doubt seriously if the books are ever given to parents.)

And to parents, the book offers this advice: "Don't make your child feel it is wrong to get high. If you oppose the use of drugs ... be prepared to forgo your own drug use as an example to your child." (A perfect lecture for a society so deeply immersed in the drug problem that it is practically impossible to point an accusing finger to any guilty party because everybody is guilty.)

Daniel M. Haigh, president of Sanford Area Families in Action, Sanford, Michigan, expressed his concern after reading the fourth edition of *Understanding Psychology*. In his letter to the Editor of Random House, Inc., he said, "With more being learned daily about the adverse effects of marijuana, and the horrible addiction potential of cocaine, I cannot understand how both of these drugs could have placed so low on your table of 'Drugs Used for Mind-Alteration from Most Dangerous to Least Harmful.' Both cocaine and marijuana should be rated very high in harm potential."

Page 170 of said book addresses marijuana in a largely positive sense, declaring: "...in general, most sensory experiences seem greatly augmented — music sounds fuller; colors look brighter; smells are stronger; foods have stronger flavors; and other experiences are more intense than usual. Users may feel elated, the world may seem somehow more meaningful, and even the most ordinary events may take on an extraordinary significance. A person who is high on marijuana may, for example, suddenly become aware of the mystical implications of a particular painting."

Page 94 of *Chocolate to Morphine* shows a striking similarity to the above passages. Drawing from those who had "pleasant trips" with LSD, Weil and Rosen talked of such experiences as "a powerful feeling of love, mystical oneness with all things, union with God, and deeper understanding of themselves ... description of vivid sensory changes ... such as seeing flowers breathe, objects shimmer with energy, and mosaic patterns appear on all surfaces." Such descriptions the authors added, "make other people, especially young people, eager to try the drug for themselves." Their additional advice includes seeking an experienced companion for the first-time user of hallucinogenic drugs. But who can find such a "companion" among the hordes of drug addicts?

Weil stated that his experience with all mind-altering drugs and marijuana gave him a source of great joy as a result of his experimentation. He cites the drug use of famous persons such as Edgar Allan Poe who used laudanum, a tincture of opium, suggesting that his macabre tales were no doubt influenced by his experiences with the drug; Aldous Huxley, British writer and philosopher, experimented extensively with mescaline; William James used nitrous oxide; Sigmund Freud took cocaine; English poets Samuel Taylor Coleridge and Thomas De Quincey both were users of laudanum.

We cannot doubt that the inclusion of such famous names is a subtle endorsement to rationalize the use of drugs. The message is loud and clear: "If they experimented and used drugs and I did it too, why not you?" Dr. Sokoloff's statement's regarding the extreme egocentrism of Freud who believed that every fact he experienced himself was applicable to others seems to be the norm of those who experimented with drugs and lived (and wrote about it).

To speak of "using drugs intelligently and responsibly" as advocated by writers of the drug culture, is a frightening statement for a society targeted by this group whose young members have yet to understand what responsibility means and what intelligent information they could gather amid the vast misinformation deliberately designed to sow confusion in their young minds.

In conclusion, we see that misinformation is a big lie, the most destructive propaganda machine ever conceived. It feeds the drug epidemic, destroys and alienates relationships among family members by "guru-follower" tactics and above all, claims many young lives and places the future of this nation in limbo.

Rosenblatt, in *A Letter to the Year 2086*, addressed this powerful encroachment in our lives. He wrote: "A huge business these days is called public relations, which in fact is concerned with the most private relations of well-trained people with information on social patterns. That enterprise has taken the expansiveness of democracy and honed it to a point from which a few manipulate the many." In his preface to *The Closing of the American Mind*, Bloom is more direct and talks about "the various impostors whose business it is to appeal to the young.

These culture peddlers have the strongest motives for finding out the appetites of the young."

To close this chapter, I believe it appropriate to include Labin's thought on the effect of the continued use of drugs:

> All of the drugs, after long usage, undermine the two principal pillars of all civilizations: in the realm of the mind, the power of reasoning; and in the realm of the soul, the will. Without the ability to think about the universe in a positive way, and without the impulse to act on it, there is no longer room for great works and, hence, there is no more real culture. That is why, should the use of drugs become permanent and universal ... it would lead to the ruin of all human civilizations.[42]

42. *Papers on Drug Abuse*, op. cit., p.15.

7

VOICES

It's extraordinary how we go through life with eyes half-shut, with dull ears, with dormant thoughts.
— Joseph Conrad, British writer

Amid the intolerable noises around us — if we really care to listen — we would find time to reflect upon the individual voices, the amplifiers for the silent voice in all of us. They are the voices of the famous and not-so-famous, the known and the unknown. Some speak of sympathy and compassion but others are angry voices that express resentment, frustration and indignation. There are thoughtful voices that offer solutions, send warnings and pose some challenges for us. We hear voices of former addicts who learned from their hard experiences. And there are the voices of the vast majority who are just concerned that "another scourge of humanity" is unsettling all of us.

They ought to be listened to — because their messages, in great part, speak of facts and realities. It could result in drawing us together into one collective force, as a community of believers, who would turn the tide of war on our side. *This must be our overriding consideration.*

We are all part of this period in history where collective voices could make a big difference, especially where drastic alternatives like the legalization of illegal drugs could prove very problematic and dangerous. We must rally, and then rely on a responsible and determined citizenry to make the needed changes, first from within and then to implement that change in all of society. We are a nation gone awry. We have become unwilling, and at times, willing pawns and puppets manipulated by sinister forces, but history has proven that we are a positive and resilient people who arose at the crises of the past to emerge victorious every time. This is another difficult moment in history but we can rely once more on this resiliency and willingness of our fellow Americans to heed yet another great voice from the past, that of John F. Kennedy, to "ask not what your country can do for you — ask what you can do for your country."

The burden is on us if we want history to judge us fairly, but as John Ruskin, a British writer, stated, "The only history worth reading is that written at the time of which it treats, the history of what was done and seen, heard out of the mouths of the men [and women] who did and saw." We have seen and we are doing something — and here are some of the voices to tell us what we feel and what ought to be told:

- ❏ Drug trafficking has become the nation's No. 1 crime. *William H. Webster, former FBI Director*
- ❏ Drug dealers and pushers are domestic terrorists. *President George Bush*
- ❏ When they sell their poisons on the streets and in the suburbs of America, the drug pushers don't check their customers' party registration. *Former Speaker of the House Thomas P. O'Neill*
- ❏ The drug business is awful. The drug business is destructive to our lifestyle and the security of this country, and we've simply got to face it for what it is: that is, a major threat. *Howard Baker, former Senator and White House Chief of Staff*
- ❏ Take a body count of how many people we've lost to Communism, and a body count of how many people we've lost to drug addiction, and I'll tell you how to measure national security. *Rep. Charles Rangel*
- ❏ Heroin and cocaine does not grow here — it's brought here. We must stop it, stop it from coming here. *Mayor Marion Barry, Washington, D.C.*
- ❏ Corruption is fueling this drug epidemic. There's so much money in the illicit drug trade. *Rene Medina, President, Lucky Tours, Inc., San Francisco*
- ❏ The United States is the most pervasive drug-abusing nation in history. *Rep. Lester Wolff*
- ❏ You know, drugs at a chic LA party, New York party, Chicago, wherever, are no different from drugs in a

back alley. It's the same thing. *Former First Lady Nancy Reagan*

❏ Go around and test all the housewives and doctors and lawyers in this country and see what you get ... This country is awash with drugs. *Steve Howe, former LA Dodgers pitcher*

❏ What can I tell you? It's a dope-ridden society. *A Police Officer*

❏ We see walking drugstore cases frequently — drivers found to have four or five different drugs in their body fluids. You wouldn't expect that a person could handle this number of drugs and still be conscious — much less driving an automobile. *Victor Reeve, Sacramento Department of Justice Crime Lab*

❏ The drug situation is no different than it was in 1956 or 1962. I was an intern in Harlem Hospital in New York in those years and I had seen rampant drug abuse. *Dionysius I. Macatiag, General Surgeon, San Francisco*

❏ Drug dealing and violence makes me sick to my stomach. *A 60-year old woman, East Oakland*

❏ I've done drugs because I wanted to and I've done it ever since I was little because my parents used them and I tried them since. *A teenager, from a TV News Report, "Lost Innocence: The Erosion of American Childhood"*

❏ A sizeable number of our young people will not mature as they should. Instead, we can look forward to a growing population of immature, underqualified adults, many of whom will be unable to live without economic, social or clinical support. *Mitchell Rosenthal, Director, Phoenix House, New York City*

❏ We're close to genocide of our young people. *Al Davis, LA Raiders owner*

❏ To many Americans today, adolescence is a mess. When alcohol and drug use are added, the mess becomes deadly. *Robert L. DuPont, Jr., M.D.*

❏ Drug use impairs memory, alertness, and achievement. Drugs erode the capacity of students to perform in school, to think and act responsibly. The consequences of using drugs can last a lifetime. Because of drugs, children are failing, suffering, and dying. We have to get tough, and we have to do it now. *William J. Bennett, former U.S. Secretary of Education*

❏ Kids can get hold of almost anything they want to get high — a joint, a snort, a vial, a pill, or a drink. They want to get high, more and more of them every day, and every year the customers get younger. *David Toma, former narcotics detective, New Jersey*

❏ You don't look into a crack-infested neighborhood and see flower children. We must be realistic. Many of our young brothers and sisters are not going to make it. *Harry Edwards, sociologist, UC Berkeley*

❏ We cannot afford the tragedy of losing our kids to drugs. *William Schumacher, member, Board of Supervisors, San Mateo County, California*

❏ Our children are our future. It is sad to see our future lie in the gutter ... hopeless, helpless, and addicted. *Anthony Villegas, United States Jaycees District 15 Governor, California*

❏ The regard for law and values deteriorates, because if you can't stop people from pumping poison into themselves, you can't do much of anything else as a society. *Rudolph Giuliani, U.S. Attorney*

❏ People have to say no to this stuff. It's a poison, it's a rat poison, it kills people. It doesn't do anybody any good. It helps foment crime in the streets. It's ruining our country. Enough! Stop! *Peter Ueberroth, Baseball Commissioner*

❏ I wish we could devote our energy to mitigating the health problems caused by unavoidable disease and accidents, rather than treating people for problems they brought on themselves. *Bruce W. Jafek, M.D., University of Colorado School of Medicine*

❏ Anybody that takes a damn straw to their nose ought to think: it can happen to me if it can happen to Len Bias. *Arthur A. Marshall, Jr., Maryland State Attorney*

❏ It's the cruelest thing I've ever heard. *Larry Bird, Boston Celtics, referring to Len Bias' death*

❏ Perhaps the most surprising evidence of cocaine's popularity is its widespread use in professional sports. Athletes, according to popular myth, treat their bodies like temples; it turns out that many treat their bodies like laboratory rats. *Authors B.J. Plasket and Ed Quillen*

❑ It scared me that so many people are using cocaine and pushing it. As far as I'm concerned, anybody who uses it is showing a sign of weakness. *Billy Martin, baseball manager*

❑ I have no sympathy for young people today who, complaining that they have no hope for the future, try to escape reality by using drugs. *Chuck Norris, actor, author of The Secret of Inner Strength*

❑ Ingesting poison, short-circuiting the impulses in your brain, sucking a chemical into a cavity in your skull where there is no lymphatic system to protect you against infection, isn't chic or modern or bright — it's stupid. *Buck Rodgers, author of The IBM Way*

❑ You're like a rat in a sewer — scurrying around; it's an emotional sewer and a physical sewer. *Anonymous*

❑ I believe, passionately, that drugs ... are foolish. I do not drink, smoke, or take drugs. I never have. When I give speeches I beg people to give up this form of self-destruction. However, if you do it, that's your choice. It's your life. I only ask, then, that you contain your self-destructiveness. Why should I be forced to watch it? *Rita Mae Brown, novelist, poet and teacher, from The Courage of Conviction*

❑ I don't think being isolated and lonely is glamorous. I think this is your life and why kill yourself? *Anonymous*

❑ Legalizing drugs? We'll be seeing a whole bunch of guys going from clinic to clinic. *David Sliptzin, pharmacist, San Francisco*

❑ Anything of mood-altering drugs, like crack, or any form of cocaine, I think is nothing short of playing Russian roulette with your health and with your life. *Anonymous*

❑ Cocaine is one of the worst drug-abuse catastrophes ever to face our nation. *Dr. Donald Ian McDonald, administrator, U.S. Alcohol, Drug Abuse and Mental Health Administration*

❑ I consider cocaine the devil on this Earth. *Keith Hernandez, New York Mets*

- ❏ PCP can't hurt? Go to the cemeteries and look at the tombstones and then say that. *Anonymous*

- ❏ Crack is more addictive than any other form of cocaine. It's the dealer's dream and the user's nightmare. *Dr. Arnold Weshton, Director of Research, National Cocaine Hotline*

- ❏ It's hard, it's uncomfortable, it's nasty. You feel degraded. This strips you mentally, morally and physically. If I could have any wish, anything I wanted in the world, if I could turn back the hands, I wouldn't ask for $2 million. I wouldn't ask for money. The thing I wish most for is that I never f——d around with cocaine. *Anonymous*

- ❏ Cocaine addicts go downhill at 200 miles an hour. We see them after they have crashed into the proverbial brick wall. *A therapist*

- ❏ Enough is never present in your reasoning. You've had enough when it's gone, and when it's gone you want some more. *Eugene Morris, former Miami Dolphin football star*

- ❏ I inhaled deeply, the way I do cigarettes or marijuana. I felt I'd been hit in the chest by a hammer. I was in shock. I couldn't feel myself breathing, my throat and lungs went numb. I was scared to death. *A cocaine user*

- ❏ PCP is no good. It's a rattlesnake and it'll kill you. Don't go near it. *Robert Blake, TV star of Baretta*

- ❏ The drug culture is an escape, a destructive cop-out. *Bill Milliken*

- ❏ When you're as well-known a junkie as I was, it's easy to get the drug dealers to come right over. They're faster than a pizza delivery. Over the years I spent millions of dollars. *David Crosby*

- ❏ But a non-user should not use a recovering addict as an example. They should use dead addicts as examples. *John Burton, lawyer and Congressman*

- ❏ "Just say no" sounds fine but an addict is a person who can't say no. It's a horrible merry-go-round, a nightmare ... I was paranoid all the time, became psychotic and was hospitalized. I couldn't function in a loving manner with my family. The pain of isolation was intense. *A recovering addict*

❑ In the beginning, I felt I was communicating with God. In the end, I thought I was God. *A recovering physician*

❑ Drug people aren't stupid. They know that if they can addict a superstar ... they can link themselves to his name, to his fame. Then they can get other people to fall in line a little easier. *Red Auerbach, General Manager, Boston Celtics*

❑ I think we have to hold out that responsibility and try to portray ourselves as good, clean human beings who have problems like anyone else but hopefully not a drug problem. *Ron Darling, New York Mets pitcher*

❑ We are accustomed to living way beyond our means. We flesh out our domestic economy with loans and credit cards. So it is almost a natural extension of this logic that we can live outside our emotional means, with drugs, and get away from it. *Mark S. Gold, M.D., author, 800-Cocaine and founder of the toll-free National Hotline for cocaine users and victims*

❑ Drugs never made anything easier to cope with. The effect wears off and the problems don't go away. I don't do drugs because I like to be in control of my life. *Madonna*

❑ How bad is the drug scene? The securities business makes us look like Mary Poppins! *Skid Weiss, communications director at Warner/Elektra/Atlantic Records*

❑ Who are people taking drugs? People avoiding unpleasantness and seeking happiness in the wrong way — escaping from their problems only to find themselves deeper into more problems. *George W. Yen, tax and financial consultant, San Francisco*

❑ Something is wrong with a lot of people — there's no meaning in their lives — that's why they resort to drugs. *Mario A. Santos, Chairman of the Board, O'Manna Financial Corporation, California*

❑ Illicit drugs enslave the user and victimize all of us. We are all innocent victims in a lot of ways. *Cas & Lucy Nacario, Amway Pearl Direct Distributors*

❑ Some people seem to use drugs casually and have few resulting problems, while others center their lives around a drug and literally follow its pleasures, however hapless or harrowing, to their graves. *Robert L. DuPont, Jr., M.D.*

❑ One of the most startling attacks on our immunity is the recreational use of drugs. Recent studies have linked drug use — including smoking and drinking — to decreased immunity. Some experts also think such drug use opens the window of vulnerability for the AIDS virus. *Bill Dunnett, editor and writer, American Health Magazine*

❑ We all think our personalities are well grounded and well formed, but it doesn't take a lot to tilt the psychological balance. *Peter Bensinger, former DEA chief*

❑ The drug user must understand the gravity of his situation and the necessity for ending his dependency; his recognition of these facts must lead to a determination to quit. Only he can make this decision. *Hardin and Helen Jones, authors of Sensual Drugs*

❑ Without chemical assistance, we can explore ourselves as much as we want. *Fred Swanson, candidate, Permanent Diaconate Program, San Francisco*

❑ If you guys don't say "no," then the country's gone. See, because I only know one way that a foreign country could knock out the United States, and that's to tear up a generation, to knock a generation out, and your generation is being knocked out by drugs. *Doc Ellis, former major league baseball player*

❑ Our high school athletes must meet other challenges separate from the pressure of competition. They must face the reality of drug and alcohol abuse in their schools. *John C. Lawn, Administrator, Drug Enforcement Administration*

❑ There's a problem because of the great demand for illegal drugs. It's definitely a people problem and people should rethink their personal values, and in a larger sense, the family values as well. *Stan Escalante, President & CEO, O'Manna Financial Corporation, California*

❏ In my experience, students who have had a serious fling with drugs — and gotten over it — find it difficult to have enthusiasms or great expectations. It is as though the color has been drained out of their lives and they see everything in black and white. *Allan Bloom, from The Closing of the American Mind*

❏ The problem of drugs can be solved by families helping one another; schools educating the children from the earliest grades possible; and, in general, making the dangers of drugs to be everybody's concern. *Purificacion B. Lazo, teacher, San Francisco Unified School District*

Teachers and parents have a great task in molding young minds. They exert tremendous influence in inspiring and motivating our young people to like themselves, and to set higher goals for themselves. A lot of us can learn from athletic coaches who are well known for great motivation. One such trainer of athletes is Carey E. McDonald, Executive Director of the National High School Athletic Coaches Association, who is convinced of the urgent need to do all that we can to win the war against the drug onslaught. He declared, "The development of an effective drug education program in each school offers a tremendous challenge to each coach and athlete at all levels of sports in America to compete in the battle for youth against drugs ... a very desperate struggle in which our final scoreboard must read WIN!"

Part Three
Toward a Drug-Free America

8

CRUSADE AGAINST DRUG TRAFFICKING AND ABUSE

This war has to be fought in the minds of the citizens of our country — it's they who spend billions of dollars consuming these drugs.

— Charles Lewis, U.S. Attorney

— War Strategies Against Supply —

The Eradication Drive. Because drug abuse is real, it requires action on several fronts. One long-held effort to stop the flow of illegal drugs is border interdiction. But the length of the U.S. coastlines and borders is more than difficult for federal agents to police. The 8,426 miles of deeply indented Florida coastline and the 2,067-mile border with Mexico, for example, pose a formidable challenge to our law enforcement agents overwhelmed by the sheer volume and magnitude of the drug traffic. It's a frustration to many of them, evidenced by the complaint of one of its agents: "It's an awful lot of border to cover and there's an awful lot of airspace and there's a lot of time available. I mean, the crooks can do it 24 hours a day, seven days a week."

A congressional study revealed that federal officials are intercepting only a small percentage of the narcotics being smuggled into the U.S. Only 6-10 percent of all drugs coming in are seized. Experts believe that though seizures are up, it points to the fact that there is a greater volume of supply, and the search for incoming drugs will always be a needle-in-a-haystack operation.

So pervasive has the drug issue become that last year 24 nations joined together in a crackdown to eradicate the growing world supply. *U.S. News & World Report* wrote that the effort paid off with the destruction of 5,046 metric tons of coca leaf and 17,585 tons of marijuana plants. It remains a fact, however, that the eradication effort is insufficient to reduce the worldwide supply of illicit drugs. An example is the cocaine now sold on the streets: it's much purer and yet its price has plummeted, giving evidence of increased supplies.

Law enforcement efforts and the continuing crackdown on drug dealers and pushers have resulted in more arrests and more convictions. The seizure and forfeiture of convicted drug trafficker's assets, funnelled to education and prevention programs, is considered a successful part of the crackdown drive. But despite the seemingly positive results, the war on narcotics on the streets is far from being won. Many contend that the war on drugs is unwinnable. And the greatest optimists have no hope of ever intercepting even half the marijuana, heroin and cocaine slipping into the U.S. and eventually landing on the streets. There are simply too many ways to bring those drugs in. This reality is best summed up in the words of a former smuggler: "Trying to stop drug smuggling is like sweeping the bottom of the ocean with a broom."

A Call for Tougher Policies.   In the current anti-drug fervor, several proposals are under study:

- ❏   The White House National Drug Policy Board proposes the development of an international police force to attack record-setting cocaine production in South America. The international force hopes to include the participation of European countries which are experiencing increased cocaine consumption. The proposed international force would provide security for institutions such as the Colombian Judiciary which is under attack by powerful cocaine traffickers.

- ❏   Another proposal was a sweeping reorganization of the government's anti-drug activities, calling for the creation of a cabinet-level national drug director or drug czar, a national drug prevention agency and consideration of an international anti-drug fleet of aircraft.

- ❏   Among the recommendations of the White House Conference for a Drug-Free America were tougher mandatory sentences for drug dealers including the death penalty for drug kingpins responsible for murders; harsher sanctions on first-time users including fines, community services, house arrest and loss of driver's license.

❏ The bulk of the anti-drug bill is aimed at bolstering law enforcement efforts. Its most notable aspects stem from a decision to go after consumers in a strict policy known as "user accountability." It includes civil fines up to $10,000 for possession of small amounts of marijuana, cocaine or other illegal drugs; a cutoff of some federal benefits, such as student loans, federal mortgage guarantees, federal grants, licenses and permits and government contracts for persons convicted of drug-related crimes; establishment of a federal capital punishment statute for some drug-related murders.

❏ A proposal by Lieutenant Governor Leo McCarthy of California suggests transferring $1 billion from the "Star Wars" funds to existing drug interdiction and law enforcement programs; cutting off foreign aid to governments found by the CIA to be involved in drug trafficking and shifting that money to U.S. anti-drug education programs; transferring assets seized in drug arrests to addict's rehabilitation programs; and providing federal money to school districts for mandatory drug education.

❏ A "Drug-Free Zone" around schools was introduced by U.S. Attorney Joseph P. Russoniello. The idea is an accompaniment to the federal government's tough "Zero Tolerance" program under which federal agents are seizing vehicles, boats and planes if traces of controlled substances are found aboard. Russoniello's plan would use existing federal laws to double the potential federal prison terms for those caught selling drugs within 1,000 feet of a school. Trafficking in drugs near a school would result in a minimum of 20 years imprisonment and a maximum of life.

Military Intervention. The White House Conference for a Drug-Free America gave no estimate of how much its more than 100 recommendations would cost. The reality is that even the best possible solutions are costly and time-consuming, and some are problematic and even unworkable as in the case of using the military. But the bitterly disillusioned are determined to send in the Marines. Previous experience, however, proved to be an embarrassment as in the case of "Operation Blast Furnace." U.S.

troops stormed and carried the drug battle to Bolivia but the search-and-destroy missions into the countryside ended in failure.

To mobilize troops in the fight against drugs, like sealing the border of Mexico, would take 90 infantry battalions, more than half of all U.S. combat units. Intercepting smugglers at sea could be just as ineffective as the U.S. lacks sufficient ships to set up a blockade across the Caribbean. Tracking drug traffickers by air is extremely difficult with tens of thousands of small-plane flights each year entering the Southern states from abroad. Even the use of great balloons packed with radar capable of peering more than 100 miles into Mexico has been challenged. Altogether the National Drug Policy Board had approved a "chain" of 16 balloons stretching from the Caribbean to the Pacific — a supposedly impenetrable "electric picket fence" that officials contended would close the entire southern border to drug smuggling aircraft. At a cost that may reach $1 billion over the next six years, this latest anti-drug weapon may be largely worthless: It has not caught a single drug plane since it began full-time operations in June 1987. The reason was that drug smugglers are using land vehicles rather than aircraft and concealing their shipments in containerized cargo. Jack A. Blum, chief investigator for the Senate Foreign Relations Subcommittee on Narcotics calls the newest anti-drug strategy "a screaming idiocy." And he wryly added, "There's a wonderful madness to all this."[1]

Using the military to solve non-military problems will not work. Critics contend that law enforcement requires a different set of values from those in combat. Thousands of soldiers would have to be trained in rules of law enforcement. Some voice concern about giving the military search-and-seizure and arrest powers. Some fear that militarizing drug enforcement could lead to further breaches in what they see as a constitutional wall between the civil state and the military.

The military involvement would have its inherent risks and limitations. The kingpins of the trade have heavily-armed drug armies and serious military arsenals to protect their business interests. We already ignited anti-Yankee sentiment with our

1. "Anti-Smuggling Strategy Doubted," *San Francisco Chronicle*, November 9, 1988.

failed assault in Bolivia. Military operations would erode restraints on military action contained in the Posse Comitatus Act of 1878 which forbids the military from civilian law enforcement. The War Powers Act of 1973 requires consultation with Congress for the deployment of troops in hostile places abroad.

Defense Secretary Frank Carlucci strongly resented the broad expansion of the Pentagon's role in the war on drugs, stating, "just because people say it's a national security problem doesn't automatically make it a defense responsibility." In short, it's a wrong task for the military to police drug trafficking.

— Clamping the Lid on Demand —

With each desperate search for a solution to the drug dilemma, we are moving further and further away from where the real solution lies, that is, in attacking the root cause of this problem — America's voracious appetite for mind-altering substances. It makes sense to shift the focus of the drug war from trying to control and cut off the supplies to reducing the demand. Consider how much we have already spent in the drug war: "Since 1981," says *U.S. News & World Report*, "76 percent of the $21 billion in federal funds has financed overseas crop eradication, speedboat chases off the Florida coast and seizures along the Mexican border."[2] The cost of keeping an AWACS in the air is about $7,500 an hour. This staggering amount could be better put to use in the prevention and education programs to reduce and eliminate the demand in the long run. We know that despite the big effort in all areas of interdiction, the payoff is meager in terms of denting the multi-billion drug business.

The real problem then isn't foreign supply but domestic demand. By creating a huge illegal market, the United States has even exported its drug culture abroad with all the accompanying miseries and social disruptions in other places as well. It's estimated that the number of regular cocaine users in Western Europe alone may reach three to four million by the mid-1990's. The United Nations study reveals that it is at the point now of endangering the very security of some nations.

Prevention and Education. It is a step in the right direction to cope with the enormous, unmet need for drug education and

2. "The Demand-Side Fix," *U.S. News & World Report*, March 14, 1988.

prevention. Nancy Reagan's "Just Say No" crusade has created an awareness and more than 10,000 clubs with 200,000 youngsters are now spread throughout the nation. The program's simple approach requires more than a pledge to be effective. It should be followed up with a vigorous and consistent educational program that should be broad-based and comprehensive involving not only the school system but parents' and teachers' groups, civic and human services organizations, police agencies and the business sector in every community. School curricula must not only include instruction on the dangers and evils of drugs, peer pressure, and the development of good self-esteem but must include *permanently* the teaching of character education. Irving Kristol, professor of social thought at the NYU Graduate School of Business and a senior fellow of the American Enterprise Institute, observes what he calls "the sad decrepitude of such habits of the mind" of present-day young students and "the growing furor over our schools' apparent incapacity to instill good habits of the heart and spirit" among the students.[3] He said that the overwhelming majority of parents would like "to see their children neat rather than slovenly, polite rather than rude, respectful rather than insolent, inclined to self-restraint rather than self-indulgence, aware that they have duties and obligations as well as rights." He pointed out that schools in contributing to the formation of such good character must not only show it by teaching but by doing it. "And contrary to much current psychobabble," he says, "most young people actually feel more comfortable in such schools, more relaxed, more at home" where there are rules and discipline to follow. He sums up his talk of character education briefly: "If a school has an ethos — a 'way of life' within the school walls — youngsters are more likely to emerge with an ethic. If not, not." [4]

In the long run, education is the only key both to rehabilitation and prevention of drug abuse. It is the only way to prevent people's madness of snorting drugs as if "they have vacuum cleaners for noses" as one DEA agent puts it.

3. "Schools Can Do This Much," Irving Kristol, *The Wall Street Journal*, September 8, 1986.
4. For more information on related topics, please refer to *The Moral of the Story* by Gary Bauer in Appendix B and *Drug Abuse Prevention* by Malcolm Lawrence in Appendix C.

Greater Public Awareness. The facts about drugs are better known today. Law enforcement-sponsored drug abuse prevention and education programs are rapidly spreading throughout the country. Two such programs are SPECDA (School Program to Educate and Control Drug Abuse) and DARE (Drug Abuse Resistance Education).

Operation SPECDA is an in-school curriculum program, jointly sponsored by the New York Police Department and the Board of Education. It operates in 154 schools, serving students and their parents from kindergarten through grade 12. It emphasizes the building of good character and self-respect; the dangers of drug use; civic responsibility and the consequences of actions and constructive alternatives to drug abuse.

The DARE Program is a joint program of the Los Angeles Police Department and the Los Angeles Unified School District. It is now operating in 405 schools. It includes a full-semester (17-week) in-school curriculum course meeting once a week for fifth, sixth and seventh grade students. Its purpose is to teach students to say no to drugs, build their self-esteem, manage stress, resist pro-drug messages and develop other skills to keep them drug free.

Another project is Lions-Quest Program, developed by the Quest National Center and the Lions Club International. It is an in-school curriculum program offering middle school students (grades 6, 7 and 8) daily sessions for a full semester by specially trained teachers in seven specific areas of need: understanding the changes of adolescence; building self-confidence and communication skills; understanding and managing feelings; improving friendships and resisting negative peer pressure; strengthening family relationships; making wise and healthy decisions, especially regarding alcohol and drug use; and setting goals for successful and healthy living. It is operated locally under the auspices of the Santa Clara County Bureau of Drug Abuse Services in California.

One program that requires sponsorship by the private sector and active participation by diverse citizens and youth-serving agencies in the community is Channel One. It is a drug abuse prevention program developed by youth for youth that helps to make the total environment a factor in learning and growth. It has expanded beyond the pilot program conducted with the Prudential Insurance Company in the Northeastern United

States in 1976 to include approximately 140 communities in more than 46 states and territories. Because so many communities have come to recognize its value for community improvement and the healthy development of youth, Channel One is beginning to have a broad impact on cities, towns, and neighborhoods throughout America. It has gained increasing acceptance among human service professionals and those in the private sector who are concerned about corporate social responsibility and business participation in community affairs.

Through Channel One young people acquire and learn many different alternatives to drug abuse. These prevention strategies are the following:

❑ VOCATIONAL SKILLS DEVELOPMENT. Any training or on-the-job experience that helps to develop specific skills. For example, carpentry, landscaping, masonry, or sales.

❑ ALTERNATIVES. Activities designed specifically to provide young people with a sense of personal fulfillment and satisfaction and to preclude the need for using drugs. For example, acting in theatrical productions, hiking, participating in sports, and working in arts and crafts.

❑ SOCIAL SERVICE. Activities through which young people have an opportunity to help others. A good example is providing escort services to the elderly or day care services to young children.

❑ EDUCATION. Learning and teaching experiences such as peer tutoring and drug education classes conducted by youth.

❑ HISTORIC PRESERVATION. Restoration or preservation of historic sites, including becoming acquainted with the history of the site and surrounding community.

❑ ECOLOGY. Projects that focus on dealing with environmental problems and restoring the environment to its natural state.

We can see the far-reaching effects of such a program. It is a model not just for drug abuse prevention but a timely creative approach to community involvement, growth and improvement. It can also be seen as a panacea for the absence of community so prevalent in our society today, brought about by too much self-preoccupation and the excessive fostering of individualism.

SPECDA, DARE, Lions-Quest, Channel One, Just Say No, Pros For Kids, Teen Alternative Program, and many others are discovering one great truth: that by being drug-free, young people are learning to harness their unlimited potential and creativity by helping themselves and others — thus, giving purpose, direction and meaning to their lives.

The Media-Advertising Partnership for a Drug-Free America. In an effort to further raise public awareness and consciousness on the issue of illegal drugs, the Media-Advertising Partnership for a Drug-Free America was created.

We have seen their advertisements in major national newspapers and magazines and on network television but few understand what the partnership is all about. It is a volunteer, private-sector coalition which aims to fundamentally reshape social attitudes about illegal drug use. Only by changing attitudes can we hope to effectively change behavior and reduce the demand for drugs.

Their objective is continuous exposure of their messages, everyday across all media. Key members of this coalition are The American Association of Advertising Agencies, Association of National Advertisers, American Advertising Federation, Ad Council, Market Research Association, the commercial production industry, plus national and local media.

Why this unprecedented effort? In a brief statement, the Partnership sums up the reason:

> We are faced with a lot of misinformation and a lot of ignorance. But not stupidity. Americans can curb their appetite for illegal drugs if they are persuaded the costs outweigh the benefits. What we need to do is to change America's attitudes about illegal drugs. Once we change the attitudes we can effect behavior. And that's the classic role of advertising ... And the people who "market" drugs are getting smarter about it all the time. We've already seen they're going for younger and younger users (median age of first use is 11.6 years). Now they're into free sample programs. In fact, 60 percent of kids age 10-15 who are users got their first drugs free. Most of the kids who try drugs don't pay for the first one! And they're into sophisticated pack-

aging. What we are doing is taking all the talent and media power that has sold detergents, jeans and toothpaste and using it to affect the attitudes of Americans about illegal drugs. We are making illegal drugs unattractive. We are going to change attitudes so that no illegal drug is acceptable. This "un-selling" effort is made even more urgent by recent findings in AIDS. It is estimated that 60 percent of AIDS-related deaths are a result of IV drug use. IV drug use is now the primary source of the spread of AIDS within the heterosexual population. So illegal drug use prevention can be the major element in AIDS prevention ... the time is right ... it only depends on how strongly we want a Drug-Free America.

We only hope that the effort and goal of the Partnership will result in "freeing" America's preoccupation with illegal drugs. We cannot truly succeed as a drug culture.

Drug Testing. Although *Time* calls it "The New Inquisition," nevertheless, it is one idea that officials at all levels of government and private business are seizing as a bright hope of abating the demand for drugs. The big question is: How effective can it be?

As drug testing proved to be a success in the military, strong opposition is expected from the civilian sector. The main argument is that the tests would violate the Fourth Amendment's prohibition against unreasonable searches and the unwarranted invasion of the privacy of people who have done nothing wrong. Many believe, in terms of economics, the procedure would be costly and problematic in many ways.

The requirement for mandatory testing, however, is fully justified for those employees who research and design the nation's nuclear weapons as well as for workers at the national laboratories dealing with programs and materials of the highest sensitivity and importance and whose jobs pose a threat to safety and national security. It's viewed reasonable to mandate drug testing for all airline employees in safety-related jobs like the more than half-million pilots, flight attendants, air-controllers and mechanics. Other occupations in which the use of drugs poses a substantial danger to those whose lives are entrusted to their steady hands and alert minds include surgeons, bus drivers and train engineers, to name a few.

Some believe that targeting the young for drug testing is the way to reduce the great demand for drugs. *Los Angeles Times* correspondent Scott Ostler sees the need for drug testing at the junior high school level and praises baseball Commissioner Peter Ueberroth's zeal in attacking the problem at the school levels "where the real drug action is," as he calls it. He encourages the drug test for kids not only in junior high but in high school and college levels where they are young, impressionable, naive and need protection.[5] DeForest Z. Rathbone, Jr. of Great Falls, Virginia recommends what he calls "diagnostic drug testing" for schoolchildren as a solution to the drug problem.[6]

— The Legalization Issue —

Amid the hullabaloo and growing frustration over the war against drugs, serious people are "thinking the unthinkable," as *Time* put it in a cover story about the legalization issue.

Advocates of legalization point to the failure of the 74 years of federal prohibition against illegal drugs since the passage of the Harrison Narcotics Act of 1914. The effort since that time, they say, has been doomed to failure as it created in its wake the staggering profits for the drug lords and kingpins. By contrast, legalization would take away the profits from the criminal elements and thus would reduce crime related to drug trafficking. *The Economist*, one of the leading weeklies in the world, has reported that the only way out of the war against drugs is to give up the fight and legalize all illicit drugs in order to "get gangsters out of drugs." The same general conclusions are advocated by many including former drug crusaders who have been bitterly disappointed with the current fight against drug trafficking. Dr. Gabriel G. Nahas, internationally known pharmacologist and consultant to the United Nations Commission on Narcotics argues with them along this line of thought:

> Most fallacious are the arguments used by the intellectuals and *literati* of the media who claim that legalizing illicit drugs will eliminate crime associated with drug traffic and use. They are mistaken. Nobody ever suggested that legalizing crime would decrease criminality. Indeed, drug use induces crime. The first victims of drug use are the drug consumer and his family because drugs kill, especially cocaine and heroin. The drug addict also kills others on the road, or by negligence, or because he has become insane as a result of drug consumption. The other major

5. *San Francisco Chronicle*, July 11, 1986.
6. See *Drug Testing and the Death Penalty* by Mr. Rathbone in Appendix D.

flaw in the argument put forward by *The Economist* and other well-meaning social reformers is their equation of legal drugs, such as alcohol and tobacco, with illegal drugs. Such comparison is akin to comparing a running faucet with Niagara Falls. Although the damaging effects of alcohol and tobacco should not be underestimated, tobacco, unlike cocaine, does not impair brain functions and does not scramble neurotransmission in such a way that the brain cannot relate in an authentic fashion with the environment. Neither does alcohol when taken in small doses. Tobacco does not drive people to madness, as do cocaine and, at times, marijuana.[7]

The opponents of legalization predict that making drugs socially acceptable would result in an increase of drug abuse with all the accompanying increases in shattered health and lives, family violence, highway accidents and suicides. Mitchell Rosenthal of Phoenix House, known for his work with addicts, believes that legalization "would give us a vast army of people who would be out of control." New York Republican Senator Alfonse D'Amato sees the transformation of the United States into a "society of zombies." With the vast hordes of addicts among us, who would control their cravings for more drugs? Who would give them gainful employment? And are they willing to hold regular jobs? Then, where are they going to get the money to pay for the drugs? Where there are none to supply them with free doses, many will continue to steal, mug, or even murder for it. We know what PCP, LSD and crack can do.

The truth is, despite legalization, many will continue to live in addiction and it is inevitable that crime will soar to an unprecedented level. The prospect of seeing crime drop, as argued by those favoring legalization, is just pure wishful thinking.

The greatest setback of legalization is "throwing out of the window" what we have already gained in the prevention and education effort. We are in effect telling everybody, especially the young people, that the only alternative to drug use is more drug abuse. It is a big blow to our educational effort. Children, who are targeted by the drug culture, would be getting con-

7. "How To Win The Cocaine Wars," Gabriel G. Nahas, M.D., Ph.D., from *Newsletter* of the Committees of Correspondence, Inc.

fusing messages (and we have already confused them enough) when we tell them it's O.K. to use drugs because the government says so and because it is socially acceptable. "You can't say drugs are bad at the same time that you are making them legal," says U.S. Attorney Rudolph Giuliani.[8]

Writing for the Committees of Correspondence, Inc. newsletter,[9] Cathy Thomas took issue with the pro-legalization advocates on another aspect of the marijuana health question:

> If a major pharmaceutical firm were trying to obtain approval from the Food and Drug Administration (FDA) to market marijuana as over-the-counter substances for adults, based on the scientific data available and the FDA's current guidelines for pre-clinical and clinical studies (to document manufacturer claims of benefits and/or provide evidence of adverse physiological effects on laboratory animals and humans) would the FDA approve marijuana and other currently non-legal drugs, even though the pharmaceutical firm would stand to make substantial profits from sale of the drug(s)?
>
> I propose that the pro-legalization advocates submit all drugs they wish to have decriminalized or legalized to the same level of intense scrutiny as all other drugs approved and intended for human use — either by ingestion, injection, inhaling, or topical use — and that all such drugs are evaluated under the auspices of the FDA. It was a mistake not to have done so with alcohol and tobacco, but FDA policies and procedures were not then as protective of human health as they are now.
>
> Let us not sink to the lowest common denominator in our approach to releasing drugs to the general public. The FDA functions as they do in the best interests of all public health ... No strictly commercial venture is qualified to provide an unbiased assessment of the risks versus the benefits of a drug it wishes to sell to the general population. So, why don't we let the FDA do its job?

The lessons of history repudiate any notion that illegal drugs are socially acceptable. It strongly documents one simple fact, that "their use is associated with a high incidence of individual and social damage," as Dr. Nahas points out.[10]

---

8. See Robert E. Peterson's articles, "Stop Legalization of Illegal Drugs," and "The White House Conference For A Drug-Free America," Final Report, June 1988, in Appendices E and F, respectively.
9. September 1988.
10. See his brief commentary on *The Lessons of History*, in Appendix G.

The answer to the drug problem can never be found in political rhetoric and posturing nor can it be found by legalizing illegal drugs. Legalization is fraught with hazards. The answer is to declare war against the common enemy of all — us. The problem is not the drugs. It is us. It's not the trafficker's problem. We created the demand for their "goods." We could beat our chests and pull our hair in frustration, shift the blame to our politicians and law enforcers but that does not do us any good. It's a problem we brought upon ourselves. That's all there is to think about.

We need a societal order to survive as a nation. We need laws to keep order. We need self-control and a firm determination to observe those laws. U.S. Attorney Russoniello sums it best:

> A society that tolerates self-indulgence among its members even when physical and economic injury to its general population inevitably occurs, is disordered and likely to disintegrate from the weight of pressure from special interests that any control of behavior, however reprehensible, must yield to individual choice.

What society wants is an end to drug abuse, not an end to law enforcement. We can start in the right places — the family, the school and each individual person. That's the only way to end the drug problem because there's no other human way possible. Let's start by giving Dr. Nahas' words serious consideration: "The original American ethic, an inspiring blend of personal freedom and strong moral fiber, is fundamentally opposed to the slavery of the mind imposed by dependence-producing drugs."

9

THE CITADEL WITHIN

Knock on your own door. Everything you need comes from inside your "house." Quit wasting time looking for what you're seeking on anyone else's doorstep.
— Katherine Cain from *Change Begins With Me*

— Family: The Starting Point —

An Ashanti proverb says: "The ruin of a nation begins in the homes of its people."

As parents we have now the biggest job of all time, as a result of the current drug plague — the job of rebuilding America. First, we have to wean ourselves from the alcohol and drug binges which have become the nation's number one pasttime. We have to set an example for the young and become part of the solution to the problem. And secondly, we must have commitment to family life.

One of the reasons why drugs are pervasive is due to the disintegration of family ties and values. When such things happen, the result is strained relationships and broken homes. One parent admits: "I was pursuing the American Dream, and I thought drugs would get me there faster. I was running through life so fast I didn't see that my role as a parent to my children was disintegrating, that my business abilities were crumbling."

We see the trauma experienced by young people when drug arrests swoop down on their family; when assault and physical abuse (violence is greater with alcohol and drug use) makes the home a "house of horrors" when parents abandon them; and when members of the family are caught up in the self-destructive and violent world of drugs, either becoming an addict, a pusher or a dealer.

We have an epidemic of children running away from home. It's possible that they are in contact with their parents. As they have learned throughout their life — the only way is through an electronic means like the telephone. And it's sad that too many were raised by remote control — too many are stranded, left without structures to hang on.

The world makes way for children who know where they are going and not running away. As parents we can lead the way and show how — without them fumbling and blind-alleying. We have to take the responsibility and make a serious commitment to do it, as we must do with anything to succeed in life. And there's never been a better time than now.

There are four vital areas we can concentrate on to strengthen our family life — the areas of coping with responsibility, commitment to each other, the importance of constant communication and the significance and primacy of a loving and caring environment. I call them the four C's of a stable family life.

Coping Not Cop-out. To raise kids in a negative world, exacerbated by the onslaught of pro-drug messages, is extremely difficult. It takes courage and conviction to cope with the negative environment around us. But the worst thing we can do to our children is to abdicate our responsibility as a parent and pass that responsibility to someone else. Turning to teachers and school administrators for solutions, for example, is the ultimate cop-out.

The drug culture's message of irresponsibility in promoting the "intelligent, meaningful and responsible use" of drugs is taking away from us the task of raising our children in a responsible fashion. Unknowingly, too many of us have been stripped of that responsibility when children are asked to experiment and alter their consciousness by taking "mood-altering" drugs as the drug culture propagandizes them. It's not the children's responsibility to decide what is dangerous for them. We cannot afford to leave such hazardous choices to them. It's our responsibility to do all in our power to provide the information and the protection to assure our children of a drug-free childhood and adolescence. We have to give them factual and updated information about the health consequences of drug use in order to reinforce their courage to stay drug-free.

We can only provide the correct information to them if we ourselves are knowledgeable about illicit drugs and their dangers. It is our responsibility to educate ourselves. The keystone for drug prevention will always be the knowledge of the serious health risks of using mind-altering drugs. And that knowledge must come from us first.

Children who are taught the meaning of individual responsibility, self-discipline and a clear sense of right and wrong are less likely to try drugs. Again it's our responsibility to set the good example we want our children to follow by not using drugs ourselves. Parents who curse the scourge of drug addiction, while asking their children to buy them a pack of beer are as AWOL in the war on drugs as any politician who is merely full of rhetoric. James Baldwin once wrote: "Children have never been very good at listening to their elders but they have never failed to imitate them."

With increasing force the argument is made that children learn their bad habits from their parents and while the drug may be different in kind from the parent's drug of choice, it is often seen that the parents are themselves either drug users or alcohol abusers. Any parent who thinks he or she can indulge his or her own dependency, whether it's alchohol or cocaine, and rear drug-free kids is deluding himself or herself. The evidence is undeniable that children whose parents abuse alcohol or drugs are more likely to develop the same destructive habit. Parents who have lost control of themselves have a poor chance of controlling their children. On the other hand, it is a fact that children who don't run into trouble with drugs are brought up by parents who are non-users and who honestly practice what they preach. There are some victims of drug abuse despite parental control and supervision because of strong peer pressure. In general, however, if the bonds of trust and affection are strong between the young children and parents, children are more open to the advice and counsel of their elders.

I believe that where there are delinquent parents there will be delinquent children. To blame the teachers for this behavioral problem is a cop-out. To leave the accountability and care of our children to our social services systems is another cop-out. David Toma pulls no punches in defining our responsibility as parents: "Your children are your responsibility — twenty four hours a day — and you can't expect anyone to share that responsibility with you."

Children are blameless when it comes to how they start their lives. Some of us may feel squeamish about this fact but it is a sobering reality we have to face. Who is to blame? Listen to a part of a poem written by Joe Woody, a high-school student at Amesbury High School, Massachussetts.[1]

> We don't peddle the drugs
> That muddle the brain
> That's all done by older folks
> Greedy for gain.
>
> Delinquent teenagers
> Oh how they condemn
> The sins of a nation
> And blame it on them.
>
> By the laws of the blameless,
> The saviour made known
> Who is among us
> To cast the first stone?
>
> For in so many cases
> It's sad but it's true
> The title "delinquent"
> Fits older folks too!

Commitment. This very broad subject runs the gamut of human relationships from commitment to responsibility to commitment to marriage, our business, work and profession, our civic and social obligations, our ministries and many others. Without commitment, it is impossible to accomplish anything worthwhile and lasting in any field of human endeavor. We can always justify and rationalize why our commitment is floundering. We can always announce our good intentions but without commitment, it doesn't mean anything at all. It is hollow and empty.

One of the most overlooked yet important factors that measures results in anything is our commitment to time. But that time should be quality time not just quantity time. Worse than the "poor time" we devote to our children is no time at all. We establish, whether deliberately or not, our relationship with them by being "invisible parents" but nonetheless showering

1. "Who Is To Blame?" by Joe Woody, March 1984, Amesbury High School, Massachussetts, presented to Otto Moulton after he presented a drug education program at the school.

them with expensive toys and countless gifts by special mail deliveries. The words of Reverend Jesse Jackson tell us what's more important, "Your children need your presence more than your presents."

"Some families," wrote Nick Stinnett and John DeFrain, "have seen commitment eroded by a more subtle enemy — work, and its demand on time, attention and energy." One Wisconsin father, they said, offered this insight: "Sometimes I feel that the time I spend with my sons could be better spent at the office. Then I remind myself that the productivity report will affect life for a few days or weeks. I must do it and it's important, but my job as a father is more important. If I'm a good father to my sons, they're likely to be good parents too. Someday — after I'm gone, and certainly after that report has rotted — my grandchild or great grandchild will have a good father because I was a good father."[2]

Isn't it the feeling of the majority among us — caught in the ambivalence about the choices we have to pursue? Which is more important — work or family? There is no reason why we cannot prioritize things despite our busy and hectic schedules. We have to find the time and pay the price for it. That means we have to give up a lot of things: our favorite television programs and some of our social commitments.

Once we have done with the commitments spent outside of the family, then we can look at the many activities we can designate as family time together — time to be looked at as something productive rather than time wasted. These activities promote stability and happiness within the family. They include eating, reading and playing together, hiking and camping, sharing household tasks — the list is endless. Outside the home, there are opportunities to be part of the community. Again, the opportunities are limitless. In this way, we are teaching our youngsters to learn to become responsible and caring young adults rather than being just onlookers.

In a sense, we are creating a oneness that can thwart the instability and fragmentation of modern family life and the erosion of the communal aspect of living brought about by the prevalent attitude of self-preoccupation.

2. "Secrets of Strong Families," by Nick Stinnett and John DeFrain, *Reader's Digest*, November 1987.

Communication. The death of communication — nothing can prevent it from happening when we start building walls so thick around us that we prevent others from coming into our lives. And the tragedy is: we may not be able to get out anymore. That means we are "dead" to those around us.

That's the lot of parents who have found addiction, not only to drugs, but to the modern conveniences of life and have no time left to communicate with family members. The result becomes tragic when each one starts to isolate himself or herself, building the walls of silence that are inimical to good communication.

When such conditions exist, the most vulnerable are our young children and adolescents. One of the saddest realities we see so frequently is the desperate effort many of our young children go through just to get our attention — only to be completely ignored. To these young people, the greatest yearning is to be listened to. They want time and attention from us. If they feel they are not listened to, they inevitably seek elsewhere the attention they crave and we have lost control of them.

It is through active listening to their concerns, interests, and problems that we can help them resist peer pressure. They need guidance and support to stay off drugs. It's our responsibility to discuss drugs knowledgeably with them to keep them from obtaining the information from their peers or on the streets. It's also worth our time to communicate with the parents of our children's friends and share our knowledge about drugs with them. It's through parents working together and educating themselves about the health hazards of drugs and alcohol that they can provide in turn correct and updated information to their families and communities.

To meet this challenge on a national level, parents have initiated the National Federation of Parents for Drug-Free Youth (NFP), a non-profit organization with a sharply focused aim: to establish a national commitment to support the efforts of parents dedicated to raising a generation of drug-free youth. We can communicate our concern by becoming a member of this worthwhile organization and find greater power through a unified effort in order to help change young people's attitudes about drugs. Children have endless potentialities for growth and creativity and it's tragic to lose them to drugs.

The pathology of today's drug addicts, especially among a vast number of our youngsters, is at root a function of the isolated life. Open communication, at best, helps break down the walls of silence and prevents the development of a full-blown crisis (like suicide). We cannot expect our children to discuss their problems with us if we don't ask and listen.

In this complex and complicated society we live in, where relationships between family members seem to be growing evermore impersonal, there is a great need for listening. When we listen to our children, more than our ears are involved — our hearts have to be engaged too. To listen in a true sense is to open ourselves to them and take their pain, troubles and confusion into ourselves. We give them the satisfaction of knowing that we truly care.

Caring. This is by far the greatest single factor in building a strong family life. In essence it spells love. We only become responsible, committed and ever-listening parents because we are concerned and we care for the welfare of our children.

The absence of love, on the other hand, is evident in the lack of discipline of children, in frequent marital violence and, at times, the heartless removal of the elderly and the handicapped members from the family. We throw away love when we feel the inconvenience of putting up with the burden of supervising and disciplining our youngsters. We throw away love when we feel it's not necessary to patch up marital differences because of foolish pride on either side. We throw it away by becoming indifferent to the plight of the helpless in the family.

This lack of concern affects the children profoundly. And if there is a lack of self-esteem among many young people today, it can be traced to the absence of a caring and supportive home environment that only the family can provide. Children need to know they are special. Dorothy Law Nolte wrote *Children Live What They Learn*, her famous advice to all parents. In part she says, "If a child lives with encouragement, he learns confidence; if a child lives with praise, he learns to appreciate ... if a child lives with approval, he learns to like himself; if a child lives with acceptance and friendship, he learns to love the world." We bring up positive children when they are treated with respect — telling them that they are special and unique individuals, gifted in so many ways although differently.

It is a self-evident truth that no child is ever going to be spoiled by having too much love. We show by demonstrating it. We cannot afford to be insensitive to the greatest of human longings of wanting to be loved especially the longings of tender hearts like those of our children. What causes us then to withhold our love? What's wrong with hugging our children and telling them, "I love you as deep as space." Are we not going to be thrilled to hear the sweetest response back, "Dad, Mom, I love you too, as deep as space." Try it and you will be surprised at the result. Children don't hold back what they feel — we only have to initiate that we care for them and listen to what they feel.

In a negative family environment where children perceive the lack of love, the situation is different. Nolte wrote that a child who lives with criticism, hostility, ridicule and shame learns to condemn, to feel guilty, violent and shy. Once these things are learned at an early age, it is extremely difficult to unlearn them because by then a child will already have become desensitized to brutality and degradation. Such a child will grow into an uncaring and unloving adult unless exposed to a positive and loving environment.

To teach gentleness and obedience to parental authority is a challenge for most parents. Because it takes effort, many parents cling to the idea that children will eventually emerge as caring, law-abiding and socially responsible adults, that is, they believe and hope that something will happen to make them come out all right. This is a dangerous assumption. We must recognize that if we take the effort, we will relish the satisfaction and great joy, greater than all the sacrifices we made, in having raised responsible children in this world. Such is the nature of love when we freely give it away.

And because we care, we can pass down to our children inspiring words that have changed the lives of millions of young men and women. The Optimist Creed or "Promise Yourself" as originally known is distributed today among young people, given out on the streets and sent in great numbers to remote corners of the globe where people are in need of a creed they can hold on to and live by. It should be in every home to guide not only young people but parents as well. It is an effective anodyne that could "win out over all our craziness and jumbled thoughts and ill intentions and neuroses and all the rest," as

Joan Baez puts it. It is "a way of life" that will change our lives forever and our family life for the better.

The Optimist Creed[3]

Promise yourself —

To be so strong that nothing can disturb your peace of mind.

To talk health, happiness and prosperity to every person you meet.

To make all your friends feel that there is something in them.

To look at the sunny side of everything and make your optimism come true.

To think only of the best, to work only for the best and to expect only the best.

To be just as enthusiastic about the success of others as you are about your own.

To forget the mistakes of the past and press on to the greater achievements of the future.

To wear a cheerful countenance at all times and give every living creature you meet a smile.

To give so much time to the improvement of yourself that you have no time to criticize others.

To be too large for worry, too noble for anger, too strong for fear, and too happy to permit the presence of trouble.

What words wouldn't inspire young people once they hear the famous hit by Whitney Houston, a song called "Greatest Love of All." The words go deep into the hearts of many children, that's why they love to sing it. A portion of it speaks of our role as parents: "I believe the children are our future; teach them well ... Show them all the beauty they possess inside. Give them a sense of pride." And we may add, give them a creed to live by.

No one could sum better what I am trying to say here than George Santayana: "Nature," he said, "kindly warps our judgement about our children, especially when they are young, when it would be a fatal thing for them if we did not love them."

And it's tragic to squander the greatest wealth of all, our family, if we place our priorities in the wrong order.

---

3. "The Optimist Creed," written by Christian D. Larson, adopted by Optimist International.

— The Ethical Self —

Imagine the Greek philosopher, Diogenes, going out in broad daylight with a lantern "in search of an honest man or woman."

What's wrong with our society today, many are bound to ask. Archbishop John F. Whealon of Hartford, Connecticut attributed this modern dilemma to what he called the "moral acid rain" that is eating up the nation's ethical roofing. In its May 25, 1987 cover story, *Time* asks, "What Ever Happened To Ethics?" The description of the story says "Assaulted by sleaze, scandals and hypocrisy, America searches for its moral bearings." Inside, articles scream with its titles: What's wrong ... betrayal and greed unsettle the nation's soul.

A poll for *Time* conducted by Yankelovich Clancy Shulman revealed that more than 90 percent of the respondents agreed that morals have fallen because parents fail to take responsibility for their children or to imbue them with decent moral standards; 76 percent saw lack of ethics in businessmen as contributing to tumbling moral standards; and 74 percent decried failure by political leaders to set a good example.[4]

Again we see beyond doubt the influence of a strong family in the development of values in a child's life and the erosion of the same in a family with a diminished sense of commitment and responsibility. As the home becomes unstable and uncaring, the children are pretty much left to themselves. Parents blame schools for not instilling values in the classrooms. Former Secretary of Education William J. Bennett laments that many U.S. public schools are "languishing for lack of moral nutrition." Many will contend however, that there already is "values education" being taught currently. But we know what it is — a new catchword that is sending many youngsters on a slippery slope, displaying a blithe lack of responsibility toward themselves and others. "What is now being promoted," says Kristol, "in the name of values education is, from an educational point of view, just another cop-out. Even the words themselves are disingenuous, since chatter about values is simply a way of not talking about morals." Even higher education, Allan Bloom charged, is

4. "Looking To Its Roots," *Time*, May 25, 1987. Findings are based on a telephone survey of 1,014 adult Americans, conducted January 19-21, 1987. The potential error is plus or minus 3%.

"a fraud — untrue to its students, untrue to itself. It has displaced moral truth with a melange of 'values' and forsaken reason for the trivial pursuit of relevance." And he observed that although students become brilliant and competent professionals later on, they emerge still as "unfinished persons." Steven Muller, president of John Hopkins University says "the failure to rally around a set of values means that universities are turning out potentially highly-skilled barbarians."[5] The late Albert Einstein was more specific as regards to an individual lack of moral training: "It is essential that the student acquire an understanding of, and a lively feeling for values ... of the morally good. Otherwise he — with his specialized knowledge — more closely resembles a well-trained dog than a harmoniously developed person."

With grown-ups in high government positions and businesses, in the ethical professions and even in churches wallowing in a moral morass — it sends a strong signal to our youngsters that to be ethical is a joke. Leaders in government, in business and professions, and in the church should set an example to the youth of this nation. However, we have seen things differently. In the wake of the drug epidemic, there's nothing that fuels the growth of the illegal drug business more than corruption. We have seen its influence upon individuals with "transaction mentality" whose motto is "Enrich Thyself." It spares no one. "A Code of Ethics is practically non-existent and there's no consideration for others but only self-aggrandizement — there is no such thing as a permanently damaged reputation anymore," observes Herb Freinberg, an insurance executive in the San Francisco Bay Area.

As the family disintegrates, society and the whole nation disintegrate under the weight of "moral anarchy." Leaders have failed to set the standard for ethical behavior and parents have reneged on their responsibility to do the same. Our educational institutions have likewise failed to assert their authority as regards teaching morals or ethics among their students. The words of Franklin Delano Roosevelt, our thirty-second president, remind us of the significance of the moral education that

5. *Raising Positive Kids in a Negative World*, by Zig Ziglar, published by Oliver-Nelson Books, a division of Thomas Nelson, Inc., Publishers, 1985, p.47.

so many of our educators have shunned to teach. No one could say it better for us — so we may know why there is rampant corruption and disregard for ethical practice to assert itself. He said, "To train a man in mind and not in morals is to train a menace to society."

Because of the apparent disregard for ethical behavior in all segments of society, I challenge everyone, especially those in positions of leadership, to think about the message of "The Incorruptible Man."[6] It is a daily reminder that we all have civic and social responsibilities to bear. I hope its message will have continuing impact on thinking people throughout the nation and the world.

The survival of America depends on the strong ethical leadership upon which this great nation was founded. "The battle over values," writes Elmer Von Feldt, former editor of *Columbia* magazine, "is one of the most crucial for the future of American civilization. Eventually the creed by which a country lives will determine the character of its people. Every American has a critical stake in this battle. He or she will be affected gravely by its outcome, particularly by the false values that can victimize his or her own children and grandchildren."

6. "The Incorruptible Man," *Newsweek*, October 10, 1966.

The Incorruptible Man

If he's in
the District Attorney's
office,
the word quickly spreads,
"No deals."
If he's in a key
position to sign
contracts,
the advice is,
"Don't tamper."
If he is sent
alligator shoes,
tickets to Paris,
or a suspicious-looking,
bulging envelope,
"He'll send them back."
His presence
gives society
a solid counterbalance
to a contemporary
who may be allergic
to what a Chief Justice
called, "The Sea of Ethics."
Without him,
civilizations collapse.
What a clean,
powerful,
satisfying,
psychological edge
you have,
if,
in your field of
endeavor,
the Incorruptible Man
is known as
you!

10

THE ONLY SOLUTION

No amount of technological progress will cure the hatred that eats away the vitals of materialistic society like a spiritual cancer. The only cure is, and must always be, spiritual.

— Thomas Merton, Trappist monk

— In God We Trust —

"When everything else fails," David Toma advises parents, "ask God for help."

To a culture that is so inwardly drained of the spirit, such advice may sound meaningless or even ridiculous. Some people don't like to hear it — it cramps their lifestyle and they like to think they are self-sufficient. To a dysfunctional society like ours, anything of a spiritual nature is a waste of time. Because we are taught to be independent, there is a strong denial of our dependence upon God's help and providence. This is viewed as a weakness and we have to grope and go around in a silly circle first before we recognize that there is a Power greater than and beyond ourselves.

Philosophers and humanists have promulgated this way of thinking — they have been telling us for some time now that "God is dead." But "what we confront today," says Erich Fromm, "is the possibility that man is dead, transformed into a thing, a producer, a consumer, an idolator, or other things." In short, if we don't believe in God, we will believe in anything. That's why we realize that without invisible means of support, it is entirely possible that we could have all the material things and yet at the same time feel spiritually impoverished.

In his commencement address at Harvard University on June 8, 1978, Solzhenitsyn's words reveal how he looked at the cause of our lack of spiritual commitment. "The constant desire," he says, "to have still more things and a still better life and the struggle to this end imprint many Western faces with worry and even depression ... This active and tense competition comes to dominate all human thoughts and does not in the least open a way to free spiritual development." And he added, "The West has finally achieved the rights of man, even to excess, but man's sense of responsibility to God and society has grown dimmer and dimmer ... we have placed too much hope in politics and social reforms, only to find out that we were being deprived of our most precious possession: our spiritual life."[1]

This spiritual deprivation has sent millions wandering aimlessly, looking for meaning in their lives, not knowing if such a thing even exists. "The increased incidence of drug abuse in all sectors of society, the fact that depression now outnumbers all other medical symptoms put together," writes Phillip L. Berman in his introduction to *The Courage of Conviction*, "seem undeniable signs that ours is a society out of balance, in need of new directions, revived hopes, greater courage." A relevant thought comes from Tom Wolfe who notes: "America now tingles with the things of the flesh while roaring drunk on the things of the spirit. We are in that curious interlude of the 20th century that Nietzsche foretold a century ago: the time of the reevaluation, the devising of new values to replace the osteoporotic skeletons of the old."[2] Pope John Paul II tells us what counts in our search for deeper meaning: "The secret of eradicating the poison of drug addiction is to cultivate intensely spiritual values. Human values which are purely on a worldly level, even though they are of fundamental importance to mankind, are not always sufficient to give deeper significance to existence ... The tranquil conviction of the immortality of the soul, of the future resurrection of the body, and of the eternal responsibility for one's actions, this is the surest way."

It is apparent and convincing that the only solution to the drug problem is the need for spiritual reawakening in the whole land. Because there is no issue in life that is without spiritual significance, then the drug problem is one issue that has left

1. *A World Split Apart*, by Alexander Solzhenitsyn, Harper and Row, Publishers, Inc., 1978.
2. "Voices from Life," 50th Anniversary Edition, *Life* magazine, Fall 1986.

many searching for deeper meaning in their lives. The spirit will always groan and seek something higher and more meaningful than the temporary "high" that drugs provide. It will always remain restless as long as the means to plug the "vacuum and holes" in our lives come from an external source and not from the inner world deep within us. As is the case, we see "spiritual suicides" committed in greater number every day as those "spiritually dead" outrank the living among us.

In this age of drugs and rootlessness, we daily witness the terrible hunger of many for spiritual life. This brings about the "zoo of beliefs" as Ivan Stang, author of *High Weirdness by Mail*, calls it. And the number is growing rapidly. Stang is genuinely not optimistic about what he sees as the growing gullibility of Americans. (We only have to be reminded of the "mass suicide" in Jonestown, Guyana.) "The kooks are our future," he says.

J. Gordon Melton, director of the Institute for the Study of American Religion in Santa Barbara, California, estimates that currently there are about 1,500 national and regional religious groups in the U.S.[3] With the advent of computers, notably desktop publishing, and inexpensive xeroxing, it has become easier to promote weirdness these days. Many unusual groups and organizations have flourished since the 1960s which, coincidentally, was the beginning of massive drug experimentation among our young people.

The need for spiritual nourishment in the lives of users and those undergoing rehabilitation and treatment is voiced by those close to the drug scene and its victims. Kathleen R. O'Connell in her book describes this great need in the lives of the addicts:[4]

> Often the biggest spiritual gift in recovery from cocaine addiction is simply to know that there is a spiritual side to existence. Many people who develop a problem with cocaine have never really given themselves time to discover the spiritual aspects of life ... They never allowed themselves to know that there is a greater purpose in life beyond individual daily existence. For some people recovery from cocaine addiction is a rediscovery of their spiritual desires and goals; for others it

3. "On The Trail of High Weirdness," *U.S. News & World Report*, November 14, 1988.
4. *End of the Line, Quitting Cocaine*, by Kathleen R. O'Connell, The Westminster Press, Philadelphia, 1985, pp. 110-111.

is a time when they learn new ways to express the spiritual side of their lives. This is important for a sense of balance in life — a sense of perspective beyond immediate needs and desires. With it comes a sense of peace and serenity.

The truth in her statement rings profoundly in the words of St. Paul to the Romans: To be spiritually minded is life and peace. Reflecting on his interaction with his patients, Hardin B. Jones tells his experience:

> Among the heroin addicts I have helped, those most successful at breaking the use-withdrawal cycle were the ones who turned to a spiritual power for help ... why an addict should still be capable of deep religious feelings when all other sensations and experiences have vanished cannot be fully explained. From my interviews with addicts, however, I have discovered that the capacity for religious response remains in spite of drug-induced sensory deprivation. Once spiritual insight has been felt, it helps the addict get off drugs and stay off and to recover his capacity for sensual gratification ... The addict needs support in his struggle to give up drugs. Religion can often fill this need. It offers the addict support and strengthens his will power.[5]

"In our modern secular society, talk of religion in relation to a drug problem or drug abuse treatment can sound old-fashioned or even narrow-minded," says Dr. Robert L. DuPont, Jr. His next words reveal how highly he regards the importance of religion as "a sturdy bridge over troubled waters."[6]

> As a physician who has spent over a decade treating drug-dependent people and their families, I am convinced that this kind of religious experience is an enormously useful part of dealing with a drug problem ... From a public health point of view, virtually all religions, other than the bizarre cult credos of individualistic and often seemingly mad leaders, are effective in helping to stop drug problems. Thus, it matters little whether one speaks of Christian or Jewish religions or of Buddhism or Islam. The point is simply that a renunciation of personal, present-tense pleasure as the ultimate goal of living, seeing that one's life is part of a larger and more meaningful shared pro-

5. *Sensual Drugs*, Hardin and Helen Jones, Cambridge University Press, 1977, pp. 176-177.
6. *Getting Tough On Gateway Drugs*, by Robert L. DuPont, Jr., M.D., 1984, p. 296.

cess, is often essential to solving a drug problem ... When it comes to preventing and curing a drug problem, the drug-burdened traveler needs a bridge over troubled waters. Religion, surely, is one of the most sturdy bridges.

One drug-weary traveler who found a sturdy bridge to a higher power was Je'Rol Gray. He was a private nurse for celebrities in Los Angeles who got hooked on cocaine and eventually found himself down on Skid Row. After playing games with himself, he went into counseling and later admitted: "I feel great. I feel good about myself. I feel alive. The most important thing I've done is open my heart and let God in. He brought peace of mind, and strength and encouragement, confidence, faith."

Stacy Keach's arrest at London's Heathrow Airport on April 3, 1984 and subsequent recovery period were "such a trauma, it brings you to your knees," the actor admitted. What helped him fight his cocaine addiction was his renewed faith in God and Bible classes he attended while in prison. It was the discovery of a greater Power than himself that restored his sanity.

A study by Father Sean O'Sullivan, director of the substance abuse program for the Miami Archdiocese, shows that youngsters are far less likely to become involved with drugs when the family has a strong religious commitment. "I've never seen anyone come back from addiction without undergoing a spiritual renaissance," says Father O'Sullivan. God is the only one who can release a person from the chains of addiction.

The misery of every human being and the death of all that is decent in our society only happens when we reject God's guidance in our affairs. That's why our Founding Fathers never forgot to put their hope and trust in God. It is such trust that gave an awe-inspiring meaning to the Declaration of Independence in which they mutually pledged their lives, fortune and sacred honor "with a firm reliance on the protection of the Divine Providence."

They firmly believed in the separation of Church and State but nevertheless believed just as firmly in God. Benjamin Franklin even suggested that they start their Constitutional Convention sessions with a prayer, since without God's help, he said, they would surely fail in their great endeavor to make the colonies into "one nation, under God, with liberty and justice for all." Thomas Jefferson said categorically that "the God who gave us life, gave us liberty at the same time." George Washington, in bidding farewell to public life in 1796, uttered these profound words:

> Of all the dispositions for happiness which lead to practical prosperity, religion and morality are indispensable supports. In vain would that man claim the tribute of patriotism, who should labor to subvert these great pillars of human happiness, these firmest props of the duties of men and citizens.

Is there still a doubt in our minds that spiritual values and adherence to ethical principles are a foundation that will stand and that will always make America great? In 1831 Alexis de Tocqueville, French statesman and writer, was sent to America and wrote his many observations. In part he talked about the richness of our fields, the vast wealth of our mines and industrial might, the abundance of our forests, the beauties of our rivers, streams, lakes and the grandeur of our mountains. He said that none of these things is the cause of America's greatness. He declared: "It wasn't until I went into your churches that I saw the reason for America's greatness. America is great because America is good; and as long as America is good, America will be great. If it ever ceases to be good, it will cease to be great."

The words of Abraham Lincoln give us another insightful look at the reason why any nation could be so richly blessed: "I recognize the sublime truth announced in the Holy Scriptures and proved by all history that those nations are blessed whose God is the Lord ... Without him, all human reliance is vain." Peter Marshall, former chaplain to the United States Senate addressed a life without God and had this to say, "Your world is a chaos of two billion souls without rhyme or reason, like ships without rudders, living for no purpose, and you are adrift in a world that doesn't make sense. If there is no Providence, then there is no meaning to life, and it remains a mystery."[7]

And it is the cause of the widespread human despair and spiritual nakedness that is prevalent today — people existing daily just to live, without purpose, without any worthwhile goal in life. The truth is: a prayerless life is a powerless life, especially against the assaults and destructive influence of illicit drugs that strip one's self-determination and dignity bit by bit until what is left,

---

7. *A Man Called Peter*, by Catherine Marshall, McGraw-Hill Book Co., 1951.

figuratively, is shell and the shadow of a nonentity. There are hundreds in the psychiatric wards of hospitals, thousands roaming our streets like zombies and robots. Why? William J. Bennett has the answer: "When we have disdain for our religious tradition, we have disdain for ourselves."

"In God We Trust" is the powerful inscription we find on all our coins. We touch those coins in our pockets and purses almost every day yet, ironically, we pay little attention or none at all to the deep meaning of those words. Opposite is inscribed yet another meaningful message: "Liberty." Both remind us that the only and truly liberating experience without chemical assistance or drug dependency, is knowing that there is a loving, dependable and gracious God who provides everything we need in life. To trust Him is to touch the source of life within us; to gain knowledge of ourselves as gifted persons in varying degrees with gifts to share with others; and to know how special we are as the words of Kahlil Gibran speak eloquently about our spiritual makeup, "The human soul is but a part of a burning torch which God separated from Himself at Creation." That divine spark and the beautiful image of God in all of us, explicitly revealed in Jesus Christ's humanity, is so vast a dignity that St. Paul spoke of our bodies as "the temples of the Holy Spirit."

To waste ourselves on reckless drug use and experimentation is to destroy our only hope for the happiness and peace that we all desperately seek. Material things can never satisfy our human desires. God is in us, not the countless little gods we foolishly fashion out in the material world and in our minds that bring chaos in our private world and, consequently, upon the country.

But order and peace is the reward of a nation that trusts in Him, as the prophet Isaiah spoke of long ago, "A nation of firm purpose you keep in peace; in peace, for its trust in you."

Part Four
An Afterthought

11

FREEDOM OR LICENSE?

The decay of the family means that community would require extreme self-abnegation in an era when there is no good reason for anything but self-indulgence.
— Allan Bloom, *The Closing of the American Mind*

Eleven years after the signing of the Declaration of Independence, our Founding Fathers wrote and signed something even more important on September 17, 1787 — the Constitution of the United States of America. Historians call it the greatest single document struck off by the hand and mind of man. The freedom unleashed by the Constitution allowed every American to develop his or her talents and abilities to the fullest and attain what is known the world over as the American Dream.

Is it a reality today for the millions affected by the drug plague? Or is it an "American nightmare" for the majority terrified night after night by back-to-back sequences of horror films on TV such as "Friday the 13th" or "Nightmare on Elm Street"? As unreality is forced upon us by the freedom guaranteed by the Constitution to the purveyors of such messages, we just sit back and watch with our children. And the brainwashing continues with the unreal messages of some television commercials. And so the reality of the drug problem becomes part of our subconscious mind as another "unreality." We shrug it off as nothing to worry about and something we expect to go away in time. But the terror and violence of the drug problem is much closer to our homes than the horror films and commercials we are watching.

We have seen in this decade how freedom is being used in the most destructive, unrestrained, and wasteful way. We have seen the staggering cost we are paying for its abuse and we can't keep track of the casualties who never knew what it means to be free.

Sometime in the distant future — 97 years from today — our great grandchildren will have the opportunity to read and learn from Rosenblatt's essay, "A Letter to the Year 2086." He wrote what he perceived was happening in the year 1986: "One secret of our age is that we are learning that democracy can kill democracy. For one thing, excessive freedoms have made it almost impossible for an ethical conscience to assert itself. People have been free to ignore social obligations, to abuse one another, to kill themselves."[1]

Governor Mario Cuomo of New York expressed his frustration over not finding the answer to people's destructive urges, especially among our youngsters: "Generations of kids are growing up learning to kill themselves better and better. The big question that none of us has answered, and perhaps none of us can, is why. But at one point we have to teach ourselves not to kill ourselves."[2]

Are people killing themselves just for the thrill of it? Are there some mysterious forces telling them to do it? Is it a phenomenon of this age? I doubt it. Adult and young alike simply lack the self-direction and self-knowledge necessary to fend off the temptation of drug use that leads to self-destruction. There are plenty of reasons, as we already know, why there is a drug epidemic and why people are hooked on drugs and are killing themselves in the process.

In a permissive society, anything can happen and everybody is "free to ignore social obligations," as Rosenblatt puts it; then it follows that we are free to do anything including the freedom to kill ourselves. But is it really freedom to do whatever we want to do or is it license? What then is the difference between the two? A simple analogy is to look at what a traffic light is for in order to find the answer. A law abiding citizen follows traffic lights to avoid accidents, prevent chaos, and to give fellow motorists respect and consideration. He or she knows that freedom includes the accompanying responsibility, account-

1. "A Letter to the Year 2086," by Roger Rosenblatt, cover story, *Time*, December 29, 1986. Rosenblatt's letter to the next century was deposited in the Museum of the Statue of Liberty in a special capsule.
2. "Cocaine Country: A National Forum," op. cit.

ability, and knowledge of the consequences of one's actions. Imagine if there's only the green light as the traffic signal. That's what license means — a "go signal" to do everything one pleases to do, unrestrained in most cases without regard to one's safety or the welfare of others.

One of the most violent films of this decade featured Chuck Norris as Matt Hunter in "Invasion U.S.A." He was a one-man army and defender of America's precious freedom after she was invaded for the first time in her history by a rag-tag group of terrorist commandos. If ever there were a redeeming value in such a fictionalized story it was the truth spoken by Matt Hunter's arch enemy, Soviet agent Rostov, in a scene where he was referring to young people kissing on the beach and some drug dealings taking place. Rostov told a fellow terrorist: "Look at them, Nikko, soft, decadent — they don't even understand the nature of their own freedom and how we can use it against them. They are their worst enemy but they don't know it."

"When people," says former West German chancellor, Helmut Schmidt, "believe that their well-being and liberty are permanently guaranteed, they feel that they themselves do not have to do anything. I think this attitude is our greatest danger."[3] As it is true to a nation, so it is true to everyone of us who feel secure in our freedom and are tempted to believe that the only way to go is the route toward complacency and laxity, and believing nothing is ever going to happen.

Someone wrote a rather amusing statement: "We should be extremely happy living in a country where we put chains on tires and not on people." Could we really admit that it is true today? In the light of the drug epidemic it becomes a sad paradox that millions of fellow Americans are voluntarily putting chains on themselves rather than on their tires. We are, as someone also remarked, two nations bitterly divided, we have liberty for some and slavery for others. And this is one of the saddest chapters in our history.

In a society where freedom is used as license, the reality of "enslaving" oneself has dramatically developed and progressed incredibly to the ranks of younger and younger segments of our population. We find the truth of what is happening before our eyes in a paraphrased statement by Jean-Jacques Rousseau:

3. "Hope for the West — And a Warning," *Reader's Digest*, September 1975.

"Man and woman are born free, and everywhere they are in chains."

To be a slave or not — this too is implicitly guaranteed under the Constitution of the United States. We all have the right to make fools of ourselves as we see fit and this right also includes the right to mismanage our affairs. We enjoy such unlimited freedom that we will never have fully appreciated its significance until we have lost it — lost it to a national disgrace called drug addiction. The greatest irony of it all is to have lost it because we have everything in America: we have never had to experience the abject poverty and dire necessity of those unlucky ones in the Third World countries; we take for granted our humane laws (that some find oppressive) and never have to face a firing squad for involvement in drugs or to confront a Malaysian or an Iranian brand of justice, that is, getting hanged on crude gallows or from posts. Or becoming a victim of mass execution as Mao Zedong's communists did to eliminate all opium smokers. We are indeed lucky to be living in the United States of America.

The drug plague, with our blind acquiescence, is wrecking the lives of many. It has helped accelerate the growth of "slavery" and the new burgeoning enterprise that says: Freedom for Sale. The issue of slavery that Frederick Douglass spoke of 136 years ago is no different from the kind of "slavery" we have today, although in another form. Forcefully he declared:

> The existence of slavery in this country brands ... your humanity as a base pretense ... It destroys your moral power ... it makes your name a hissing and a byword to a mocking earth. It fetters your progress, it is the enemy of improvement; the deadly foe of education; it promotes vice; it shelters crime; it is a curse of the earth that supports it, and yet you cling to it as if it were the sheet anchor of all your hopes.[4]

The unbridled pursuit of drugs is like a volcano that lays waste all living things in its wake. Drugs do the same thing, devouring honor and whatever vestige of self-esteem is left in the addict. Drug dependence becomes the worst form of self-imposed imprisonment. Nowhere is this statement expressed with greater finality than by Stacy Keach: "There is no greater

---

4. "The Meaning of July 4th for the American Negro," an address by Frederick Douglass, Rochester, New York, July 5, 1852.

imprisonment than that of being dependent on any chemical substance for one's existence." Rousseau in *The Social Contract* wrote quite bluntly: "For to be subject to appetite is to be a slave, while to obey the laws laid down by society is to be free."

Restrictions, like laws, are seen as limiting freedom or allowing no freedom at all. If every act, in fact, were subject to the rule of law, we would be free. Without restrictions we will see rampant abuses worse than we are seeing today. There will be anarchy as a result of unrestrained freedom. We see it already in places where drug dealing is rampant with its accompanying corruption, violence,and murder sprees.

This can happen to a society like ours lacking in self-control; our foundation is constantly shifting and shaking and we are on it. Our feet keep sinking in and we are losing our balance. We simply don't think or care anymore. "Attention," advises Mortimer B. Zuckerman, "must be given by everyone to the first law of holes: When you are in one, stop digging."

The freedom to choose from a host of alternatives that is almost unlimited becomes incapacitating if not paralyzing to many of us. This is so when "destructive and irresponsible freedom has been granted boundless space," says Solzhenitsyn.

In one's life, significant new beginnings occur either for the better or for the worse. It's freedom of choice that makes this possible. It is the burden of being responsible for the self one chooses to be; it is commitment to purpose in every aspect of living; it is the arduous task of knowing what to do with one's freedom. True freedom, I believe, is acting on our rights and privileges as free men and women in a sane and rational manner in making our choices, knowing that such choices have consequences, and that we alone are responsible and accountable as a result of our actions.

When we are under the influence of mind-altering chemicals, we are not acting rationally and we compromise our precious freedom and hurt ourselves and society as well. We are accomplices and as responsible as those who supply us with death-dealing drugs. This dependence on chemicals for one's existence is a voluntary resignation that is self-imposed and is the cause of rampant drug abuse. Lorin McMackin describes this total lack of restraint in his book, *Thoughts on Freedom: Two Essays*:

Man can be an egoistic and useless creature, but he can never be happy when he has lost his way. In this unnatural condition, his confusion is commonly so great that he can imagine no cure for the illness save the aggravation of his infection. In single-minded, insatiable drive, he demands to augment his already hopeless autonomy and insists upon casting off even the few remaining threads to the source of his guidance and comfort. Satisfaction is impossible for him! He can never get enough of that which he has never needed. But he thinks to ease his wretchedness by distending its cause. And he drives on to press license into perversion and perversion into insanity.[5]

This condition and attitude tend to exalt individual freedom without any limitation. And it's a challenge for us to temper such destructive tendencies. Former Chief Justice Warren E. Burger once said: "The very opportunities within our reach mean that we Americans bear a great burden of accountability for the kind of society we live in."

We made it and we are the only ones who can unmake it. Our future is in our hands.

History records a sad cycle of great civilizations that thought nothing could bring them down — except themselves. "And if the United States," wrote Paul Harvey, America's favorite radio commentator, "ever does succumb, here too it will have been by our own hand."

Should we fail to act now, then we have accepted a prescription for the suicide of another great civilization. And nothing can prevent it from happening as the truth in the words from *The Rubaiyat of Omar Khayyam* speaks to us like the writing on the wall with absolute certainty:

> The Moving Finger writes; and
> having writ, moves on. Nor all your
> Piety nor Wit shall lure it back to
> cancel half a Line, Nor all your Tears
> wash out a Word of it.

---

5. *Thoughts on Freedom: Two Essays*, Lorin McMackin, Southern Illinois University Press, 1982.

Appendices

SPECIFIC DRUGS AND THEIR EFFECTS

— CANNABIS —

EFFECTS

All forms of cannabis have negative physical and mental effects. Several regularly observed physical effects of cannabis are a substantial increase in the heart rate, bloodshot eyes, a dry mouth and throat, and increased appetite.

Type	What is it called?	What does it look like?	How is it used?
Marijuana	Pot Grass Weed Reefer Dope Mary Jane Sinsemilla Acapulco Gold Thai Sticks	Dried parsley mixed with stems that may include seeds	Eaten Smoked
Tetrahydro-cannabinol	THC	Soft gelatin capsules	Taken orally Smoked
Hashish	Hash	Brown or black cakes or balls	Eaten Smoked
Hashish Oil	Hash Oil	Concentrated syrupy liquid varying in color from clear to black	Smoked — mixed with tobacco

Use of cannabis may impair or reduce short-term memory and comprehension, alter sense of time, and reduce ability to perform tasks requiring concentration and coordination, such as driving a car. Research also shows that students do not retain knowledge when they are "high." Motivation and cognition may be altered, making the acquisition of new information difficult. Marijuana can also produce paranoia and psychosis.

Because users often inhale the unfiltered smoke deeply and then hold it in their lungs as long as possible, marijuana is damaging to the lungs and pulmonary system. Marijuana smoke contains more cancer-causing agents than tobacco.

Long-term users of cannabis may develop psychological dependence and require more of the drug to get the same effect. The drug can become the center of their lives.

— INHALANTS —

Type	What is it called?	What does it look like?	How is it used?
Nitrous Oxide	Laughing gas Whippets	Propellant for whipped cream in aerosol spray can Small 8-gram metal cylinder sold with a balloon or pipe (buzz bomb)	Vapors inhaled
Amyl Nitrite	Poppers Snappers	Clear yellowish liquid in ampules	Vapors inhaled
Butyl Nitrite	Rush Bolt Locker Room Bullet Climax	Packaged in small bottles	Vapors inhaled
Chlorohydro-carbons	Aerosol sprays	Aerosol paint cans Containers of cleaning fluid	Vapors inhaled
Hydrocar-bons	Solvents	Cans of aerosol propellants, gasoline, glue, paint thinner	Vapors inhaled

EFFECTS

Immediate negative effects of inhalants include nausea, sneezing, coughing, nosebleeds, fatigue, lack of coordination, and loss of appetite. Solvents and aerosol sprays also decrease the heart and respiratory rates, and impair judgment. Amyl and butyl nitrite cause rapid pulse, headaches, and involuntary passing of urine and feces. Long-term use may result in hepatitis or brain hemorrhage.

Deeply inhaling the vapors, or using large amounts over a short period of time, may result in disorientation, violent behavior, unconsciousness, or death. High concentrations of inhalants can cause suffocation by displacing the oxygen in the lungs or by depressing the central nervous system to the point that breathing stops.

Long-term use can cause weight loss, fatigue, electrolyte imbalance, and muscle fatigue. Repeated sniffing of concentrated vapors over time can permanently damage the nervous system.

— STIMULANT: COCAINE —

EFFECTS

Cocaine stimulates the central nervous system. Its immediate effects include dilated pupils and elevated blood pressure, heart rate, respiratory rate, and body temperature. Occasional use can cause a stuffy or runny nose, while chronic use can ulcerate the mucous membrane of the nose. Injecting cocaine with unsterile equipment can cause AIDS, hepatitis, and other diseases. Preparation of freebase, which involves the use of volatile solvents, can result in death or injury from fire or explosion. Cocaine can produce psychological and physical dependency, a feeling that the user cannot function without the drug. In addition, tolerance develops rapidly.

Type	What is it called?	What does it look like?	How is it used?
Cocaine	Coke Snow Flake White Blow Nose Candy Big C Snowbirds Lady	White crystalline powder, often diluted with other ingredients	Inhaled through nasal passages Injected Smoked
Crack or Cocaine	Crack Freebase rocks Rock	Light brown or beige pellets — or crystalline rocks that resemble coagulated soap; often packaged in small vials	Smoked

Crack or freebase rock is extremely addictive, and its effects are felt within 10 seconds. The physical effects include dilated pupils, increased pulse rate, elevated blood pressure, insomnia, loss of appetite, tactile hallucinations, paranoia, and seizures.

The use of cocaine can cause death by disrupting the brain's control of the heart and respiration.

— OTHER STIMULANTS —

Type	What is it called?	What does it look like?	How is it used?
Amphet-amines	Speed	Capsules	Taken orally
	Uppers	Pills	Injected
	Ups	Tablets	Inhaled through nasal passages
	Black Beauties		
	Pep Pills		
	Copilots		
	Bumblebees		
	Hearts		
	Benzedrine		
	Dexedrine		
	Footballs		
	Biphetamine		
Methamphet-amines	Crank	White powder	Taken orally
	Crystal Meth	Pills	Injected
	Crystal	A rock which resembles a block of paraffin	Inhaled through nasal passages
	Methedrine		
	Speed		
Additional Stimulants	Ritalin	Pills	Taken orally
	Cylert	Capsules	Injected
	Preludin	Tablets	
	Didrex		
	Pre-State		
	Voranil		
	Tenuate		
	Tepanil		
	Pondimin		
	Sandrex		
	Plegine		
	Ionamin		

EFFECTS

Stimulants can cause increased heart and respiratory rates, elevated blood pressure, dilated pupils, and deceased appetite.

In addition, users may experience sweating, headache, blurred vision, dizziness, sleeplessness, and anxiety. Extremely high doses can cause a rapid or irregular heartbeat, tremors, loss of coordination, and even physical collapse. An amphetamine injection creates a sudden increase in blood pressure that can result in stroke, very high fever, or heart failure.

In addition to the physical effects, users report feeling restless, anxious, and moody. Higher doses intensify the effects. Persons who use large amounts of amphetamines over a long period of time can develop an amphetamine psychosis that includes hallucinations, delusions, and paranoia. These symptoms usually disappear when drug use ceases.

— DEPRESSANTS —

Type	What is it called?	What does it look like?	How is it used?
Barbiturates	Downers Barbs Blue Devils Red Devils Yellow Jackets Yellows Nembutal Seconal Amytal Tuinals	Red, yellow, blue, or red and blue capsules	Taken orally
Methaqualone	Quaaludes Ludes Sopors	Tablets	Taken orally
Tranquilizers	Valium Librium Equanil Miltown Serax Tranxene	Tablets Capsules	Taken orally

EFFECTS

The effects of depressants are in many ways similar to the effects of alcohol. Small amounts can produce calmness and relaxed muscles, but somewhat larger doses can cause slurred speech, staggering gait, and altered perception. Very large doses can cause respiratory depression, coma, and death. The combination of depressants and alcohol can multiply the effects of the drugs, thereby multiplying the risks.

The use of depressants can cause both physical and psychological dependence. Regular use over time may result in a tolerance to the drug, leading the user to increase the quantity consumed. When regular users suddenly stop taking large doses, they may develop withdrawal symptoms ranging from restlessness, insomnia, and anxiety to convulsions and death.

Babies born to mothers who abuse depressants during pregnancy may be physically dependent on the drugs and show withdrawal symptoms shortly after they are born. Birth defects and behavioral problems also may result.

— HALLUCINOGENS —

Type	What is it called?	What does it look like?	How is it used?
Phencyclidine	PCP	Liquid	Taken orally
	Angel Dust	Capsules	Injected
	Loveboat	White crystalline powder	Smoked — can be sprayed on cigarettes, parsley, and marijuana
	Lovely	Pills	
	Hog		
	Killer Weed		
Lysergic Acid Diethylamide	LSD	Brightly colored tablets	Taken orally
	Acid	Impregnated blotter paper	Licked off paper
	Green or Red Dragon	Thin squares of gelatin	Gelatin and liquid can be put in the eyes
		Clear liquid	
	White Lightning		
	Blue Heaven		
	Sugar Cubes		
	Microdot		
Mescaline and Peyote	Mesc	Hard brown discs	Disc—chewed, swallowed, or smoked
	Buttons	Tablets	
	Cactus	Capsules	Tablets and capsules — taken orally
Psilocybin	Magic mushrooms	Fresh or dried mushrooms	Chewed and swallowed
	Mushrooms		

EFFECTS

Phencylidine (PCP) interrupts the functions of the neocortex, the section of the brain that controls the intellect and keeps instincts in check. Because the drug blocks pain receptors, violent PCP episodes may result in self-inflicted injuries.

The effects of PCP vary, but users frequently report a sense of distance and estrangement. Time and body movement are slowed down. Muscular coordination worsens and senses are dulled. Speech is blocked and incoherent.

Chronic users of PCP report persistent memory problems and speech difficulties. Some of these effects may last six months to a year following prolonged daily use. Mood disorders — depression, anxiety, and violent behavior — also occur. In later stages of chronic use, users often exhibit paranoid and violent behavior and experience hallucinations.

Large doses may produce convulsions and coma, heart and lung failure, or ruptured blood vessels in the brain.

Lysergic acid (LSD), mescaline, and psilocybin cause illusions and hallucinations. The physical effects may include dilated pupils, elevated body temperature, increased heart rate and blood pressure, loss of appetite, sleeplessness, and tremors.

Sensations and feelings may change rapidly. It is common to have a bad psychological reaction to LSD, mescaline, and psilocybin. The user may experience panic, confusion, suspicion, anxiety, and loss of control. Delayed effects, or flashbacks, can occur even after use has ceased.

— NARCOTICS —

EFFECTS

Narcotics initially produce a feeling of euphoria that often is followed by drowsiness, nausea, and vomiting. Users also may experience constricted pupils, watery eyes, and itching. An overdose may produce slow and shallow breathing, clammy skin, convulsions, coma, and possibly death.

Tolerance to narcotics develops rapidly and dependence is likely. The use of contaminated syringes may result in diseases such as AIDS, endocarditis, and hepatitis. Addiction in pregnant women can lead to premature, stillborn, or addicted infants who experience severe withdrawal symptoms.

Type	What is it called?	What does it look like?	How is it used?
Heroin	Smack Horse Brown Sugar Junk Mud Big H Black Tar	Powder, white to dark brown Tar-like substance	Injected Inhaled through nasal passages Smoked
Methadone	Dolophine Methadose Amidone	Solution	Taken orally Injected
Codeine	Empirin compound with Codeine Tylenol with Codeine Codeine Codeine in cough medicines	Dark liquid varying in thickness Capsules Tablets	Taken orally Injected
Morphine	Pectoral syrup	White crystals Hypodermic tablets Injectable solutions	Injected Taken orally Smoked
Meperidine	Pethidine Demerol Mepergan	White powder Solution Tablets	Taken orally Injected
Opium	Paregoric Dover's Powder Parepectolin	Dark brown chunks Powder	Smoked Eaten
Other Narcotics	Percocet Percodan Tussionex Fentanyl Darvon Talwin Lomotil	Tablets Capsules Liquid	Taken orally Injected

— DESIGNER DRUGS —

EFFECTS

Illegal drugs are defined in terms of their chemical formulas. To circumvent these legal restrictions, underground chemists modify the molecular structure of certain illegal drugs to produce analogs known as designer drugs. These drugs can be several hundred times stronger than the drugs they are designed to imitate.

The narcotic analogs can cause symptoms such as those seen in Parkinson's disease — uncontrollable tremors, drooling, impaired speech, paralysis, and irreversible brain damage. Analogs of amphetamines and methamphetamines cause nausea, blurred vision, chills or sweating, and faintness. Psychological effects include anxiety, depression, and paranoia. As little as one dose can cause brain damage. The analogs of phencyclidine cause illusions, hallucinations, and impaired perception.

Type	What is it called?	What does it look like?	How is it used?
Analogs of Fentanyl (Narcotic)	Synthetic Heroin China White	White powder resembling heroin	Inhaled through nasal passages Injected
Analogs of Meperidine (Narcotic)	Synthetic Heroin MPTP (New Heroin) MIPP PEPAP	White powder	Inhaled through nasal passages Injected
Analogs of Amphetamines and Methamphetamines (Hallucinogens)	MDMA (Ecstasy, XTC, Adam, Essence) MDM STP PMA 2, 5-DMA TMA DOM DOB	White powder	Taken orally Injected Inhaled through nasal passages
Analogs of Phencyclidine (PCP) (Hallucinogens)	PCPy PCE TCP	White powder	Taken orally Injected Smoked

— EFFECTS OF ALCOHOL ON THE BODY —

Site	Observable Signs and Symptoms
The Brain and Nervous System	Impaired memory, judgment, and concentration
	Confabulation (imaginary story-telling to fill gaps in memory)
	Loss of control over drinking
	Ataxia — more often in lower extremities
	Numbness, tingling, or prickly sensations in the extremities
	Temporary nerve palsies — usually radial — ulnar or peroneal
	Malnutrition (related to polyneuritis)
	Fatigue
	Depression
	Reduced libido
Liver	Hepatic pain (right upper quadrant abdominal pain)
	Jaundice
	Ascites
	Spider angiomata (on trunk and face)
	Palmar erythema (redness of palms)
	Peripheral edema
	Bruising
Gastrointestinal System	Poor eating habits
	Heartburn — gas, distention
	Nausea and vomiting
	Gastric pain
	Irritation or inflammation of the mouth, throat or oesophagus
	Alternating diarrhea and constipation
	Weight loss or gain
	Malnutrition
Respiratory System	Diminished cough reflex (depression of central nervous system)
	Difficulty in expectorating (heavy smoking pattern usual)
Cardiovascular System (Alcoholic Cardiomyopathy)	Elevated pulse
	Shortness of breath
	Decreased exercise tolerance
	Transient chest discomfort
	Distended neck veins
	Peripheral edema
	Spasmodic shortness of breath during sleeping hours

SOURCES FOR SPECIFIC DRUGS AND THEIR EFFECTS

Drug Enforcement Administration. *Drugs of Abuse*. U.S. Government Printing Office, 1985.

Mann, Peggy. *Pot Safari: A Visit to the Top Marijuana Research in the U.S.* New York, N.Y.: Woodmere Press, 1985.

National Institute on Drug Abuse.

Cocaine Use in America: Epidemiologic and Clinical Perspectives. ADM 85-1414, 1985.

Drug Abuse and Drug Abuse Research. ADM 85-1372, 1984.

Hallucinogens and PCP. ADM 83-1306, 1983.

Inhalants. ADM 83-1307, 1983.

Marijuana. ADM 83-1307, 1983.

NIDA Capsules, various issues.

Opiates. ADM 84-1308, 1984.

Phencyclidine: An Update. ADM 86-1443.

Sedative-Hypnotics. ADM 84-1309, 1984.

Stimulants and Cocaine. ADM 84-1304, 1984.

Newsweek. March 17, 1986, p. 58.

Tobias, Joyce. *Kids and Drugs*. Annandale, VA: Panda Press, May 1986.

THE MORAL OF THE STORY
How to Teach Values in the Nation's Classrooms

— Gary Bauer —

In the past decade, it has become the conventional wisdom in the academic establishment that moral education is illegitimate because it constitutes "indoctrination." As a result, teachers have approached the subject in a diffident manner. And our children are growing up with very confused and sometimes dangerous notions of what it means to act morally and responsibly in today's society. The problems of alcoholism, drug abuse, vandalism, promiscuity, and simple lack of common decency which pervade our schools are clearly related to the terrible state of moral education in the American classroom.

Until very recently, the idea that values or morality were part of the educational process was unchallenged. Indeed, it has been at the core of the educational philosophy of Western civilization since the time of the Babylonians. Both Plato and Aristotle believed that virtue was the highest form of wisdom and it was the duty of elders and educators to transmit such knowledge to their students. Irving Babbitt in *Literature and the American College* maintained that a large component of learning is ethical and there is no such thing as education without moral education. These ideas guided American public education from the outset. The governing philosophy was that students should not just be taught about the world but also about themselves — how they could be better persons, how they should behave in a civilized society. The great *McGuffey Readers* embodied the approach of distilling clear moral lessons from texts like Milton and Shakespeare, which children read in the original.

Moral education fell into disrepute for several reasons. The first is that several of the values that were previously taken for granted came to be challenged. For example, many psychologists came to think that sexual restraint was not necessarily the best option for children, that moderate drug use could be salutary, that some forms of destructive behavior served a therapeutic function, or at least constituted "self expression." The second is growth of the fact/value dichotomy, a brainchild of positivism, and the concomitant notion that if education aspired to be a science, it could only teach empirically verifiable propositions and not subjective values. Finally, it was recognized that the values being taught in schools were intrinsically connected with the Jewish and Christian religions; educational philosophers wondered if moral education was simply a means to impose theological beliefs on children.

In recent years, a new system of values education has gained enormous influence in the teacher training schools. "Values Clarification" is rarely taught as a separate course to students; rather, it is a methodology of learning that is aggressively promoted in courses that prospective teachers take. Thus, it greatly influences teacher attitudes toward moral education — attitudes that express themselves in courses ranging from literature to government to history to philosophy. From being a marginal element in values education theory, Values Clarification has become the mainstream. This is alarming, because although it claims to be a theory of moral education, in fact Values Clarification is a repudiation of moral education.

— Choosing Dishonesty —

The standard Values Clarification text is *Values and Teaching* by Louis Raths, Merrill Harmin, and Sidney Simon. It argues that teachers should not try to "impose values" on students. Even to teach such fundamental values as honesty or compassion is to be oppressive. "All the traditional methods of moral education have the air of indoctrination, with some merely more subtle than others." Teachers should try to "flush out" or clarify students' own value systems; they should "be concerned with the process of valuing and not particularly with the product."

The fact that Values Clarification focuses entirely on procedures and is indifferent to outcomes is part of its appeal. It sounds so scientific, individualistic, and nonjudgmental, all phrases congenial to the progressive orthodoxy. And yet what are its practical results?

In one Values Clarification class, students congenially concluded that a fellow student would be foolish to return $1,000 she found in a purse at school. The teacher's reaction: "If I come from a position of what is right and wrong, then I am not their counselor." In *Values and Teaching*, Raths, Harmin, and Simon provide a case to illustrate what happens when Values Clarification conflicts with classroom rules.

> **Ginger:** Does that mean we can decide for ourselves whether we should be honest on tests here?
>
> **Teacher:** No, that means that you can decide on the value of honesty. I personally value honesty and though you may choose to be dishonest, I shall insist that we be honest on our tests here.

The problem with this is that it leaves students with the impression that attempts to enforce values such as honesty are totally arbitrary. The teacher is allowed to impose his will only because he is in possession of the means of compulsion. The implicit moral lesson here is that values should be followed not because they are right but because they are backed by coercion.

In fact, the general presumption behind Values Clarification is that there are no reliable standards of right and wrong—each person develops a morality which is right "for him." But under such a radically subjective approach, how can we justify holding our children to any consistent standards at all? C. S. Lewis in *The Abolition of Man* notes the irony that

> We continue to clamor for those very qualities we are rendering impossible.... We make men without chests and expect of them virtue and enterprise. We laugh at honor and are shocked to find traitors in our midst. We castrate and bid the geldings be fruitful.

— Parents vs. Educational Theorists —

Undoubtedly parents want values taught in school. The problem is that the confidence of teachers in performing this task is constantly undermined by the educational theorists who write the textbooks and dominate the teacher training profession. Teachers are given the impression that moral education is unscientific, unprofessional, and oppressive. They are constantly reminded that if they teach values they are entering into the unconstitutional domain of religion. Our public school teachers are no longer sure of what values to teach and how to go about teaching them.

The vacuum created by this uncertainty has resulted in the introduction of numerous courses in the public schools which amount to little more than political indoctrination. The educational materials distributed by the National Education Association on nuclear war claim to be neutral and unbiased, but in fact they are rife with propaganda for disarmament and the nuclear freeze. The entire enterprise of "peace education" largely consists of political values creeping into the chasm created by the abandonment of moral education. This is ironic, because on political issues there are frequently multiple points of view which should all get a hearing, whereas on many moral questions — especially the basic ones — there is very little ambiguity.

This is not to say that a return to moral education in the public school classroom would be an easy task. Russell Kirk has reminded us that we cannot expect "abrupt reform and speedy results." And yet "if there is no education for meaning, life will become meaningless for many. If there is no education for virtue, many will become vicious." We have got to face these difficult questions and come up with satisfactory answers.

As usual, the past provides clues to the solutions that exist. We know from history that all good educational systems, from Roman times, have taught the rising generation loyalty to parents and family, a sense of responsibility to the public order, duties to the community, a high value for human life, respect for nature and its creation, love of beauty and truth. A modern catalog of desired virtues that parents and teachers could agree on would be quite similar.

At a recent conference on education, Clark University professor Christina Hoff Summers was pressed to identify some clear issues of right and wrong by academicians who clearly felt that no such things exist. She replied:

> It is wrong to betray a friend, to mistreat a child, to humiliate someone, to torment an animal, to think only of yourself, to lie, to steal, to break promises. And on the positive side, it is right to be considerate and respectful of others, to be charitable, honest and forthright.

She met with a very skeptical reaction.

Of course, exceptions can be found to rules such as these. The problem with modern approaches such as Values Clarification is that they mistake the exception for the rule. A typical model problem that Values Clarification advocates use on children is: what do you do if you have no money and your mother is dying of starvation — is it all right to steal? Another common example is to ask children whom they would throw overboard if they were in a lifeboat with six people and could only stay afloat with five. These are interesting mind-bending dilemmas, but the vast majority of life's situations do not involve starving mothers and sinking lifeboats. They involve such mundane things as learning how to live in a family, showing up on time for work, displaying courtesy to fellow citizens, discharging responsibilities to the community and country. For these tasks, fairly simple rules should suffice.

In a recent speech, Mark Curtis, president of the Association of American Colleges, argued that today "there is a pervasive sense that values are private, personal matters, rising from individual subjective preferences or even prejudices, not from widespread agreement on the basic ends and means to be used on the conduct of our life and dealings with others." But our "commitment to pluralism," Curtis said, should not "obscure the possibility that certain values can unite rather than divide us."

The most important unifying values that our public schools must teach, I believe, are the fundamental principles that are the basis for our free society and democratic government.

Such documents as the Mayflower Compact, the Declaration of Independence, and the Constitution embody the values of our Western heritage. They teach such things as the inviolability of the individual, the rule of law, and the rights and duties that citizens incur when they enter into civilized society with the purpose of protecting themselves, promoting the general welfare, and enjoying freedom. In today's society, we are very conscious of "rights," whether they be civil rights or human rights. But as de Tocqueville said, "The idea of rights is nothing but the conception of virtue applied to the world of politics." Ironically, while rights multiply in our society, we have lost our common vision of what values undergird those rights and make them worth having.

Cicero writes in *De Res Publica* that "Our age inherited the Republic like some beautiful painting of bygone days, its colors already fading through great age, and not only has our time neglected to freshen the colors of the picture, but we have failed to preserve its form and outlines." This is our predicament today. We cannot subsist forever on the moral capital of the past. It is not just social continuity or personal happiness — it is the very future of our political system, of democracy and freedom — which require that we be alert to moral values, and pass them on to our children.

Moral education is not the same thing as religious education, and teachers in public school classrooms are not permitted to teach theology. But constitutional prohibitions on promoting sectarian religious beliefs should not be used as an excuse to avoid teaching about the role of religion in our history and culture. Professor Paul Vitz in an Education Department study documented a shocking bias against religion in textbooks commonly used in our schools. The Pilgrims, for example, are identified as "people who make long trips" and Christmas as "a warm time for special foods." Not only is this a form of censorship, but it severely damages our children's moral development because so many of the values Americans can agree on have as their source the Judeo-Christian ethic.

Here, for example, is a lesson from McGuffey's *First Reader*, a very popular textbook in public schools until quite recently, "Always do to other children as you wish them to do to you. This is the Golden Rule. So remember it when you play. Act upon it now, and when you are grown up, do not forget it." Suspicious lawyers for the American Civil Liberties Union might detect that this sounds alarmingly like something Christ once said. But what if it is? To teach about the values of the Jewish and Christian religions (as distinct from the doctrine) is to teach love, dignity, forgiveness, courage, candor, self-sacrifice — all the highest manifestations of what it means to be alive and to be human.

In our effort to identify values that can be taught in public schools, we should attempt to discover a common body of ethical knowledge that, even if it has a religious origin, serves the purpose of maintaining and strengthening devotion to our country, to democratic institutions, to fellow citizens, to family members, and finally to an ideal of human dignity.

— The Role of Literature —

Once we can agree on the values that are to be taught, there remains the question of how to teach them. I do not think that the best approach is to preach to students or to ask them to write "I will not lie" a hundred times on the blackboard. Obviously there is a place for propositional teaching — setting forth a set of moral propositions and getting students to memorize them. But there are other ways to transmit values that are more effective over the long term.

Perhaps the method of moral education that would harmonize best with the existing curriculum would be to demonstrate the working out of moral rules through experience. Several courses in the humanities and the social sciences provide teachers with the opportunity to view such principles in action. Sometimes conflict in the areas of history or literature provides a wonderful dramatization of moral ideals set against each other. This not only exposes students to the relevant ethical criteria, but it complicates the issue by making them choose, as indeed in real life we frequently have to do.

In literature, we have the example of Raskolnikov in Dostoyevsky's novel *Crime and Punishment.* Here is a very intelligent young man who has developed a great deal of pride and some very strange theories. He convinces himself that he is justified in murdering an old woman and stealing her money because he is a superior person to her, and because she — being ugly and miserly — does not deserve her possessions. Surely Raskolnikov can do more good with her money than she is doing now, he reasons, his pride leaning on a defiant utilitarianism.

Yet through the fabric of the novel, Dostoyevsky illustrates the disastrous consequences of this thinking. He gives the reader, with great force, a sense of the urgent need for moral norms which transcend cost-benefit analysis, the need for a principle which affirms the moral dignity of the human being above considerations of what they look like and what they are "worth." Because we are creatures of God, Dostoyevsky shows, we are equal in His image. *Crime and Punishment* is many things, but it is an excellent example of moral education.

Naturally very young minds might find Dostoyevsky too complex. But there are numerous alternatives. The fables of Aesop, the legends of Hans Christian Anderson, and the works of the Brothers Grimm, all make sharp distinctions between good and evil in a context that the child's mind finds exotic and appealing. Even films like *Star Wars* illustrate the benevolent force and the evil force in conflict. In my own childhood, I remember reading Rudyard Kipling's *Jungle Book*. Then, of course, there is Kipling's fascinating and moving poem "If," which consists of wise and timely advice from a father to his son, advice from which all young children could benefit immensely.

Recently *U.S. News and World Report* asked the American Federation of Teachers for some simple moral lessons that could be derived from children's texts. The A.F.T. provided the example of the Bible: "And the Lord said to Cain: where is Abel, thy brother? And he said: I know not. Am I my brother's keeper?" This can be used to teach responsibility. In the *Story of Pinocchio* we read, "Lies, my dear boy, are found out immediately because they are of two sorts. There are lies that have short legs and lies that have long noses. Your lie, as it happens, is one of those that have a long nose." This can be used to teach honesty. Finally, in *To Kill a Mockingbird* by Harper Lee we read, "You never really understand a person until you consider things from his point of view...until you climb into his skin and walk around in it." This can be used to teach compassion and empathy.

As students grow older and are exposed to more sophisticated works, they can understand moral principles of a higher order. *Hamlet* is not just a morality tale which says you should not commit murder and incest; it is about the paralysis of indecision in the face of moral obligation. *King Lear* is about the ingratitude of the young, but it is also about the imperiousness of the old. Moral principles can be stated with clarity at a young age, then refined in higher grades. Patriotism can be presented in the first grade as a virtue, but later students must be taught not to be uncritical of their country. "For us to love our country, our country ought to be lovely," as Edmund Burke remarked.

Our children will retain their moral principles only when they have been thoroughly explored and students have had an opportunity to see them challenged and successfully defended. Even the good people in the classics didn't always behave well. Achilles was pompous and cruel, Saint Peter was cowardly, Lancelot and Guinevere committed adultery. But these stories leave no doubt about how they should have acted, and the heavy price of their misdeeds is outlined. Children need to see that immoral actions have serious consequences — that virtue is not something you just talk about, but something you do.

I have great confidence in the power of stories to teach. Flannery O'Connor once said that "A story is a way to say something that can't be said any other way — you tell a story because a statement would be inadequate." The literary device of showing instead of telling is a very effective way to convey truths to young minds.

Then there are the lessons of history. Recently I read a very disturbing comment by Richard Hunt, a Harvard professor who teaches a course on the Holocaust. Professor Hunt reports that over half his students felt that Hitler and the Nazis were not to blame for their atrocities. The students believed that Hitler's rise was "inevitable," that it was impossible for Britain and France to have resisted German imperialism, and that no one was really responsible for what happened in the end. "No-fault history" is the term Hunt used to describe his students' refusal to ascribe moral responsibility to historical actions.

Most of these students seem to have been influenced by theories like determinism and behaviorism, even though they may not know it. It is important for those who teach history in the public classroom to convey clearly the notion that historical events and conflicts are rife with moral meaning, that the human beings who took part in them chose actions which had consequences, and that many similar moral choices are before us today.

From Napoleon and Hitler who were finally destroyed by their blind ambition, students can see where the totalitarian instinct leads. From the Roman wars, students can learn about great valor but also about conceit and cruelty — this great civilization held slaves and treated them inhumanely. Of course, evil is not always extinguished in history — Stalin, after all, died in bed — but by making itself known, it incurs the harsh judgment of posterity and becomes a lesson in what successive generations should abhor and avoid.

Our goal in teaching values is not merely the transmission of a desired set of beliefs. Rather, it is a process, integrated into the general curriculum, which provides students with a clear articulation of the norms and concepts that have sustained this free and democratic society since its founding; which informs the student, at appropriate stages of development, of alternative value systems; which encourages a comparison between them; which gives the student the tools to examine and defend personal beliefs; which brings students into contact with the moral circumstances of the past; which gives the student the justification and the equipment to participate in the conservation and improvement of this civilization of ours.

C

DRUG ABUSE PREVENTION
The Role of the Schools

— Malcolm Lawrence —[1]

A major contributing factor to the tolerance of illicit drugs and narcotics in America is that many of our schools are sending out weak and confusing messages. Since the early 1970s, educators have been brainwashed by permissive pundits and curriculum developers to believe that scare tactics and facts about drugs are counter-productive and that the solution to the drug abuse problem for students is to use a values clarification approach, apply compassion, give counseling, set up hot lines, and at all costs avoid using the word "don't" when discussing drugs. The fashionable approach in drug education has been to let the children examine all aspects of their feelings, attitudes, values and societal pressures and then make their own decisions about whether to use drugs.

In point of fact, our schools never really did use scare tactics or give adequate factual information about the serious effects of drugs on the body, the brain and the genes. Those who say that scare tactics and facts have failed are usually the ones who make the ridiculous argument that law enforcement has failed, the implication being that we have to give up law enforcement and try something else. As any sensible person in the drug battle knows, we need all the help we can get.

In my 17 years of experience in dealing with the drug problem, I have read much drug curriculum and talked with many parents. I have yet to come across any good, solid, effective educa-

---

1. Former special assistant for international narcotics control matters, U.S. Department of State. Excerpts from testimony delivered to House and Senate Committee hearing on Children, Youth and the Family, Washington, D.C.

tion. I have, however, become acquainted with some poor curriculum. Let me cite some examples.

Heading the list of wrong-headed education is the values clarification approach exemplified by the widely used by highly controversial kindergarten through 12th grade curriculum called, "Here's Looking at You, Two." This misguided package dwells on stress, fear, anxiety and unpleasant situations, but does not teach about the real dangers of illicit drugs or that taking drugs is wrong.

Another curriculum that misses the mark is called "Ombudsman," which was developed with funds from the National Institute on Drug Abuse. "Ombudsman" has very little information about drugs, but exposes 5th through 10th graders to such things as role playing, encounter activities, feelings charades, warm fuzzies, love lists, self portraits, personal questionnaires, the trust fall, the human knot, who shall survive exercises, gravestone statements and death notices.

Even children in grades 1 through 6 have to suffer through a values clarification course called, "The Me-Me Drug Prevention Education Program," developed 11 years ago with U.S. Office of Education Title III funds. Little 6- and 7 year-olds learn all about their full potential, self concepts, decision making, peer pressure, Mr. Yuk, and developing positive feelings toward their teachers. Unfortunately, "Me-Me" and "Ombudsman" are still being promoted by the National Diffusion Network of the U.S. Department of Education.

There are elementary level drug courses that classify all kinds of substances into the harmful basket category — coffee, tea, soft drinks, aspirin, tobacco, cough syrup, beer, marihuana, heroin, cocaine, pills of all sorts, etc. — conveying the notion that the differences are minor. To a small child, if something is bad, it is bad. This type of education presents a real problem for the 7-year-old who may tend to equate drinking a cup of coffee with shooting heroin.

Some schools give 2nd and 3rd graders an assignment to explore the family medicine cabinet and take inventory of what they find. It is amazing how curriculum developers try to encourage curiosity in children well beyond their maturity levels. It is even more amazing that school boards approve such curriculum. Showing a small child where mom's sleeping pills are can be the same as handing him a loaded gun.

About the most asinine approach I have come across is from the 7th grade drug curriculum in my own community, Montgomery County, Maryland, which opens as follows:

> Currently, community concern regarding drug misuse is centered on today's youth. They are growing up in a world full of problems for which they see no immediate solutions. Young people in adolescence undergo bodily changes with related emotional pressures. Superimposed on this is peer pressure, accompanied by the "fad syndrome." It is not surprising, therefore, that many young people are seeking an escape through drug experimentation.

This message implies that earlier generations did not experience bodily changes, emotional pressures, fads and peer influences and were able to solve all of their problems. Therefore, those people didn't need drugs. Such rationale is not only stupid, but is an open invitation for 12 year-olds to enter the drug culture.

It is no small wonder that drug abuse education in our schools is getting such a bum rap. It is also no small wonder that there are 20 million persons admitting to using cocaine, five million regular cocaine users and up to one million cocaine addicts, as well as half a million heroin addicts and countless millions of abusers of marihuana, PCP, and other illicit drugs. Will crack get as strong a hold on our youth as marihuana has?

My observations may be limited, but I have reached the conclusion that our wishy-washy approach on the demand side of the drug problem has been a major contributing element to addiction and death among our youth. In a word, our schools are not tough enough. The solution is not more values clarification and situation ethics, but factual instruction backed up by a no-nonsense school policy....

It seems clear to me that the reasons for the enforcement measures in the area of drug abuse should form the basis of our educational approach. Indeed, the message to be emphasized in the home, in the schools and by the media should be the straightforward extension of the findings of the medical and chemical experts as well as the justifications for the laws.

A massive supply of drugs and narcotics has slipped into our midst within the past two decades, but this does not mean we should in any way foster the notion promoted in our schools that each person be permitted to make an independent analysis and decide whether or not illegal drugs are the thing for him. It cannot be viewed as a civil right and a privilege for any individual to dabble in such substances and in the process drag others with him down the road to addiction and crime. It is nothing short of ridiculous to devote so many of our resources to cutting off the supply of drugs and at the same time carry on with a soft, compassionate approach at the demand end.

We are not trying to curtail the supply simply to give enforcement officials something to do. There is a much better reason, and that is to keep the drugs and narcotics from the end-users. If the abusers and the prospective abusers do not understand this, then perhaps the message should be put across much more emphatically than it has in the past. We should stop teaching the reasons why children take drugs and instead teach them the very basic and perfectly clear reason why children should not take drugs. The message should go to young and old alike; the young do not have a monopoly on self-abuse.

Drug abuse education can only be effective if it is done correctly, if it tells the practical truth. There is no need for a pro-and-con debate. Drug abuse is bad. It can destroy the mind and kill the body. In a word, it is stupid. This is a very simple truth, a sad one reported daily in the newspapers. Hence, we should moralize about the subject. We should say it is wrong to abuse drugs and to abuse yourself. We should say, "Don't."

Let's face it. A large percentage of our youth has been suckered into a drug-oriented cult, whether on a street corner, in a schoolyard or at a rock festival. At the same time, many otherwise clear-thinking adults have been duped into believing that a vast range of social and psychological pressures has forced children to rely on a crutch to soothe their natural and normal growing pains, a crutch which is preventing a portion of our youth from maturing, facing reality and earning a decent place in society.

To correct the situation, we should cease agonizing over the problem and adopt a constructive policy in every community. This can be done by the implementation of some very simple preventive measures to complement the efforts of the law enforcement authorities....

Dealing with the drug problem in the schools calls for much more than "busting" students and throwing them out of the system. Rather, every board of education should formulate a Policy Statement on Drug Abuse which for all practical purposes should apply to the middle school through senior high levels.

The Policy Statement should be a community education document. Thus, sufficient copies should be printed and disseminated to parents, students, religious leaders, civic clubs, and other interested groups.

The Policy Statement should condemn the abuse and distribution of drugs and narcotics as defined under the law and implement a constructive action program to combat the problem during school hours and on school property. Specifically, it should do the following:

1. Outline the scope and dangers of drug abuse;
2. Define the penalties under county, state and federal laws for the abuse and distribution of drugs and narcotics, including the penal procedures for juvenile offenders;
3. Identify the principal types of drugs and narcotics as well as the symptoms to look for in persons under or suspected of being under their influence;
4. Spell out the administrative measures to be implemented by school authorities on an area-wide scale to curtail the illegal use and transfer of drugs and narcotics on school property, including school vehicles;
5. Indicate the precise procedures to be followed by school personnel when drugs and narcotics are found on school property and when students are determined to be or suspected of being under their influence ....

I wish to re-emphasize that the Policy Statement on Drug Abuse should go to all school personnel, parents and students so that everyone in the system is aware of the rules.

In addition to its regulatory function, the school's Policy Statement should provide the basic thrust for the drug abuse curriculum in the classroom. Instruction should be factual, uniform and uncomplicated. It should be included in routine fashion with the treatment of other health hazards such as alcohol and tobacco and handled in a matter-of-fact way as a component part of the health education instruction. Students should be tested on their knowledge of the subject matter to ensure proper understanding. There should be no glamorization of the topic of drug abuse, no soppy mysticism and soul-searching seminars on the deep-rooted causes and significance of the drug phenomenon in our society. There should be an absolute minimum of films, and those shown should be selected with the greatest of wisdom.

I am firmly convinced that if drug abuse education is over-done, it will not only bore the students, but will expand the base of the problem. Student exposure to all aspects of drug abuse on a kindergarten through 12th grade basis would not represent a panacea; it would instead only increase curiosity and lead to greater experimentation with drugs and narcotics. School authorities would do well to keep the instruction within the limits of an informative message and not treat drug abuse as a behavioral science by putting it on a psychological altar. In my view, the 6th grade would be the appropriate starting level for most school areas.

The adoption of a constructive policy by the school system of each community in our nation would have a profound influence on the local population in the following ways:

❑ The subject of drug abuse would be placed in proper perspective, and the current cloud of frustration that tends to mark the reliance on drugs as a predestined curse on the young would drift away.

❑ The healthy, hardy, fun-loving "in" groups of abusers would be ostracized by their peers and would no longer be considered either fashionable or tolerable.

❑ The youth of the community would become far too wise to serve as legal guinea pigs for the older libertines and libertarians who dedicate themselves to the worship and use of marihuana, LSD, PCP, cocaine, heroin and other illegal substances.

❑ The cop-out mentality would disappear because the children would realize that whatever they might want to do, they could do it better without drugs.

❑ Parents would begin to look to their own life-styles and appraise themselves as examples to their children.

❑ Gradually the community would learn that the supply of drugs, whether legal or illegal, does not necessarily create its own demand. When these things happen, youngsters will no longer use drugs because they are there, because they will know better.

(For a copy of the complete text of this speech, write to Committees of Correspondence, Inc., P.O.Box 232, Topsfield, MA, 01983, or call (619) 774-2641.)

D

DRUG TESTING AND THE DEATH PENALTY
The Solution to the Drug Problem

DeForest Z. Rathbone, Jr.

Under the twin-driving forces of human greed for wealth and human lust for instantaneous sensual pleasure, the drug holocaust rages out of control throughout much of America. After nearly two decades of a no-win "war on drugs," assured of its no-win status by all the corruption $500 billion in illegal revenues can generate, the problem remains firmly entrenched for the indefinite future.

Enormous social problems have either been directly caused by drugs or greatly aggravated by them. A fact that best describes the net human costs of the drug epidemic is this awful statistic: the only age group in America today which has an increasing death rate (all others are getting healthier and living longer) is the age group from 15 to 24, primarily due to their compulsive use of drugs. Tragically, recent statistics show that age group declining toward the 12 to 20 age bracket.

Somehow many of our citizens seem to have missed the obvious connection between the drug problem and the increase of those enormous social problems whose development has closely tracked that of the drug problem. While many suspect that the increase in driving accidents and street crime may be drug-related, few have attributed to drugs the inordinate increase in teen suicides, teen pregnancies, sexual abuse of children, AIDS, the proliferation of "street people," murders of infants by parents and babysitters, murders of parents by children, schoolchildren murdering each other, commuters shooting each other over minor traffic incidents, and the increase in fatal plane, train, and bus crashes.

One shudders to think that the entire class of the 60's and 70's, constituting in large part the dope generation, is out there operating and maintaining our planes, trains and buses, building our atomic power plants, building and repairing our cars and homes, educating our children and, as we now see from the example of the dope-smoking Harvard law professor who became a Supreme Court nominee and as further evidenced by the resistance of some U.S. Justice Department attorneys to taking drug screening tests, entrenched throughout our judicial system as well.

Americans who have suffered through the drug epidemic of their children's generation are now facing the anguish of seeing this plague destroy the minds and lives of their grandchildren. And there is no end in sight!

Unless we are willing to use the legislative equivalent of atomic warfare on this "war on drugs," our children will continue to be sacrificed for the benefit of the wealthy dope merchants and their corrupt co-conspirators among public officials, lawyers, and business interests who profit so greatly from the continuation of this vile trade.

Just as Truman's atomic bombs stopped World War II and saved many GI lives which otherwise would have been lost, so will the following legislative "atomic bombs" stop the drug-related slaughter of America's children. These vital weapons are the death penalty for kingpin drug traffickers and diagnostic drug testing for schoolchildren.

Both are essential. And both will work! But without both being adopted and fully utilized, we can expect to see the personal hell and the social hell of drug abuse continue the devastation of our families and our communities. These two simple tools are *the* solution to the horribly destructive epidemic of drug abuse.

— Drug Testing —

Drug testing is needed to reduce the demand for drugs by eliminating the vast market created by introducing vulnerable young children to drugs in their schools. And the death penalty is needed to reduce the supply of drugs by creating the ultimate disincentive to profiting from the illegal drug trade.

Drug education by itself has been only partially effective, interdiction of trafficking at our limitless borders and shorelines is impractical, law enforcement agencies in many areas are completely overwhelmed by drug-related crime, and punishment under the ACLU-influenced judiciary system is widely perceived as a farce. Although we must continue to try in all those areas, none has been very successful to date in reversing the drug/crime wave.

Specific legislation will be needed to authorize diagnostic drug testing and the death penalty, but with the certainty of the dope generation having infiltrated legislative bodies at both the state and national levels, enactment of those laws will not be easy. Widespread and intensive support for those measures among the citizenry will be needed in order to induce legislators to enact the appropriate laws.

Following are separate rationales supporting the need for such legislation.

But for the Grace of God and drug testing, New York Mets star baseball pitcher Dwight Gooden might have ended up like Len Bias or David Kennedy or John Belushi, or any of the huge number of other young persons whose lives have been destroyed by drug abuse. Gooden is now recovering from his addiction and is once again performing up to his gifted potential as a professional ballplayer, primarily due to the benefits of drug testing.

Gooden completed his 1987 baseball season as the reliable and effective pitcher he once was before his enslavement to cocaine. Drug testing enabled Gooden to face the reality of his failing condition during the time when his brain was chemically blocked from believing that a problem could even exist. Drug testing saved Dwight Gooden and it can save schoolchildren too!

By treating drug abuse — particularly among schoolchildren — as the contagious disease it is instead of treating it as a behavioral problem, drug testing becomes an appropriate and effective diagnostic tool to identify for treatment and rehabilitation kids who have become enslaved to mind-altering substances and who subsequently feel compelled to pressure their classmates to use drugs.

To eliminate the "privacy rights" issue ACLU liberals use to disparage diagnostic drug testing, additional legislation will be required prohibiting the use of drug testing for disciplinary or criminal prosecution purposes for children below the age of 18. Thus, drug testing for children would join TB testing, etc., as strictly a medical, and therefore perfectly legal, diagnostic tool.

This would facilitate the early identification and treatment of drug-abusing children which in turn would subsequently assure that the remaining clean but vulnerable population of school kids would not be exposed to classmates with that dangerous and highly communicable disease of chemically induced emotional instability, drug abuse.

As schools are cleaned up of drugs, in time we should expect to see a commensurate reduction in drug abuse among the adult population, thus a significant reduction in the demand side of the drug-abuse equation.

— Death Penalty —

The only feasible solution to the supply side of that drug-abuse equation is the death penalty for kingpin drug traffickers. I wish to accentuate the term "Kingpin" which is defined in current federal legislation as "major drug trafficking organizational leaders" whose ill-gotten profits number in the millions of dollars. I also wish to accentuate that the death penalty is *not* appropriate for the small-time pusher who is often as much of a victim of the wealthy drug lords as are the hapless addicts.

In addition to being responsible for the drug-related carnage among America's youth, kingpin drug traffickers have been responsible for the murder of a great number of public officials such as judges, legislators, prosecutors, DEA agents, and police officers who are our first line of defense in combating their evil enterprise.

It is strongly suspected that the enormous profits of drug trafficking which are often used to corrupt public officials (or intimidate them through acts of violence) are a major driving force behind the refusal to date of politicians to enact the death penalty for kingpin traffickers. Many suspect that this same economic incentive is also the impetus behind the opposition to such legislation by lawyers who stand to profit so greatly from their share of the nearly $500 billion world-wide commerce in illegal drugs as defense attorneys, legal advisors, etc.

Because of the enormity of this economic incentive, it is going to take massive political pressure by parents and other citizens to reverse that corruption-induced legalistic resistance to that death penalty.

Those who oppose the death penalty on religious or moral grounds should consider that by protecting kingpin drug traffickers from the death penalty, we are in fact sentencing our own children to the death penalty imposed upon them by those traffickers. It would seem that as long as people are going to die anyway from the flourishing illegal drug trade, it would be better that those who die be the kingpin drug traffickers themselves rather than our own children and our honest public officials.

Whether America can enact such laws to protect our citizens from the ravages of drug abuse remains to be seen. Opposition from the liberal lawyers' lobby, the ACLU, is virtually certain. And their influence is substantial. However, unless the American people can be persuaded that the health and safety of their kids, their families, their elderly, and their communities are more important than any slavish adherence to the ACLU's perverted view of the Constitution which presently favors the drug criminal over the ordinary citizen-victim and favors the drug culture over traditional civilized values, the drug holocaust among America's children will continue unabated.

Millions of frustrated Americans are in for a continuation of the heart-breaking destruction of our kids by drugs unless we are willing to bite the bullet and make use of such effective weapons as will guarantee the end of this drug nightmare: drug testing and the death penalty.

Therefore, I propose adoption of such legislation at both the state and federal level without further damaging delay.

And I further propose that all concerned citizens join the effort to get these laws enacted as a major step needed to turn this continuing no-win war on drugs into an unconditional victory for our children and for our country.

STOP LEGALIZATION OF ILLEGAL DRUGS

— Robert E. Peterson —
Deputy Attorney General,
Commonwealth of Pennsylvania

The argument that the only solution to the drug problem is to legalize illicit drugs has resurfaced with a fiery vengeance. This time it is not only NORML and the usual group of drug lobbyists calling for marijuana decriminalization. Legalization proponents now include conservatives such as William F. Buckley Jr., commentator Andy Rooney, and the mayors of Baltimore and Washington, D.C. Economist Milton Friedman says that the harm caused by drugs is caused by the fact that drugs are illegal, and he maintains that if crack was legal, there would be no crack epidemic!

Following Baltimore Mayor Kurt Schmoke's appeal for a national debate on legalization to the U.S. Conference of Mayors, the media swiftly launched the legalization issue back into the public domain. The *Sunday New York Times* placed the issue on the front page, a *Time* magazine cover blazingly asks "Should Drugs Be Legalized?", and *Nightline* and *Crossfire* ran televised discussions on the issue. Even though the vast majority of Americans adamantly oppose drug legalization, and 99.9% of the true experts in the drug field know it's a destructive idea, the debate is once again here. Those involved in fighting drug abuse must be prepared to deal with the issue.

Just asking the question "Should drugs be legalized?" sends a confusing mixed message to young people. One class of 14- and 15-year olds wrote a letter to the *New York Times* regarding drug legalization and they correctly stated that "... America is in a 'moral rut' and ... drug abuse is one of the main causes." (*New York Times*, May 7, 1988) The students concluded that "[l]egalizing drugs is not the answer." Don't these kids have enough pressure trying to resist drugs and say "no" to their peers and the pushers every day? It should not be their responsibility to also try and keep the message from adults clear and consistent.

Many of those advocating drug legalization do not realize the damage they are doing. They have never talked with the kids who bravely refuse to use or to the young addicts struggling to recover a shattered life. As Congressman Rangel angrily states, to many people the legalization issue is "idle chitchat as cocktail glasses knock together at social events." It is our duty and responsibility to speak out for those who often cannot speak for themselves. We must publicly challenge every assertion that drugs should be legalized.

This article is intended to provide factual data to refute the legalization position. It is up to you to use this material in editorials, letters to the editor, interviews and other communications to help silence legalization proponents who, either intentionally or unintentionally, are beginning to whisper to our children and our nation "just say yes."

— Why Legalize? —

There is both an old school and a new school of thought on why drugs should be legalized. The old school dates back to the hippy era and argues that drug use should be allowed as a matter of individual liberty and that people should have the right to use whatever drugs they want, regardless of the consequences to society. The old liberal school will support almost any argument to legalize drugs, such as: claiming drugs are not that dangerous; or that there is a compelling medicinal need for illicit drugs; or that drug laws are an evil plot by big brother government; or that people only use drugs because they are illegal. This group has generally lost ground over the past ten years as the marijuana decriminalization push stagnated and public concern about the drug issue mounted.

America has grown increasingly intolerant of illicit drugs as the destructive impact of these substances has expanded. Ironically, in the midst of increasing drug intolerance, a renewed cry for drug legalization is being heard. This call for drug legalization is primarily based on fear and frustration. The inability of law enforcement to single-handedly solve

America's drug problem is cited as evidence of the futility of imposing legal prohibitions on drugs. The costs of enforcement, it is argued, outweigh the benefit society derives from such enforcement. Faulty economic theory is simplistically applied to bolster the legalization position.

I call such economic theory "blind-side economics" because it overlooks historical experience, neglects social and economic realities, ignores the biological and pyschological effects of illicit drugs, and misinterprets lessons from our recent experience with these deadly substances. The frustration of those concerned about the drug issue is understandable. The call for drug legalization is not.

The legalization argument sounds deceptively logical when viewed as an abstract theory or when coupled with distorted analogies or facts out of context. However, the argument completely self-destructs when it is placed in the context of human experience and history, and then examined in conjunction with the scientific biological nature of illicit drugs. The major questions raised by pro-legalization proponents are addressed below.

— Can We Win The War On Drugs? —

The advocates of drug legalization claim that the war on drugs cannot be won and we must withdraw now and cut our losses. In support of this claim they cite the fact that drug availability, drug consumption, and drug-related violence has increased in spite of stronger law enforcement efforts and tougher drug laws.

Factual Analysis:

History and the experience of other nations reveal that the most effective means of solving a drug epidemic is to apply strong enforcement in conjunction with a public education and user rehabilitation campaign.

China overcame a severe opium addiction problem through a tough law enforcement and education program. (See historical accounts of Opium War).

Japan routed an amphetamine epidemic after WW II and a growing heroin problem in the late fifties and early sixties through aggressive law enforcement and the stigmatization and rehabilitation of users. (*US News and World Report*, May 16, 1983, p.57; *Wall Street Journal*, December 9, 1987, p.34).

Great Britain discovered that allowing doctors to prescribe heroin created a large black market and led to an increase in drug problems. (*The Economist*, April 18, 1987, p.55; *New York Times*, April 11, 1985).

Amsterdam is rethinking liberal drug policies as defacto legalization has led to an increase in certain crimes. (*Time*, August 31, 1987, pp.28-29; *Forbes*, February 27, 1984, p.46).

Spain relaxed drug laws in 1983 and has experienced a recent spurt in cocaine and heroin addiction. A crackdown on drug pushers is now underway. (*The Economist*, April 18, 1987, pp.45-46).

The experience of other nations indicates that applying tough law enforcement measures in conjunction with public education and rehabilitation efforts is the only way to successfully solve a drug crisis. Liberalizing drug laws only brings about an increase in drug use, drug addiction, and drug-related criminal activity. It is true that law enforcement cannot win this war alone and prevention, education and treatment efforts have only just started to work in conjunction with enforcement.

The fact that certain aspects of a battle are going poorly does not lead to the conclusion that surrender is inevitable. There are areas in which we are gaining ground. Among high school seniors and young adults drug use of all types (except alcohol) appears to be down according to annual statistics. The public is more concerned about drugs and has a more negative attitude toward drug use than ever before.

Tough drug enforcement, detection, and education in the military brought about a 62% drop in drug use in the Navy.

We have only really begun to fight drugs in the past eight years. Prior to that we had a President who talked of legalizing marijuana and drug researchers who claimed that "recreational" cocaine use was harmless! A problem that developed over 25 years will require a long-term, serious effort to overcome.

We still have not committed the resources to wage a serious fight against drugs. More federal money is put into public transportation subsidies than drug enforcement. There are more police personnel committed to protecting the members of Congress than there are federal drug agents.

As Pennsylvania Attorney General LeRoy S. Zimmerman wrote in the *New York Times*, the drug war "... is a fight for the hearts, minds and futures of our children. And there is no place to which we can withdraw."

— Would Legalization Reduce Crime? —

Legalization proponents say that if drugs were legal and made less expensive then illegal drug trafficking would cease and crimes committed by drug users would dramatically decline. They also claim that various schemes of governmental regulation of drugs could be tried. In defense of this claim they analogize the current drug laws with alcohol prohibition and assume that drug users only commit crimes to pay for high-priced drugs.

Factual Analysis:
Drug Trafficking

Legalization proponents use the alcohol system analogy to demonstrate the problems of prohibition, but they often call for a system of drug legalization that does not resemble the alcohol model. Some have argued that a restrictive government regulatory system could be implemented to control drug purity and price. This notion does not conform with logic, reason, or experience.

A strong black market in illicit drugs will persist unless all drugs of all potencies are competitively manufactured and marketed. The reason that we do not have a strong black market in alcohol products is that consumers can easily obtain a beverage with the taste, potency and cost of their choice. In the Soviet Union, where alcohol product quality and quantity is controlled by the government, illegal alcohol production and the consumption of dangerous substitutes is rampant. Drugs are easier to smuggle and manufacture than alcohol and government-approved cocaine could quickly be converted into deadly pellets of crack. Great Britain found that allowing limited distribution of heroin to addicts resulted in a stronger black market.

To eliminate the illicit drug market, pure cocaine, crack, PCP and heroin would have to be readily available at low cost. The black market in drugs would disappear, but a black plague of drug addiction, overdose deaths and crime would sweep the nation.

Drug Legalization and Street Crime

A popular misconception among legalization proponents is that drug users commit crimes solely to support expensive drug habits. This misperception leads to the false conclusion that lowering the cost of drugs would reduce the level of drug-related crime. In reality, cheaper legal drugs would increase the level of violent and property crime.

Drug users will commit crime to obtain drugs regardless of drug price. Crime levels have dramatically risen in areas where drug prices have dropped. In areas where crack now sells for only $3 per dose (a price that a legal, taxed market would find hard to beat), violent crime has skyrocketed. Amsterdam has found that defacto legalization and readily available low-cost drugs have led to a wave of theft and vandalism. Drug abusers who formerly sold drugs to support their habit would now steal to buy legal drugs. The amount of drugs consumed by addicts also would rise with falling drug prices.

Dr. Robert Gilkeson, M.D., a pediatrician, neuropsychiatrist, and director of the Center for Drug Education and Brain Research, states that "drug use [is] actually the cause of sociopathic and 'criminal' behavior." Drug users commit crimes that are totally unrelated to the cost of the drug. In Philadelphia, 50% of the child abuse fatalities involve parents who heavily use cocaine. Cheaper legal cocaine would result in more children murdered and more babies born addicted. Bizarre sexual behavior, youth suicides and murder are committed because drugs impair normal thought processes. Over 80% of criminals arrested for violent felonies were on drugs when they committed their crime according to the Department of Justice. Rapes, assaults, and murders that are unrelated to a need for drug funds are included in these statistics.

By removing legal sanctions and lowering drug cost, a broader and more frequent demand for drugs will be created. Increased drug use will result in a surge in incidents of random violence and higher crime rates.

— How Would Drug Legalization Impact On Drug Demand? —

Many legalization advocates admit that there would be at least a temporary rise in drug use if legal prohibitions were removed. This factor is mitigated by a blind faith belief that some "natural level" of use would be reached and a proposal to use the money "saved" on law enforcement for education to prevent drug use and treatment. Most legalization proponents would continue to prohibit drug use by youth.

Factual Analysis:

Experience shows that one cannot be pro-legalization and hope to discourage drug use by youth. Over half of the high school seniors had smoked marijuana, and 11% got stoned on pot every day during the period in which some states decriminalized the drug and support for anti-marijuana laws was at a low. Today, criminal penalties for pot are strongly backed and the use of marijuana among high school kids has dropped, with daily use down to 4%.

Our experience with alcohol proves that a drug that is legal for adults cannot be kept from kids. Among high school seniors, over six times more students have drunk alcohol, which is legal for adults, than have tried cocaine, which is illegal for everyone. Cocaine and most other illicit drug use has started to decline among high school students, while alcohol use has remained relatively stable. This would be the worst point in history at which to legalize drugs.

Dr. Mitchell Rosenthal, of Phoenix House treatment center, estimates that 75% or more of all regular illicit drug users become addicted, while 10% of the nation's drinkers are alcoholics. Research has demonstrated that those who drink alcohol to become intoxicated are more prone to alcoholism than those who drink and avoid intoxication. Illegal drugs are used solely for their intoxicating effect. Drugs such as crack can enslave the user almost immediately.

Cultural and social factors also contribute to how an intoxicating substance will be used. In American society, where instant relief and pleasure is demanded, illicit drug use and dependence is higher than that of any other developed nation. Drug legalization will result in more people experimenting with drugs, more experimenters becoming regular users, and more regular users becoming addicts.

Our drug laws do deter people from using drugs and have turned users to a drug-free lifestyle through mandatory treatment. 70% of the high school students in New Jersey and about 60% of the students in California said that fear of getting in trouble with the law constituted a major reason not to use drugs. Mature adults are even more risk aversive. The majority of our citizens do not use illegal drugs.

— Which Is More Costly, Drug Legalization Or Drug Prohibition? —

Drug legalization proponents claim that by taxing drugs and saving on the cost of drug law enforcement, additional funds for drug education, prevention and treatment could be raised. Again, the alcohol example is cited as evidence.

Factual Analysis:

Japan, Sweden, Spain, Great Britain, China, and the Netherlands have all found the cost of permissive drug laws to be too high and have implemented or are implementing strong drug laws and stricter enforcement. Drug legalization is a costly proposition.

The cost imposed by alcohol abuse on society exceeds $100 billion annually. This cost is not met by the $5.6 billion collected yearly in federal alcohol tax revenues. Each day approximately 600 people die from alcohol-related deaths. Do tax revenues cover these costs? Illegal drug abuse costs society approximately $26 billion annually and only $6-8 billion is spent on enforcing drug laws. Legal cheaper drugs would raise the cost of drug abuse to an intolerable level.

The major danger and cost of alcohol use results from using alcohol to the point of intoxication. Illegal drugs are always used for the purpose of intoxication and the users pose an even greater risk of causing death from accidents, suicide, and criminal behavior. The only reason that the death rate from illicit drugs is lower than that caused by alcohol abuse is that such drugs are illegal. Our current system of drug prohibition actually saves thousands of lives and billions of dollars in economic resources.

Drug education and prevention is most effective when it is backed by strong laws and law enforcement. Alcohol, a legal drug for adults, is by far the drug of choice among young people. Moreover, attitudes toward illicit drugs have become far more negative than teenage attitudes toward drinking. We have yet to determine how to keep over 90% of our high school seniors from taking a drink. It is ludicrous to think that the temptation of trying legal cheap drugs could be overcome solely through educational efforts.

— Is Illicit Drug Use The Moral Equivalent —
Of Alcohol And Tobacco Use?

Many of those who support drug legalization claim that illicit drugs cause fewer deaths than alcohol and tobacco and that it is wrong to ban some drugs and allow these other dangerous substances to be legally used.

Factual Analysis:

Simple arithmetic reveals that one costly hazardous substance plus another costly hazardous substance will not become safer or less costly by adding a new group of costly and hazardous chemicals.

There is no such thing as "responsible use" of illicit drugs. If every time someone had a drink they became inebriated, that person would be labeled a drunkard and an abuser of alcohol. Illicit drug users only take drugs for one reason — to get high. The inevitable intoxicating effect of illicit drugs distinguishes these substances from alcohol and tobacco. It has been found that the ability of airline pilots to perform certain maneuvers remained impaired 24 hours after smoking one joint of marijuana. Alcohol abuse and tobacco use are not to be condoned, but there is an important distinction that can be made between these and illicit drugs. The reason that there is no such thing as responsible use of alcohol by kids is that, as the teens themselves tell us, they drink *to get high* with their friends. And more teens die from alcohol and drug-related accidents than any other single cause.

It is difficult to conceive of how one can justify distributing dangerous and addictive drugs to those that desire them and at the same time require a prescription for potentially helpful medicines such as antibiotics. If cocaine and heroin are approved for public consumption, what will the FDA's standard be for approving any drug offered by the pharmaceutical industry? Unless we make the drug manufacturers and distributers immune from damage lawsuits from the inevitable death and destruction caused by these products, will any company risk selling these substances? It is difficult for legalization proponents to make these distinctions and to find any realistic approach to legalization.

Alcohol prohibition failed because a popular legal substance, with a long cultural and social history, was banned without the moral consensus of the people. Today, less than 18% of the public favors a return to alcohol prohibition and over 85% favor a 21-year-old drinking age. On the other hand, public support for our drug laws and strong drug law enforcement has never been stronger. Over 73% of the public oppose legalizing marijuana, and tough drug laws are overwhelmingly favored. The few vocal proponents of legalization inaccurately conclude that the nation does not have a moral consensus on this issue. Few other laws receive such strong support from the American people as those that prohibit illegal drug use.

Some legalization proponents advocate that the United States experiment with various forms of legalization. The truth is that once a legal drug market is created, a strong drug lobby will make repeal of that experiment almost impossible. The tobacco and alcohol industries exert tremendous influence in Washington and cocaine growers and manufacturers would quickly form their own organization to fight for an expanded legal market.

All laws are expressions of the moral will of the people. However, laws cannot make a wrong into a right. Laws that allowed slavery did not make slavery right or just. Illicit drug use is wrong. It enslaves the user and victimizes all of society. The current law reflects our overwhelming recognition of that fact. In a democratic society, the will of the people, expressed through a system of laws, is the rule of the land.

— What Impact Would Legalization Have —
On Foreign Relations And Policy?

The illegal drug traffic has brought about tremendous problems for drug producing nations. Legalization supporters argue that a legal drug market would eliminate drug-related corruption and violence in these countries and ease tensions between the U.S. and supplier nations (especially those in Latin America).

Response:
The United States would be in violation of international treaty if it created a legal market in cocaine, pot and other drugs. In 1961, the United States joined the Single Convention on Narcotic Drugs and agreed with other members of the United Nations to control and penalize drug manufacturing, drug trafficking and

drug use. The United Nations has recently engaged in new efforts to help coordinate global efforts to reduce the supply of, and demand for, illicit drugs. The United States would betray these efforts by legalizing drugs, cause an increase in drug availablity in other nations, and lose credibility by its double-minded approach.

Latin American governments have called on the United States to make tougher attempts to limit drug demand. Legalization would increase drug use. Unless drugs were legalized throughout the world — and there is no reason to believe other countries would follow our folly — a strong black market would persist. Producer nations are already facing their own drug abuse crisis and that would worsen if drug production is legitimized. Criminal drug lords would dominate the legal market and run large plantations and exploit peasant workers. An aristocracy of former drug outlaws would foment new political instability and corruption.

— Conclusion —

Almost every American has been personally affected by the drug abuse problem. But none have suffered as much as our youth. Whether it's a baby born addicted, a child murdered by drug-crazed parents, or a teenage abuser destroying his mind and future, the young have paid dearly. And the kids that lack families, the kids that are poor, the kids that have limited opportunity — they suffer disproportionately.

The kids are not to blame. They inherited the drug problem. The drug epidemic began in the permissive era of the late sixties and early seventies. If we didn't know it then, we know it now — freedom is not free. Responsibility, self-control, and self-sacrifice are necessary to maintain it. Our free society cannot survive if we continue to sit idly by as our children unwarily enslave themselves. We must set limits and raise standards. We *are* our brother's keeper and each of us must do his part.

F

THE WHITE HOUSE CONFERENCE
for a Drug Free America

— Final Report – June 1988 —

Although most of the recommendations made by the White House Conference for a Drug-Free America fit into a distinct category, a number apply to many different categories. These recommendations are referenced in the individual sections but addressed in this section.

> **Recommendation 1.** Legalization of illicit drugs must be vigorously opposed by government at all levels and by all segments of society.

In recent months, there has been increasing clamor in the news media and by some public figures for the legalization of drugs. At first glance, it would appear that this debate is not serious — after all, why would anyone actually espouse eliminating controls over something so destructive? But the proponents of legalizing drugs assure us that they are serious — that legalization would be a good way to eliminate crime and criminal organizations. It seems an exercise in futility to suggest that crime can somehow be eliminated by redefining it — as if a criminal act had no inherent danger other than that derived from its placement in the law books of our Nation. But illicit drugs are indeed a destructive force with which we must reckon.

We are learning more and more about the devastating effects that drugs have on the minds and bodies of users. Depending on the drug, the heart, liver, lungs, and kidneys as well as the reproductive and immune systems can all be damaged. In fact, it would be hard to find an organ or a system in the body that is not damaged by illicit drugs. Cocaine increases the likelihood of heart attack and stroke as early as the first use. Heroin ingestion can lead to suppression of respiration sufficient to cause suffocation. Damage to the drug user's mind may be even more frightening. The user under the influence of drugs is not the harmless, sleepy soul we once thought he was. During drug use and after, people are changed, they do not think clearly, they are filled with anger, fear, paranoia and a host of emotions they have never experienced or had to keep in check. Memory deprivation, organic brain damage, and psychosis are among the recognizable consequences of such use.

Although it was not long ago that many people thought marijuana and even cocaine were not addictive or particularly harmful, most advocates of legalization do not try to argue that illicit drugs are safe. Instead, they try to defuse the issue by pointing out that alcohol and cigarettes, two legal substances for adults, kill many more people than illicit drugs. Ironically, this is probably the strongest argument *against* legalization that they could make. Alcohol and cigarettes are not inherently more dangerous than illicit drugs. A given dose of cocaine or its derivative crack is far more dangerous than a drink. A joint of marijuana is far more carcinogenic than a cigarette, and it negatively affects the mind as well. Alcohol and cigarettes kill more people than illegal drugs precisely because they *are* legal — because so many more people use them. We have more public health problems than can presently be handled as a result of alcohol and cigarettes. Legalized drugs would overwhelm our public health system.

A related argument that proponents of legalization have relied upon is libertarian: that people should be allowed to take whatever substance they desire, and that users are hurting no one but themselves — they are committing a victimless act. Although this argument has a certain simplistic appeal, it is not only factually incorrect but it has also been repeatedly rejected in this country.

Regardless of what we once thought, we now know that illicit drug use is not a victimless crime. Whether we are family members or co-workers of addicts, passengers on airplanes or trains piloted by users, victims of brutal and wanton violence induced by mind-altering drugs such as PCP or speed, travellers facing the menace of drugged drivers on our highways, or simply taxpayers, we are all victims of illicit drug use.

We take great pains to protect the public from harmful drugs. Even medically useful drugs are tested for years before they are allowed on the market, and then they are carefully regulated, requiring prescriptions from licensed physicians. It is only because of their medically beneficial effects that they are allowed. What possible beneficial effect is there from marijuana, cocaine, LSD, PCP, or heroin to justify legalizing them?

It seems clear that most of the present fascination with legalization is born from a sense of frustration at the high level of violent crime associated with drug trafficking, and at our seeming inability to eliminate that violence even through increased expenditures for law enforcement. Legalize drugs, so the argument goes, and we will eliminate drug-related violent crime and save money at the same time. While this argument has some appeal on its surface, it fails to stand up to scrutiny. Even if we were to legalize drugs, we would still need drug law enforcement because even most proponents of legalization do not advocate legalizing drugs such as crack, LSD, or PCP, and because drugs would remain illegal for minors. We would thus continue to have drug-related crime and illegal drug distribution organizations that would continue to push drugs on our youngsters. We would also have much higher costs associated with increased health care and lost productivity.

In the final analysis, legalization is wrong because drugs are wrong. To legalize behavior is in large measure to condone it. Do we want to say as a Nation that it is acceptable to ruin one's mind and body, to tolerate as recreation an activity which imposes such risks on every one of us, and to consign a larger proportion of our population to incapacitation and dependence on society? We should be aware that other countries have tried legalization and that policy has failed. Illegal markets with their attendant criminal problems continue to exist. Legalization ensures that the government condones and often ends up supporting an intoxicated lifestyle for a larger number of its people.

We can be certain that if we legalize drugs, the number of users will increase dramatically. The fact that we cannot deter all users of illicit drugs by criminal laws does not mean that we should discard those laws, any more than the fact that we have robbery means that we should make robbery legal.

With all these articulable risks and dangers, how could one possibly argue that legalization makes sense? The only conceivable answer is to admit that the criminal justice system has been overrun and that the drug thugs are threatening to swamp us. Two responses are apparent. First, as discussed elsewhere in this report, we have not given the criminal justice system adequate resources to tackle the problem, and pinning our hopes to end the crisis of illegal drugs solely on prevention and treatment would be an ill-fated gamble with our Nation's future. Second, it has never been part of the American character to capitulate to criminals.

Recommendation 2. Use of illicit drugs must not be considered a victimless crime.

All citizens must speak out against the common myth that illicit drug use is a victimless crime. The victims of illicit drug use are everywhere: residents of drug-infested neighborhoods, citizens against whom criminal acts are perpetrated by users and traffickers, the business community, and society at large through taxes supporting prisons, law enforcement, medical services, and increased insurance rates.

The enormous profits generated by the illicit drug industry in the United States have attracted some of the most violent criminals to the trade. There is no innocent use of illicit drugs. People who use these drugs as a form of "recreation" do not see themselves as hurting anyone, because they did not rob or steal to obtain their drugs. What these people do not understand, however, is that their use of illicit drugs is helping to fill the pockets of drug dealers with ill-gotten gains and to support violence. The people who "casually" use cocaine are accomplices in the deaths of foreign leaders assassinated by drug cartels, of innocent inner-city children and elderly people who are caught in the crossfire of rival drug gangs, and of law enforcement officers who risk their lives to protect us in our homes and in our communities.

We must be absolutely unyielding in our opposition to illicit drug use. We must be as adamant about "casual" users as we are about addicts. And whereas addicts may also deserve our help, "casual" users deserve our condemnation. These persons must accept responsibility for the brutality and corruption which they help finance.

THE LESSONS OF HISTORY

Gabriel G. Nahas, M.D., Ph.D.

Records of history show that when dependence-producing drugs are socially acceptable and easily available, they are widely consumed, and their use is associated with a high incidence of individual and social damage.

The use of cannabis in the Islamic-dominated world surfaced only in the eleventh century when the Moslem Empire extended from the Atlantic to the Indian Ocean. Arabic historians of the twelfth to the sixteenth century have clearly documented the damage done by the widespread use of hashish in the Moslem world. A scholarly account of their voluminous writings has been compiled by Dr. Franz Rosenthal, Sterling Professor of Near Eastern Languages at Yale University, in his book *The Herb: Hashish Versus Moslem Medieval Society*. The reader learns that a controversy similar to the one raging today divided the ancient Islamic world. For several centuries the partisans of the "grass which gives joy and repose" battled the detractors of the "weed which impairs body and mind, and damages society." At one time, in the first years of the fifteenth century, restrictions against hashish were set aside, resulting in general availability, acceptance, and abuse. The historian of the era, Al Magrizy, wrote that as a result, a general debasement of the people was apparent. Finally all the scholars and religious leaders of the time condemned the weed — not from religious fervor, but because of the harm it had done to their society. It was too late. Says Rosenthal: "The conflict between what was felt to be right and socially good, and what human nature craved in its search for play and diversion went on..." until this day.

In Peru, the chewing of the coca leaf by the Indians and their leaders the Incas, was limited by religious ceremonies. After the Spanish conquest, this habit spread among the farmers and laborers who were paid in coca leaves that they chewed nearly continuously. As a result they were in a state of continuous low-grade intoxication. They have since maintained this custom. The farmers and miners of the Andes thus are able to work under most adverse conditions with only limited food intake. As a result, their social condition has not changed in centuries and their general health and life expectancy are poor.

In 1858, the legal trade of opium and the Opium Wars were imposed on China by British mercantilism. By 1900, ninety million Chinese were addicted to opium. It took a national revival and the support of the United States and the international community, as well as fifty years of coercive measures, for the country to become opium-free. Today opium and other dependence-producing drugs are banned from mainland China as well as from Nationalist Taiwan and Socialist Singapore.

In the 1920's, the unrestricted commercial availability of cocaine and heroin in Egypt resulted in a massive epidemic abuse of these drugs which, as in China, was also curtailed in the thirties following national and international interdiction, and punitive measures meted out to all addicts.

In the 1950's Japan experienced a major epidemic of intravenous and amphetamine use involving a half million addicts. A national campaign aimed at restricting demand and supply with sanctions applied against users and traffickers brought the number of addicts down to a few thousand within four years. An epidemic of heroin was curtailed in the same manner in the sixties.

In contrast, the British adopted, in 1925, a medical model allowing physicians to prescribe heroin to heroin addicts, which was dubbed "the British system." It worked satisfactorily as long as addicts were few in number: 500 per year between 1930 and 1960. It became unmanageable after 1960 when heroin had to be dispensed to more than 1,000 users of the drug. Indeed, each addict had to be provided with daily doses of heroin as well as the syringes and needles required for administration of the drug four to six times a day. Because of this logistics problem and because of the potential for diversion of the drug to non-registered addicts which is inherent in such a scheme, heroin began to be progressively replaced by methadone maintenance (methadone, a long-lasting opiate, needs to be absorbed only once a day, by mouth); in 1980, six percent of the 2,800 registered British addicts were treated with heroin compared to the thirty-one percent of the 1,400 addicts in 1973. In 1985, there were an estimated 80,000 heroin addicts in Britain. Despite this failure of the "British system," it is still advocated by some in the U.S.

The lessons of history are clear: the social acceptance of dependence-producing drugs appears to exacerbate rather than alleviate all of the problems associated with drug addiction.

RECOMMENDED BOOKS FOR READING

General

Marijuana Alert, by Peggy Mann, published by McGraw-Hill Book Company, 1985. You can consider this your "bible" on marijuana — all you need to know is in this book. A 526-page, three-part book. Available from PRIDE: 1-800-241-7946.

Getting Tough on Gateway Drugs, by Robert L. DuPont, Jr., M.D., published in 1984 by American Psychiatric Press, Inc., 1400 K Street, N.W., Washington D.C. 20005. This book offers much-needed support to families troubled with teenage drug abuse. This complete guidebook focuses on the three drugs which open the gates to dependence for American youth: alcohol, marijuana, and cocaine. A 332-page book, available from PRIDE: 1-800-241-7946.

Keep Off The Grass by Gabriel G. Nahas, M.D., Ph.D., 1985, Third Edition. A 285-page book that describes the dangers of marijuana use from documented medical, pharmacological, and scientific evidence. Available from PRIDE: 1-800-241-7946.

Sensual Drugs, by Hardin and Helen Jones, published by Cambridge University Press, 1977 & 1981. Readable account of mind-altering drugs, their effects, the consequences of their chronic use, and how to help the user. One of the best single resources for counselors, teachers, and adults interested in the action of drugs on human behavior. Available from PRIDE: 1-800-241-7946.

Raising Positive Kids in a Negative World, by Zig Ziglar, published by Oliver Nelson, a division of Thomas Nelson Publishers, 1985. An inspirational book that will help create a better family unit. A required reading for everyone who wants to raise children in today's society.

Toma Tells It Straight With Love, by David Toma with Irv Levey, published by Dell Publishing Co., 1 Dag Hammarskjold Plaza, New

York, N.Y., 10017, Revised 1988. It discusses how high school kids get pressured into using drugs. It will help you to know whether your kids are using drugs and how to help them stop their drug use, or prevent them from starting in the first place.

The White Stuff, by B.J. Plasket and Ed Quillen, published by Dell Publishing Co., 1 Dag Hammarskjold Plaza, New York, N.Y. 10017, 1985. The book tells everything you want and need to know about cocaine: its history, its chemistry, how it's handled from the fields to the streets, its ups and downs and what to do if it becomes a costly and dangerous habit.

Some Suggested Anti-Drug Materials

A booklet listing drug-prevention resources is available from The Committees of Correspondence, Inc., 57 Conant Street, Danvers, Massachusetts, 01923, (617) 774-2641.

Boy Scouts of America offers a four-color, 24-by-36-inch body chart showing how illegal drugs affect body organs. Drug Abuse Task Force, S200, 1325 Walnut Hill Land, Irving, Texas 75038-3096.

What Works: Schools Without Drugs is a 77-page booklet produced by the Department of Education and available free from Schools Without Drugs, Pueblo, Colorado 81009.

Just Say No Foundation provides free information on setting up a program in your area. Just Say No Foundation, 1777 N. California Blvd., Walnut Creek, CA 94596. 1-800-258-2766; in California 415-939-6666.

Medical Education Research Foundation publishes *Marijuana: The Myth of Harmlessness Goes Up in Smoke*. 1100 Waterway Blvd., Indianapolis, Indiana 46202.

NATIONAL ORGANIZATIONS

These national non-profit membership organizations need your monetary support in membership dues and contributions to carry on their most important work of informing the American public about the health hazards associated with illicit drug use.

COMMITTEES OF CORRESPONDENCE is a quarterly newsletter written on specific subjects relating to drug awareness. Extra mailing sent when urgent issues need letter-writing attention. C of C targets the detection and exposure of drug-culture proponents who have undeservedly been "legitimized" in various sectors of our society and who act as a resource center to disseminate "accurate" and warn about "inaccurate" information. $15.00 Send for material list.
57 Conant Street, Room 113, Danvers, MA 01923 (617) 774-2641

FAMILIES IN ACTION is a 12-page quarterly newsletter with updated information on drug and alcohol use issues. It is an accurate and dependable source of what is going on and what people are trying to do about it. They operate a national drug information center which is ready to assist those in need of any information on substance abuse issues. $15.00 yearly.
Drug Abuse Update, Suite 300, 3845 North Druid Hills Road, Decatur, GA 30033 (404)323-5799

NFP (National Federation of Parents) was formed as a national "umbrella organization" for the parent groups throughout the nation. Its principal objective is to assist in the formation and support of local parent groups. Group membership offers a non-profit status for the member. $15.00 individual, $35.00 groups (tax-exempt status).
NFP, 8730 Georgia Avenue, Suite 200, Silver Spring, MD 20910 (1-800-554-KIDS)

PRIDE (Parents' Resource Institute for Drug Education) is a resource information, conference and training organization that serves the community concerned about adolescent drug abuse. PRIDE has developed a program which includes the dissemination of accurate health information as well as the formation of parent and youth networks. It functions as a clearinghouse and reference source to the nation. $15.00 yearly.
PRIDE, Volunteer Service Center, Suite 1216, 100 Edgewood Avenue, Atlanta, GA 30303 (404) 658-2548 or (800) 241-7946

RID-USA, INC. (Remove Intoxicated Drivers) is a quarterly national newsletter and helps support the RID National Victims' Hotline. Newsletters keep you informed of national drunk driving issues and encourage letter-writing to show citizens' support to effect the necessary changes that must be made. $10.00 yearly.
RID-USA, Inc., Doris Aiken, President & Founder, P.O.Box 520, Schenectady, NY 12301

THE MINNESOTA INSTITUTE ON BLACK CHEMICAL ABUSE (MIBCA) is an excellent organization with many services: family counseling, adult intervention, aftercare, family violence, co-dependency series, youth program, community education resources and training, annual conference.
MIBCA, 2616 Nicollet Avenue, Minneapolis, MN 55408 (612) 871-7878

NCADI (National Clearinghouse for Alcohol and Drug Information) is the national headquarters of 50 statewide networks. Through NCADI, individual State clearinghouses receive information and services to meet special needs at the local level. Members of the public can obtain information from NCADI on how to contact the clearinghouse in their state. Its information resource, *Prevention Pipeline*, contains the latest information about prevention research, resources, and activities in the field. This service is must reading for those operating or planning community programs, educators, researchers, information specialists, administrators, and policymakers.
NCADI, P.O.Box 2345, Rockville, MD 20852 (301) 468-2600.

THE NATIONAL INSTITUTE ON DRUG ABUSE (NIDA) is a national information service of the U.S. Department of Health and Human Services that provides technical assistance to individuals and groups wishing to start drug prevention programs. Currently, the program focuses on the establishment of the "Just Say No To Drugs" clubs. 1-800-638-2045

Hotlines

THE NATIONAL INSTITUTE ON DRUG ABUSE HOTLINE provides confidential information and referrals to direct callers to cocaine abuse treatment centers in the local community. Free materials on drug abuse are also distributed in response to inquiries. 1-800-662-HELP

THE NATIONAL INSTITUTE ON DRUG ABUSE HOTLINE for Managers and CEO's: 1-800-843-4971

COCAINE HELPLINE is an around-the-clock information and referral service. Reformed cocaine addict counselors answer the phones, offer guidance, and refer drug users and parents to local public and private treatment centers and family learning centers. 1-800-COCAINE

Youth Organizations Against Drugs[1]

PRIDE has developed an in-school program that draws its strength from involving hundreds of high school students in an all-day educational sense of self-performance workshop. This program brings parents, students, and community together at an evening performance and empowers them to make a difference in their community. America's Pride Project includes program goals, samples of song and dance programs, and materials for education and communication between friends and families. America's Pride, 100 Edgewood Avenue, N.E., Suite 1002, Atlanta, GA 30303, 800-241-7946 or (404) 658-2548

CAMPUSES WITHOUT DRUGS is a drug prevention organization that is independent from the academic institutions; through students, faculty and staff, it provides an on-campus forum for anti-drug activities. Educational information, drug policy and enforcement reform, local community interaction, and drug-free campus entertainment are campus chapter activities supported by the national office. College students reinforce their own commitment to a drug-free lifestyle by getting peers in-

---

1. All of these organizations have a strong "no use" message.

volved in a Campus Chapter and by speaking to local high school students and teachers, parents, businesses, and community groups about the personal and national consequences of drug use on the campuses and in our society. Major emphasis is placed on college students connecting with high school students as drug-free role models who offer a "bridge" to drug-free alternatives in college.

Campuses Without Drugs, Arlene B. Seal, Ph.D., Founder, 2530 Holly Drive, Pittsburgh, PA 15235, (412) 731-8019

REACH AMERICA (Responsible Educated Adolescents Can Help America) provides training seminars for high school students about the effects of drug use preparing them to serve as positive role models to elementary and middle school students. Each student attending the seminar is provided with a *Training Manual for Drug-Free Student Groups* ($15.00) which serves as an easy reference source for information that relates to drugs and health. Special emphasis is given to positive peer pressure and alternative activities. There is a 12-member national board of students. The cost of this program is $1,000 for two days of training. This can be a joint effort between school systems in your area to financially share this cost and show unity among drug-free youth. For recommendations about the program call for programs that have been done in your state.

Reach America, c/o Mrs. Billie Avery, NFP Director, 14325 Oakwood Place, NE, Albuquerque, NM 87123, (505) 296-6798

KIDS SAVING KIDS The key to success in creating a drug-free majority in America lies in elementary education by teenagers. Adolescents provide tremendous role models for growing children, especially those children about to become teenagers themselves. Use of the nationwide program REACH America by a group of young people who call themselves "Kids Saving Kids" located at Hempfield High School in Lancaster, PA, has given the children of that community a unique opportunity to discuss and learn about the dangers of drug and alcohol use. KSK is comprised of totally drug- and alcohol-free high school students who are committed to educating their younger peers about this problem.

Kids Saving Kids, Katie True, Director, 2962 Kings Lane, Lancaster, PA 17601, (717) 898-7710

THE STOPP COMMUNITY ACTION PLAN (Students to Offset Peer Pressure) is a safe, proven approach to preventing drug abuse. By providing alternative activities for youth that are planned, organized and run by their peers, youth take ownership of their own program and make a personal commitment towards insuring its success. Rather than preaching to their peers, youth are given the opportunity to let their actions speak for them. The STOPP Community Action Plan is a program run by youth, supported by adults, and sponsored by the community at large. In addition to providing alternatives to drug and alcohol abuse, it is a source of income designed to insure solid educational programs. Write for information.
Students to Offset Peer Pressure (STOPP), Community Action Plan, P. O. Box 103, Hudson, NH 03051-0103, (603) 889-8163

WYAD (World Youth Against Drugs) is an organization run by young people for young people who share the common goal of drug-free youth. Quarterly WYAD Newsletter and notice of local, national and international meetings. It was founded in 1986 at the International PRIDE conference in Atlanta, and now has members in 35 countries and an International pen-pal program involving thousands of drug-free young people.
World Youth Against Drugs, 100 Edgewood Avenue, Suite 1216, Atlanta, GA 30303, (800) 241-9746

YOUTH TO YOUTH is a teen substance abuse prevention program that was started to support and encourage teens to be drug-free. There is a national-level conference in Ohio once a year to train youth in leadership roles to go back to their community with structured series of activities. Send for their excellent material.
Youth to Youth, 700 Bryden Road, Suite 321, Columbus, OH 43215, (614) 224-4506

WHAT IS THE COMMITTEES OF CORRESPONDENCE?

The original Committees of Correspondence was founded in Boston, Massachusetts by Samuel Adams in 1772 and put Boston at the head of what soon became the most formidable public-pressure machine in the American colonies. Within three months, Massachusetts had a network of eighty such committees. They wrote letters on important issues which were carried by men on horseback to other Committees in other towns. It accomplished what was intended and united the thirteen original colonies. In 1774, the Committees summoned the First Continental Congress which led to the signing of the Declaration of Independence in 1776.

Our nation is again threatened — this time by pervasive drug abuse. Motivated by the concerns of many parents throughout the country, a new Committees of Correspondence was founded in 1980 to reactivate the effectiveness of the original committees, and to exchange information and ideas on drug abuse issues. The Committees of Correspondence is a non-profit national organization which publishes a quarterly newsletter on specific drug awareness issues. It is affiliated with the National Federation of Parents for Drug-Free Youth State Networkers, PRIDE, and Drug Abuse Update. Members are provided with professionally reviewed, current, and credible drug information — materials, referrals, and critical analyses of literature and films. A computerized mailing list is maintained of all paid yearly subscribers to insure future contact when important issues need urgent letter writing attention. An important part of its work is the detection and exposure of drug culture proponents who have been "legitimized" in various sectors of our society and the correcting of the misinformation on marijuana and cocaine that has pervaded the media.

A new membership includes receiving over 55 articles, pamphlets, resources and past newsletters for your educational reading and puts you on the national computerized mailing list.

The single most important thing each person can do is to become educated on the subject and become involved to make sure the correct laws are passed, the correct material is being used in the school system, and the correct medical research information is being disseminated throughout the media.

You can make a difference! Be part of the solution!

Get involved — stand up and be counted — write letters!

We are networking America with knowledgeable citizens whose active involvement will help combat the deadly epidemic of drug abuse.

Write to: 57 Conant Street, Danvers, MA 01923 (617) 774-2641

Index

Index